Are You Ready to Buy a House?

Your Action Plan to Make It Happen

· · · · ·

By the Editors of Socrates.com

SOCRATES™
KNOW HOW TO DO MORE
AND SAVE

Socrates Media, LLC
227 West Monroe, Suite 500
Chicago, IL 60606
www.socrates.com

Special discounts on bulk quantities of Socrates books and products are available to corporations, professional associations and other organizations. For details, contact our Special Sales Department at 800.378.2659.

This publication is designed to provide accurate and authoritative information in regard to the subject matter covered. It is sold with the understanding that the publisher is not engaged in rendering legal, accounting or other professional service. If legal advice or other expert assistance is required, the services of a competent professional person should be sought.

From a Declaration of Principles Jointly Adopted by a Committee of the American Bar Association and a Committee of Publishers and Associations.

ISBN 10: 1-59546-251-1

ISBN 13: 978-1-59546-251-0

This product is not intended to provide legal or financial advice or substitute for the advice of an attorney or adviser.

Printing number 10 9 8 7 6 5 4 3 2 1

Are You Ready To Buy a House?

Your Action Plan to Make It Happen

. . . . .

Special acknowledgment to the following:

Ann Kepler, Managing Editor; Steven Pincich, Associate Editor; Chip Butzko, Production; Jeannie Staats, Product Manager; Peri Hughes, Editor; Sarah Woolf, Editor; Kristen Grant, Production Associate; Edgewater Editorial Services, Inc.

Get the most out of

Are You Read to Buy a House?
Your Action Plan to Make It Happen

The enclosed CD contains a read-only version of this book, the Socrates Real Estate dictionary as well as instructions to link to the dedicated resource section of **Socrates.com**:

www.socrates.com/books/ReadyHouseActionPlan.aspx.

Use the seven-digit registration code provided on the CD to register your purchase at **Socrates.com**. Once registered, you will have access to more than $100 worth of FREE forms, checklists and additional material.

Your registration also provides you with special discounts on selected Socrates products, designed to save you time and money with your Personal, Business and Real Estate matters.

Table of Contents

·····

Chapter 3: Deciding How Much You Can Afford 31

Optimize your buying power by figuring how much you can spend

Chapter 4: Preparing to Hunt for a Home 41

Decide which resource people you want to work with during this process

Chapter 15: Closing the Deal 183

Decide which type of insurance coverage you need for your home

Chapter 16: Moving In 195

Create checklists and plan ahead for a seamless move into your new home

Section One

.....

Are You Ready to Buy?

Introduction

· · · · · ·

Preparing to Make a Decision

The decision to buy a home is one of the most important–and exciting–decisions you will ever face. Making the actual decision and beginning the process may seem overwhelming to you as a first-time home buyer because of both emotional reactions and financial consequences.

Before you rush out to look at houses, take some time to evaluate your motives honestly. Does buying a first home really fit your personal situation at the moment, or do you think you have to keep up with your friends who are buying homes? Remember that your home is a place where you can live comfortably, perhaps raise children and plan for your future. But owning a home is a responsibility. If you are not comfortable in taking on the financial or time commitment of owning your own home, you may be wise to wait. Of course, there are advantages to home ownership, including potential tax breaks, building equity and pride of ownership. But these should not necessarily be the primary reasons for buying a home. Instead, you should assess your housing needs and lifestyle before buying into the assumption that everyone must own a home.

For example, do your personal circumstances warrant moving? The following factors are strong motivators to consider before buying and making a move:

- I need extra space because there is a baby on the way or my mother is moving in.
- My job is changing, and my commute will be too long if I stay here.
- I make more money now and can afford to buy and maintain a home.
- I also have the funds to pay for moving expenses, for repairs to the new house if they are needed immediately and for decorating the new place.
- I am tired of paying rent and getting nothing for it.

Also, be honest with yourself about taking on the responsibilities of owning a home. If the following statements accurately reflect your situation and abilities, you can financially afford to buy a home:

- I have a good job that I intend to keep; it is a reliable source of income.
- I pay my bills on time every month.

- My other long-term payments are a car payment or child support or other specific debt.
- My credit history is good.
- I have the money saved to make the down payment.
- I also can pay the closing costs of at least 5 percent of the home's price.
- I will make my mortgage payments and not incur late payment penalties.
- I know my mortgage payment will be more than the rent I now pay.
- I will pay property taxes, insurance and utilities.
- I will pay to maintain the house—for example, if it needs a new roof, I am ready to pay for it.

If you have some doubt about any of these statements, you should consider that you may be better off not moving from your current residence. The costs, stress and hassle of buying at this point may not be worth it. On the other hand, if you feel ready to make the investment in your first home, you can begin the process.

The First Steps

If you decide that you are ready to think about buying a home, you need to gather more information. Much of the final decision is based on how well–or how poorly–you are prepared to make the purchase. Here are some preliminary steps to help you focus on what you really want to do:

- **Analyze your current income and budget**—Finances will always dictate what kind of housing you can select. If you do not have a personal budget, now is the time to construct one. As a start, ask yourself the following questions:
  - How much do I currently spend on housing, utilities and maintenance?
  - What other living expenses do I have?
  - What expenses do I anticipate in the near future? For example, will my child require tuition payments within the next year or so, or will I have to replace my car soon?
  - Do I have a personal savings plan?

- **Determine what kind of home you can afford comfortably**—With your budget in hand, decide the type of home that fits your financial situation. Be careful to distinguish between needs, which are required, and wants, which are desired. Do not fall into the trap of becoming house poor by overspending on a house that overtaxes your budget just to maintain.

- **Investigate the mortgage process**—Find out about the types of mortgages available and the sources of mortgage loans. Look into mortgage preapproval. Most lending institutions will be happy to evaluate your financial information and tell you–without obligating you to a specific lender or loan–how big a mortgage they would give you. This provides you with a range of how much you can spend on a house. You also can learn what your monthly mortgage payment might be after figuring in the purchase price, the down payment and the interest rate on the mortgage. Compare this amount with what you are now spending in rent or on other housing expenses.

Avoiding Mistakes

Now that you have assembled the preliminary facts, you are ready to look at houses. This is the fun part of buying your first home. But do not jump in so quickly that you make some of the more common mistakes of first-time home buyers. Be careful to avoid:

- **Making premature decisions**—House hunting before doing your homework can lead to problems. You may see a house that at first glance seems to fit all your criteria. You mentally move in and even sign a contract. On reflection, you realize that the house really does not fit your family or your finances. It is too large; it is too small. Or you see another house you like better. But remember, if you sign a contract to purchase a home, you will not be able to break the contract easily. Think twice before signing anything.

- **Working with inadequate representation**—Be certain that the agent you decide to work with really represents you and not the seller. Find out exactly what an agent does and where an agent's loyalty lies. An agent who advertises a house owes allegiance to the seller, and if you contact that agent, you cannot expect impartial representation of your interests. In addition, if you try to represent yourself to save money, you may lack leverage to negotiate a favorable deal. Plus, you will not have the advantage of an agent's analysis of the market and a realistic selling price.

- **Becoming house poor**—A house that eats most of your income can lead only to stress. It may be beautiful from the outside, but the inside is bleak because you cannot afford to furnish it. If you extend yourself to your financial limits, you become especially vulnerable if your income level changes or the national economy weakens. Buy within your means.

- **Skipping the mortgage preapproval process**—Mortgage preapproval is more than just a fact-finding exercise. Today, preapprovals and prequalifications are a necessary part of the home buying process. These not only will help you avoid buying more than you can afford, they also will add strength to your offer for a new house.

- **Setting unrealistic goals**—Some first-time buyers wait for the perfect house, one that meets all of their needs and wants. This can lead to their bypassing perfectly acceptable houses only to settle finally–in exhaustion or impatience–on a house that meets few of their requirements. Even more disheartening, waiting for the perfect house allows time for market prices to climb and force buyers to select less desirable homes in order to stay within their financial range.

- **Bypassing the inspection process**—A first-time buyer often resists spending the money for a professional inspection of a prospective house. This is dangerous; you run the risk of missing potentially dangerous defects or expensive repairs in a home. A professional inspection that costs a few hundred dollars is not an extravagant expense when you are considering one of the most expensive investments you will ever make.

- **Disregarding the future**—There are two costs you need to consider when buying a home: the actual price of the house and the resale value. Look at the size of the house. Is it too small or too large for the neighborhood? You will eventually face a difficult resale if the house is too small or pay for size you cannot recover if the house is too large. Location is also important; are people in the area beginning to move out into the suburbs or returning to the city? Are long commutes a factor in the area? Maybe you should buy within a reasonable commuting distance. What about the style of house? Is it part of a trend that may look outdated at the time of resale, or is it a classic design that is flexible? Always bear in mind your future needs—either as a resident within the home you buy or as the seller at a later date.

Summary

All of these topics are discussed in detail in the remainder of this book. The information is presented in four distinct sections that will lead you step by step through the many decisions you will have to make during the home buying process. Each section includes chapters with important points, helpful tips and checklists are highlighted as quick references or sidelights of additional information. Beginning with the pros and cons of owning a home and ending with strategies for moving in, this handbook can be your reference guide for one of the biggest investments you and your family will make.

- **Section One: Are You Ready to Buy?**—Introduces the preliminary issues you need to consider before you buy a home.

- **Section Two: Starting to Search**—Explains the necessary steps you should take before you begin your search to find the home that is right for you.

- **Section Three: Finding the Right Home**—Guides you through the process of making an offer on a home and finding the right mortgage.

- **Section Four: Making it Yours**—Explains what you need to do once your offer has been accepted.

Free Forms and Checklists

Visit **Socrates.com** and register to receive a variety of useful FREE forms, letters and checklists. See page iv for details on how to register (you will need the seven-digit registration code provided on the enclosed CD).

1

· · · · · ·

Buying Your Own
Home—Or Not

In This Chapter

- Discover the financial advantages and disadvantages of buying a home.
- Learn what it costs to maintain a home.
- Evaluate the differences between renting versus owning.

Deciding you are ready to buy and then actually buying a home are such major decisions that you have to approach the situation in a practical, straightforward manner. You will do yourself a great disservice if you do not evaluate the advantages and disadvantages of taking this step. There are both pros and cons to owning a home.

> **Note**
>
> Throughout this book, any reference to home may mean single family home, condominium, co-operative, townhouse, manufactured home, multiple family home or any other dwelling you are considering buying.

Advantages of Home Ownership

Investment Value

Financially, home ownership is a sound investment. Home ownership allows you to build net worth and take advantage of an automatic savings plan as the value of your home increases. It increases your financial options; for example, you are eligible for a home equity loan as the rising market value of your house enables you to build equity. It also allows you the pleasure of living in and using your investment as it increases in value.

Furthermore, assuming financial obligations, such as a monthly mortgage payment, helps build personal financial stability. If you keep an eye on the value of your real estate and on the trends in your area, you can use your first home as a stepping stone toward financial security and stability.

Building Equity

Building equity is a major advantage of home ownership. Equity is the difference between a home's current value and the loan balance. For example, if the mortgage balance is $250,000 and the current market value of the house is $300,000, the $50,000 difference is the equity.

Equity can increase or decrease, depending on the local real estate market. Remember that real estate value is cyclical. If you buy at the top of the market, there is always the chance that equity and real estate market values will decrease if the market drops. On the other hand, equity and investment value may increase if the market value goes up after you buy.

In most cases, however, you will own a piece of property whose value will increase over time. Within a few years, you may be able to sell this property and make a profit. While you are enjoying the benefits of living in your own home, its market value continues to increase. After a period of time, you will be able to borrow against your equity at favorable interest rates because your property secures your loan. This is a desirable financial option. You can use a home equity loan to remodel the house, pay for your child's college expenses or provide cash after you retire.

Tax Breaks

An important plus in owning a home is the tax advantage. The Internal Revenue Service (IRS) allows homeowners to deduct mortgage interest, which reduces the total amount of tax you pay to the U.S. government every year. During the early years of a mortgage, most of the mortgage payments go to pay off interest, and this interest can be deducted from your total tax bill. For example, on a $1,200 monthly mortgage payment, your interest may be around $1,000. Deducting $1,000 per month reduces your yearly taxable income by about $12,000.

To determine the dollar value of this deduction, multiply your monthly mortgage interest payment by your tax bracket. If your interest payment is $1,000 per month and you are in the 28 percent tax bracket, the mortgage interest deduction is worth $280 per month. To look at it another way, that $1,000 actually costs you 28 percent less, or $720. To realize this benefit, you either can wait for a big tax refund after filing your income tax return, or you can adjust what is withheld from your paycheck each month.

In addition to this significant tax advantage, you can deduct property taxes from your taxable income. In the year you buy your home, you also may be able to deduct closing costs and moving expenses, especially if you changed job location and residence but were not reimbursed for the household moving costs.

Tip
Itemize your tax return rather than taking the standard deduction when your mortgage interest, property taxes and other deductions exceed your standard deduction. Visit **Socrates.com** for more information.

Other Financial Advantages

There are additional financial advantages to owning a home besides the tax breaks and equity. Beginning with a first home and moving up two, three or more times, you may wind up owning your ideal home with no mortgage or at least a significant amount of equity. Along the way, you will find that:

- you can leverage a small down payment into a large return—if you make a $5,000 down payment on a $200,000 house, your $5,000 controls a $200,000 asset; as your house's value increases, so does the worth of your down payment, leading to an increased return on your initial investment of $5,000;

- you have established a forced savings plan–to finance college for the children or save for your retirement–because for several decades, land and home values have steadily increased;

- you personally can increase a home's value by making wise improvements;

- you can count on the same monthly payment with a standard mortgage— rents may go up; and

- you are building financial stability and a cushion against financial setbacks.

Furthermore, when you sell, there is a significant tax advantage: married couples can take the first $500,000 in capital gains profits tax-free on home sales, while singles can take $250,000 in tax-free gains. The only stipulation is that you must have lived in your home for 2 of the past 5 years.

Other Real Estate Tax Deductions

In addition to standard mortgage interest and real estate taxes, you should talk to your accountant about the following deductions:

- principal residence acquisition mortgage fee–a loan fee, usually called points, paid to the mortgage lender–to be taken during the year you buy the house; use your closing statement for the amount of your loan fee payment to obtain a home mortgage;

- prorated mortgage interest in the year of purchase for the month the sale closed if you assumed or purchased subject to the existing mortgage; use your closing settlement statement where the buyer's and seller's shares are calculated;

- prorated property tax in the year of purchase; again, use your closing settlement statement as proof of your payment based on the number of days you owned the home during the tax year;

- moving costs if your job required relocation or if you changed jobs and were not reimbursed for moving expenses;

- casualty loss if you sustained a sudden, unusual or unexpected loss, such as fire or flood, but were not reimbursed by insurance; however, slow losses, such as termite damage, erosion, mold or dry rot are not deductible, and you must qualify–the loss must exceed 10 percent of your adjusted gross income–and provide proof of loss; and

- ground rent payments if your home is on leased land and you have at least a 15-year lease with a purchase option to buy the land; this often applies to owners of mobile homes who rent a lot on which their home stands.

Explore your eligibility to take these deductions. They can amount to a substantial savings—yet another tax advantage to owning your home. Visit **Socrates.com** for more information about the tax forms you will need.

Disadvantages of Home Ownership

Financial Risks

Just as there are financial advantages to owning your home, there are also financial risks. The reality is that owning a home is an enormous responsibility, something that many first-time buyers push to the backs of their minds.

Defaulting on Your Mortgage

If you find that you cannot pay your mortgage, you run the risk of:

- losing your entire down payment, which can equal as much as 5 percent to 20 percent of the price of the house; or
- foreclosure, where the lender can reclaim the property and sell it to pay off the loan. Lenders who are forced to foreclose are under no obligation to sell the property for its full market value in order to refund your down payment. What the lender wants to do is sell the house at a price high enough to cover the outstanding balance on the mortgage.

Most lenders do not want to take either of these actions. They began their transactions with you in good faith and would like to see you succeed in keeping the house. Most will work with you to restructure the loan in order to lower your monthly payment. If you have credit card or other debt, they may offer credit counseling to help you regain control of your financial situation. But their main concern is recovering the money you borrowed to buy the house, and sometimes foreclosure is the only step they can take.

Liability

You can be held liable for anything that happens on your property. For example, if someone takes a shortcut through your property and breaks a leg after tripping over a tree root in your yard, he or she can sue you, even though you never gave permission for anyone to use the shortcut. Of course, you should have liability insurance for just this sort of occurrence, but the situation still will cost you time and maybe even money.

Accidents

A summer thunderstorm strikes a tree and blows it onto your roof, destroying your picture window and the living room furniture, or days of unremitting rain flood your basement. A pipe in the upstairs bathtub bursts, damaging an interior wall all the way to the first floor. These may be accidents, but they are emergencies, often requiring an immediate outlay of money.

These examples illustrate one of the biggest fears a homeowner faces: the unexpected. No matter how carefully you plan, you cannot always anticipate your fate. This is one of the reasons most experts strongly recommend that you not financially overextend yourself when selecting a house. You must have some monetary resources in reserve to meet these kinds of emergencies.

Homeowners insurance is your first fallback solution for these problems. However, your insurance may not cover everything, particularly if you have been trying to keep monthly premiums down by reducing coverage.

Home Maintenance

If this is your first home, you may not have given a thought to the time, energy and money that are necessary to maintain the property.

What it takes to maintain the outside of the home as well as the lawn and garden is often a shock to first-time homeowners. At the very least, you have to mow the grass in warm weather and clear snow in the winter. Do you have a lawn mower, other gardening tools, a snowblower, brooms, hoses or rakes? Do you have time to fit this regular maintenance into your schedule, or do you plan to hire someone to take care of the yard? If so, how much will that cost? Some communities also require that you shovel snow from the sidewalk in front of your home, and failure to comply may result in a fine.

There are other less regular outside chores that are costly and time consuming. A clapboard house needs to be painted every 5 to 7 years. Even if you purchase a brick or siding-clad home, you still may have to repaint the trim regularly. Putting on storm windows in the cold months, screens in the hot months and washing windows all year long takes time and energy—and money if you hire someone to do the work. You also may need to invest in landscaping, plants or garden supplies.

Inside, there are similar chores that also take time and money. It may seem that there is always a room that needs to be painted. Annual inspections of furnaces and air conditioning systems cost money. Spending $100 here and several hundred dollars there adds up, and these are expenses that simply maintain your quality of life without adding any value to the property. If you have never had to budget funds to cover home maintenance, you may be very surprised.

In contrast, you may have anticipated major expenses–roof repair, furnace replacement, rewiring–yet you may not realize that you have little or no control over when or how these problems are solved. You cannot put off some repairs until you save up the money. Repairing or replacing a malfunctioning or nonfunctioning furnace in the middle of a cold snap cannot be delayed. Nor can you plan to make all repairs yourself to save money. First, you may not be capable of making the repair, and second, you do not want to diminish the value of your home by doing or paying for shoddy work. This means that you have to have some financial reserve at all times to keep your home in good repair. One study has found that maintaining a typical home up to legal and aesthetic standards for 30 years can cost up to four times the purchase price of the home.

Typical Costs of Home Ownership

The list of common time and/or money expenses below outlines what you can expect when you own a home. You probably will not encounter all of these items and certainly not all in 1 year. However, the list may point out some costs you have not anticipated as you think about home ownership.

General Costs

- mortgage payment
- private mortgage insurance
- property taxes
- homeowners insurance
- homeowners, condo or co-op association dues and assessments
- special assessments—often unexpected
- water and sewer services
- utilities
- trash/garbage pickup
- monthly house security alarm fees
- extermination fees

General Maintenance

- furnace service contract
- air conditioner unit maintenance
- plumbing maintenance—clearing drain pipes and septic tank systems of tree roots and debris
- changing water and furnace filters
- pump replacement and repair—for wells

Exterior Maintenance

- grass mowing
- snow shoveling
- gutter cleaning
- leaf raking
- window washing
- spraying for pests
- landscaping
- sealing/resurfacing driveway
- house painting

- roof repair/replacement
- tuck-pointing
- chimney sweeping

Interior Maintenance

- painting
- routine plumbing and electrical repairs
- wall-to-wall carpet replacement
- bathroom tile repair/replacement
- repair/replacement of major appliances

The Downside of Taxes

Although tax breaks are a major advantage of buying a home, there are instances in which taxes can be a problem for homeowners—aside from simply having to pay them.

In many areas, the local government can increase your property taxes without your approval. Just when you have set up your budget to accommodate your tax payments, you may find your property taxes have gone up. You cannot refuse to pay because you run the risk of the local government that imposes the tax seizing your home and auctioning it off to anyone who is willing to pay your taxes.

For example, a developer buys the rolling farmland adjacent to your community and proceeds to build a condominium complex. Suddenly, your town faces increased traffic and congestion as well as crowded schools because of this new development. This means increased taxes to pay for better roads, more sewers, new schools and additional teachers. Again, you may have little choice in the matter because opposing the development or the new taxes will cost you money and may upset some of your neighbors and local merchants who benefit from having the new development.

Even though as a homeowner you can deduct property taxes from your income tax returns, it can be very disconcerting to realize that you have little control over such basic expenses as property taxes.

10 Year History of Tax Increases on One Property			
2004	$8,108	1999	$3,905
2003	$6,700	1998	$3,039
2002	$6,175	1997	$2,880
2001	$6,093	1996	$2,707
2000	$4,040	1995	$2,620

Owning vs. Renting

After reviewing both the advantages and disadvantages of owning a home, you are ready to take the final step in deciding if you are ready to buy: comparing owning to renting.

Most financial planners advise that you should buy a home as soon as you can so that you can start building equity, enjoy the tax breaks and establish financial security. Despite the initial expenses of buying a home, you do own the property, a definite benefit when property values increase. The investment in your home generally pays off when you sell the home.

On the other hand, when you rent, you do not have an ownership interest in the property. In addition, you cannot count on the fixed monthly housing payment of a standard mortgage because the rent continually goes up. When the landlord raises your rent, you are paying off his or her mortgage more quickly. When you are ready to move, you have nothing to show for all those rental payments.

Owning a home also can provide you with peace of mind. You can repair, replace, decorate or change your home without worrying about your landlord withholding part of your security deposit. In addition, if your landlord dies or sells your building, you may face a large rent increase or, even worse, a conversion to condominiums. Either scenario can cause unexpected expenses or a costly move. Owning your home offers a sense of security and a feeling of control.

There are good reasons to rent, however. If you plan to be in a location for only a short time, it is wiser to rent. If your company transfers you or you decide to move to a new area, you may want to rent for a year or so to become acquainted with the community and the housing market. For example, if the new area appears to be declining in value, you may want to rent until you can find a more desirable neighborhood. If you are uncertain about your length of stay in an area, renting allows you to leave at the end of your lease or even sublet your unit. Homeowners must either rent their home or sell, options that can become problematic if you want to move quickly.

Rental units are maintenance-free for the renters. You do not have to mow the lawn, clear the snow, paint the building, maintain the heating plant or fix the roof. Your free time is not devoted to household chores and upkeep. People who like to travel probably would be happier renting. They can leave for extended periods without worrying about home upkeep.

Deciding to Rent or Buy?

	Advantages	Disadvantages
Renting	No maintenance	No buildup of equity
	Flexibility to move	Rent increase outpaces inflation
	Invest money elsewhere	
Buying	Tax breaks	Property taxes
	Buildup of equity	Mortgage costs
	Stability, security	Inflexibility to move
	Freedom to decorate, renovate	Maintenance cost and time

Summary

Despite the costs and disadvantages of buying a home, the positive financial and emotional benefits of owning a home almost always outweigh the negatives. Anyone who is ready to settle down should consider buying instead of renting as soon as he or she is able and willing. Buying your own home, especially your first home, is an exciting experience, particularly if you approach it in a thoughtful, informed way. If you are eager to begin your search, then the next step is to determine how much house you can afford. From there, it is only a matter of learning all you can to make your home buying adventure satisfying and profitable.

What You Have Learned

- How to build equity and the tax advantages of owning a home.
- The financial risks of home ownership.
- The costs of maintaining a home and the downside of property taxes.
- The differences between owning and renting.

Discounts on Other Socrates Products

In addition to a variety of free forms and checklists, you will find special offers on a variety of Socrates products. Visit **www.socrates. com/books/ReadyHouseActionPlan.aspx** for more information.

2

· · · · · ·

Assessing Your Assets

In This Chapter

- Learn how to prepare a budget.
- Evaluate your credit history and get your credit score.
- Discover how to save for a down payment.

Before making a final decision about buying a home, it is essential that you put your finances in order. Evaluating your finances and constructing a financial plan, such as a comprehensive budget, are tasks you will have to undertake before searching for a home and a lender to help you pay for it.

This initial evaluation will enable you to review your spending and saving habits and to develop some short- and long-term goals. Buying a home is part of planning for your future, and neither can be accomplished without you taking charge of your money, which is the basis of financial control.

Constructing a Household Budget

The best way to get a clear picture of your finances is to prepare a budget schedule that shows where you spent your money during the past 12 months. It is advisable to use a monthly budget schedule because expenses will fluctuate greatly from month to month. For example, if you have children in private school or college and the tuition is due twice a year, then those months will require additional cash.

Collecting Information

In your budget schedule, include all your monthly expenses. These expenses range from home mortgage payments to vacations to doctor bills. When preparing the schedule, keep in mind the expenses that could be reduced or eliminated if necessary.

Preparing the actual budget form is not as time-consuming as you might think if you have gathered all the necessary information first. The information you need includes:

- past 3 years' income tax returns
- recent bank statements

- monthly income records from all sources, including pay stubs and records of supplementary income
- rent receipts
- all monthly loan payments, including car payments, alimony, child support, school loans, credit cards or any other long-term loans
- all other fixed monthly expenses, such as child care, trash removal, cable hookup or dues
- records of variable monthly expenses, such as utilities, food, household maintenance/repair and postage, for the past 12 months
- car expenses, including insurance, maintenance, license/fees, gas and oil and repairs
- other insurance payments, such as homeowner or tenant insurance and life, health and disability insurance
- records of annual or semiannual costs, such as taxes, tuition or insurance
- records of professional fees, such as physician, dentist, attorney, medical specialists, veterinarian, hair stylist/barber
- medical expenses
- clothing and dry cleaning or laundry costs
- itemized lists of personal entertainment expenses, including eating out, vacations, travel
- contributions or gifts
- savings and investments

Try to be realistic as you estimate your expenses. Allow for increases that probably will be inevitable—insurance, taxes, school tuition. As you gather your records, take the time to apply for a free credit report to evaluate your indebtedness as well as discover problems or discrepancies that could interfere with receiving additional credit.

Tip
If you are self-employed and are thinking about applying for a mortgage, you will need tax returns for the past 3 years and all business records. The mortgage lender will ask for these records, so you should collect them while you are gathering the other information.

At this point, you may realize that you have not saved enough records to draw up a realistic budget. What can you do? First, gather all the records you do have; do not forget itemized credit card bills and canceled checks. Then, save every scrap of information for several months: all incoming bills; receipts from groceries, hardware stores, gas stations, restaurants, movie theaters, parking garages or any establishment where you spend cash; and personal notes itemizing tips, tolls or other fees. After 6 months, add up the total and try to estimate your monthly expenses from all of your records. Add in the fixed monthly, semiannual and annual expenses and begin to develop your budget.

Preparing a Budget

Once you have assembled the pertinent records, you can build a budget. Begin by categorizing all expenses as necessities or luxuries. The objective is to identify those items that are the most financially and personally rewarding and thus worthy of the expense. In the process, you will recognize which expenses can be cut or reduced.

This also may be the time to analyze how a home purchase will affect your budget. You can use your monthly rent as the basis of your housing expenses but add in some estimates of insurance, taxes, repairs and maintenance. Think about budgeting for an emergency fund to repair a broken furnace or fix a leak in the roof. This analysis will be only a ballpark figure, but it will be a starting point for developing a more detailed breakdown after you have talked with a mortgage lender.

Include income and expenditures on a household budget form that is divided into months. A sample budget form appears on the next page. As you classify information by income source and expense category, sort the corroborating documents into individual files with clear labels. An accordion file folder with labeled tabs is a good way to store the records. In fact, setting up a new file at the beginning of each year is a helpful way to sort papers and bills. This will help you maintain a running record of your budget that is always up-to-date.

Monthly Budget Planner

	Party 1	Party 2	
Average Salary	_____	_____	
Average Commission	_____	_____	
Benefits	_____	_____	
Investment Dividends	_____	_____	
Retirement Plans/Profit Sharing	_____	_____	
Other (_____)	_____	_____	
Total Monthly Income	_____	_____	_____
			Joint Total

	Present	Proposed	
Rent/Mortgage Payment	_____	_____	
Electricity	_____	_____	
Water	_____	_____	
Phone	_____	_____	
Cable	_____	_____	
Trash Pickup	_____	_____	
Lawn Service	_____	_____	
Property Tax	_____	_____	
Homeowner's Insurance	_____	_____	
Auto Payments	_____	_____	
Auto Maintenance	_____	_____	
Auto Insurance	_____	_____	
Food	_____	_____	
Clothing	_____	_____	
Child Care	_____	_____	
Education	_____	_____	
Child Support	_____	_____	
Alimony	_____	_____	
Entertainment/Vacation	_____	_____	
Pet Expenses	_____	_____	
Life/Health Insurance	_____	_____	
Medical/Dental/Optical	_____	_____	
Credit Cards	_____	_____	
Loans	_____	_____	
Other (_____)	_____	_____	
Other (_____)	_____	_____	
Total Monthly Spending	_____	_____	_____
			Joint Total

© 2005 Socrates Media, LLC
K311-7 • Rev. 05/05

Setting Goals

Use your budget to set some goals. In fact, a budget becomes more meaningful and useful if it incorporates short- and long-term financial goals. It is best to start with an attainable goal that can become the first step to a pattern of long-term goal setting. For example, think about how to trim spending to save enough for a family weekend trip without using the credit cards. Then start thinking about money objectives for the next 2 years, 5 years, even 10 years. Looking at the budget in a holistic way helps you prepare for long-term goals—college expenses or retirement plans, for example.

Evaluating Your Financial Condition

When you think about buying a home, you have to view yourself and your financial situation in the same way a lender would. Begin by answering the following questions:

What are my sources of income?

- hourly wage/seasonal pay/salary
- unemployment compensation
- veteran benefits
- military pay
- social security
- interest from bank accounts
- alimony
- child support
- retirement pension payments

What debt do I have?

- car payment
- credit card debt
- child support
- alimony
- education loans
- medical bills
- debt that has gone to collections

What expenses do I pay regularly?

- housing expenses (rent)
- utilities
- groceries
- personal and real property taxes
- Child care costs

- health care costs not covered by insurance, including copayments, doctors' fees, prescriptions, eyeglasses and dental care
- school activity and other fees
- car maintenance and annual inspection fees
- lunch on workdays

How much of my savings is accessible to me?

- savings account
- checking account
- money market fund
- stocks, bonds, trusts

Use this information to analyze your current financial state: where the money comes from and where it goes. Once you know your income, debt, regular expenses and savings and/or investments, you can determine your basic net worth—your total assets minus your total liabilities. This, in turn, helps you and your lender decide how much you can spend on a home.

Monthly Gross Income Worksheet			
Item	Borrower	Co-borrower	Total
Base income	$	$	$
Part-time, second job			
Overtime*			
Bonuses*			
Commissions*			
Dividends/interest			
Alimony, child support			
Unemployment compensation			
Pension/Social Security			
Public assistance			
Veteran benefits			
Other income			
Total gross monthly income $_____			

* If your overtime, bonuses or commissions do not fall into 12 equal monthly payments, divide them to spread this income over 12 months. You will need a 2-year history of receipts for this income to count.

Credit History

One of the most important pieces of information you can have is your current credit report. A good and accurate credit report is an essential financial asset. In addition, a credit report can reveal discrepancies or inaccuracies that could impair your request for additional credit. It is always better to correct a problem in the credit report before applying for a mortgage loan than it is to try to correct it after applying.

The U.S. Congress has authorized free credit reports once a year. Under the Fair and Accurate Credit Transactions Act (FACT Act), consumers can request and obtain a free credit report once every 12 months from each of the three nationwide consumer credit reporting companies: Equifax, Experian and TransUnion.

Under the law, you can monitor your credit reports for free by ordering a report from one bureau, waiting 4 months before ordering another report from another bureau and then waiting 4 more months before ordering from the third bureau. That way you can monitor your credit every 4 months while taking advantage of the yearly free report mandated by the law.

It is entirely your choice whether you order all three at the same time or order one now and others later. The advantage of ordering all three at the same time is that you can compare them. However, you will not be eligible for another free credit file disclosure for 12 months. The advantage of ordering one now and others later is that you can keep track of any changes or new information that may appear.

If you do find legitimate mistakes in your credit reports, correct them as quickly as possible. The credit reporting companies post their dispute procedures online, and it costs nothing. Each agency will suspend the negative or incorrect report while it investigates your request. You will need to provide proof to correct mistakes and explanations to resolve any problems. Be sure that all three credit reporting companies correct any errors and that mortgage lenders who have earlier reports receive the corrected update.

Tip
The Fair Credit Reporting Act (FCRA), under the auspices of the Federal Trade Commission (FTC), gives you the right to correct an error in your credit report. Visit **www.ftc.gov** or call 877.382.4357 for information on how to correct errors.

To obtain your credit report, you can click on **www.annualcreditreport.com**, a centralized service for consumers to request annual credit reports. It was created by the three nationwide consumer credit reporting companies and is the only service authorized by all three for this purpose. The service also provides options to request reports by telephone and by mail. You also can request a free annual credit report by phone or mail through the Annual Credit Report Request Service in your state; the report will be mailed within 15 days. As a security precaution, you should never provide your personal information to any other company or person in connection with requesting free annual credit reports under the FACT Act.

You also can contact the three major credit reporting agencies directly:

- Equifax at 800.685.1111 or **www.equifax.com**
- Experian at 888.397.3742 or **www.experian.com**
- TransUnion at 800.888.4213 or **www.transunion.com**

Credit File Disclosure

A credit file disclosure provides you with all of the information in your credit file maintained by a consumer reporting company that could be provided by the reporting company to a third party, such as a lender. A credit file disclosure also includes a record of everyone who has inquired or received a report about you from the consumer reporting company within a certain period of time. In addition, the credit file disclosure includes information such as the inquiries of companies for preapproved offers of credit or insurance and account reviews, and any medical account information that is suppressed for third party users of consumer reports.

Credit Score

A credit score is a complex mathematical model that evaluates many types of information in a credit file. It is often referred to as a FICO score after Fair Issac Corporation, the company that initiated credit rating technique. The model generates a score ranging from 300 to 850 that is used by a lender to help determine whether a person qualifies for a particular credit card, loan or service. Most credit scores estimate the risk a company incurs by lending a person money or providing them with a service—specifically, the likelihood that the person will make payments on time in the next 2 to 3 years. Generally, the higher the score, the less risk the person represents.

You can purchase a credit score by contacting one of the nationwide consumer credit reporting companies when you request your free annual credit report, or you can visit **www.myfico.com** to obtain your FICO score and other information about improving your credit.

Credit Clinics

The FTC cautions consumers to be wary of companies that make claims regarding credit repair for a fee. These companies, commonly called credit clinics, do not do anything for you that you cannot do for yourself at little or no cost. Beware of any organization that offers to create a new identity and credit file for you. Following are some warning signs that might indicate that you are dealing with a credit clinic:

- An organization guarantees to remove late payments, bankruptcies or similar information from a credit report.
- An organization charges a lot of money to repair credit.
- A company asks the consumer to write to the credit reporting company and repeatedly seek verification of the same credit account information in the file, even though the information has been determined to be correct.
- An organization is reluctant to give out its address or pushes you to make a decision immediately.

For more information about credit clinics, request the brochure "Credit Repair: Self-Help May Be Best" from:

Federal Trade Commission
Consumer Response Center
Room 130
600 Pennsylvania Ave. N.W.
Washington, D.C. 20580

Or visit **www.ftc.gov/credit** for more information.

Tip

Debt control before seeking a home loan. First, pay off as much credit card and other high-interest consumer debt as soon as possible, even at the expense of saving for the down payment. Pay this off first so that your debt load does not limit the amount you can borrow but do not switch debt from one card to another; that is merely shuffling debt, not paying it off.

Next, do not assume new debt, especially in the 6 months before buying a home. Mortgage loans are based on debt-to-income ratios–the amount you pay out monthly versus the amount you bring in–so new debt could change the ratio and hinder the chances of obtaining a mortgage.

Finally, pay all bills on time.

Job History

Your job history is an important factor in your financial picture. Having a steady job will enable you to pay back a mortgage loan. You are considered to have steady employment if you have been working continuously for 2 or more years.

A lender will want to know about your job history and will use the information to determine whether or not you qualify for a loan. However, loan approval does not always depend on your having held a job for 2 years. Job moves that result in equal or higher pay and continue to use proven skills are a plus for you.

If you have been working for fewer than 2 years, the mortgage lender will want an explanation. There may be a good reason:

- You may have just finished school or been discharged from the military.
- Your work may be seasonal, and you may have work gaps between seasons.
- You may have been laid off because of a plant closing or illness.
- You may work in an occupation that customarily has frequent job turnover.

If, despite any of the above reasons, you have been steadily employed and have maintained a regular, consistent income, you will have a good chance of getting a mortgage loan.

On the other hand, if you have been fired for cause such as excessive absences, have long gaps in your employment record or have drops in your income that are difficult to explain, you should probably wait to apply for a mortgage until you can establish and demonstrate that you have a stable work history.

Fiscal Responsibility History

Do you pay your bills on time each month? How you have paid your bills in the past tells the lender how you will pay your bills in the future.

When you apply for a mortgage, the lender will ask for a list of all your debts, the amounts of the monthly payments and the number of years left to pay on the debts. The lender will then order a credit report to verify the information that you give and to check on how well you have kept your promises to repay. Credit reporting companies have access to a great deal of financial information about you, and they make it available to lenders who review your loan application. That is why it is important that you disclose all debts and any difficulty you may have had in the past in repaying them. It is also imperative that you do not omit any information about money you owe. The credit reporting company will reveal such information, and the lender may then question your veracity in reporting all debts.

Remember, sometimes credit reports are inaccurate. This is a good reason to request your credit report before beginning the loan application process. If there are any inaccuracies or errors, you can correct the report before talking with a mortgage lender.

If your credit report reveals that you do not have a good credit history, you probably should delay trying to buy a home and take steps to improve your credit history. For example, you may have too many debts, or you may pay some loans late each month. If this is the case, you should work to bring your payments up-to-date and to pay off some of your debts. Even if your debts are current, you may not be considered a good candidate for a loan if you have consistently made your monthly payment after the due date. After you have reduced the amount you owe and can show a 2-year history of making payments on time, you can begin to think about looking for a home.

The 2-year waiting period also applies to bankruptcy. If you have declared bankruptcy within the past 10 years, that information will be revealed in your credit report. The lender will want you to explain the circumstances surrounding the bankruptcy. This does not mean that you can never own a home. Lenders usually prefer that you wait 2 years after the discharge of the bankruptcy before taking on a large debt, such as a mortgage. This gives you time to reestablish credit and show that you are able to manage your financial affairs again.

Bill Payment Scores

You can now use your Bill Payment Scores (BPS) and your Payment Reporting Builds Credit (PRBC) history report to augment or improve your FICO scores. These reports use nontraditional credit records—for example, your rent paying history; status of payments for child care, utilities or insurance; paycheck advance repayments; or other unreported, credit-related information.

Under the Equal Credit Opportunity Act (ECOA), you now have the legal right to have your BPS and your PRBC payment history be considered along with traditional credit reports and scores to evaluate your credit for a mortgage loan. Lenders will be able to see that you have paid your bills on time during the previous 3 years and that you show a history of fiscal responsibility that improves your creditworthiness.

PRBC will maintain your bill payment history for 7 years. Basic services, including enrollment and credit reports, are free. Visit **www.prbc.com** for more information.

> **Tip**
>
> You can quickly calculate how much mortgage you qualify for by doubling your annual household income. For example, a couple with a combined income of $75,000 would qualify for a $150,000 mortgage. If the couple has around $20,000 for a down payment, they can more or less afford a home with a sales price of $170,000.

Saving for a Down Payment

Planning to buy a house forces you to look at your household budget and take stock of your financial assets. You need to save money for a down payment in order to obtain a mortgage. While the amount of your down payment may vary depending on the lender, you nevertheless will have to make a down payment that equals at least 5 percent of the purchase price of the home. The higher the down payment the sounder your deal will be. You also will need money for closing costs. Furthermore, you want to establish a permanent savings program so you will always have a financial cushion for when you encounter the unexpected costs associated with homeownership.

Remember, spending less means saving more. Sit down, as you did when you constructed a budget, and brainstorm ways to save money. Here you can itemize your needs to see where you can save money. Start with big expenses, such as a car, and move to less expensive purchases, such as clothing. Combine savings on large items with more moderate savings on smaller items to form the beginning of a savings account that you can use for a down payment and for future plans.

> **Note**
>
> Most people spend 10 percent more than they earn. You may know how much money you make each month, but do you know how much you spend? By using credit cards, debit cards and automated teller machines, you do not even see your money, and it easy to spend more than your earn. This is how credit card debt grows.

Following are some guidelines for saving money:

- **Adopt the motto, spend less and save more**—Approach every new purchase with this thought in mind.
- **Distinguish between needs and wants**—Basic needs sustain your existence: food, shelter, education, transportation and clothing. Wants are often items that enhance your lifestyle. For example, you may need a car to

get to work, but does it have to be a $50,000 SUV, or will a $15,000 sedan do? This does not mean that you cannot have what you want, but you should not deceive yourself into thinking that what you want is really what you need.

- **Rethink your idea that bigger is always better**—Do you think that something must be better because it costs more? Look at how you plan to use your purchases; the smaller or less expensive item may be all you need. You do not have to pay for a fancy brand name to get the best use from an item.

- **Try a product before you buy one**—If possible, rent or borrow a product before you invest in one for yourself. The trial period may show you that you either do not need the article or would have limited use for one. The money you save more than makes up for the rental fee.

- **Look at what you already own**—Do you have a car that no one uses very often? Could you trade in your car on a smaller or newer model that would cost less to maintain? Do you have workout equipment or hobby tools that you never use? Is it time for a garage sale?

- **Evaluate your insurance policies**—When did you last do comparison shopping on car or household insurance? Did you know that you can reduce your household insurance premiums by installing security equipment, such as burglar alarms, deadbolt locks or smoke detectors? You also can save by increasing your deductibles on both household and car insurance. Some insurance companies will discount car insurance to motorists who drive a predetermined minimum number of miles each year.

- **Reduce your debt load**—Rein in the use of credit cards and eliminate those cards with high interest rates. Budget a monthly stipend to pay against credit card debts. Rather than pay just the monthly minimums, increase your payments to make a real effort at debt reduction. Remember, compounding has a negative effect on credit—the longer you have the debt, the more interest you pay. On the other hand, the longer you have savings, the higher the return. Convert debt to savings.

- **Learn how to save on food**—Food is a need, but that does not mean you cannot save money on this necessity. Try the following:
  - Take the time to clip coupons and read store ads. You may be surprised at how much you can save by using coupons and taking advantage of two-for-one specials.
  - Buy in quantity, but not more than you can use before the food spoils and not something that you seldom use.
  - Try generic or store brands, which are often more than adequate substitutes.
  - Shop at stores that consistently offer lower prices or consider discount clubs or warehouse stores.
  - Avoid buying convenience foods, which are always more expensive.
  - Plan ahead; if you think about menus before you shop, you are less likely to buy impulsively.

- **Look for bargains in clothing**—Here are some ideas:
  - Buy clothing out of season. You can save a lot of money by buying next summer's clothing at the end of this summer.
  - Coordinate outfits. Buy clothes that can be combined with other clothes and accessories to make new outfits.
  - Buy basic fashions and avoid expensive trends.
  - Select children's clothing that can be replaced cheaply. Children will outgrow and wear out clothes rapidly.

- **Shop around for savings on your telephone service**—Many plans combine local and long distance service. Others include unlimited long distance minutes for one flat, monthly rate or may offer more basic service for less than you are paying now. You can change your local phone service without losing your current phone number and with no loss in service. Visit **www.lowermybills.com** for more information.

- **Use the Internet**—Comparison shopping is easy and convenient online. You do not have to go from store to store or make numerous phone calls to find the best price on an item. Many retailers offer online buying and even special online sales that you cannot take advantage of in the store. eBay® is a good source for hard-to-find items, many of which sell for bargain prices. You also can find travel bargains and packages on the Internet. Try sites such as **www.travelocity.com** and **www.lowestfare.com** for airfares, car rentals and hotel reservations. Sites like **www.eversave.com** offer savings on all kinds of goods and services.

Summary

Now that you have evaluated your financial status, constructed a budget, reviewed your credit history, set some short- and long-term financial goals and established a savings program, you are equipped to decide if you are financially ready to buy a home and, if so, how much you can afford. You will now use all of the forms and information you have gathered to search for a mortgage lender and pinpoint just how much of a financial commitment you can make.

The groundwork you are laying ultimately will culminate in your selecting a home that fulfills your needs without emptying your pockets. In the long run, you will be glad that you have done all the tedious paperwork and have made the hard choices about saving money and reducing debt.

What You Have Learned

- How to evaluate your financial condition and create a budget.

- How to set up financial goals.

- How to get your credit score and evaluate your credit history.

- How to save money to help save for a down payment.

3
· · · · · ·
Deciding How Much
You Can Afford

In This Chapter

- Find out how to get prequalified or preapproved by a mortgage lender.
- Learn about the factors that will affect your buying power.
- Determine how much you can spend on a home mortgage.
- Estimate the closing and moving in costs.

The biggest mistake most home buyers make is to begin looking at homes or even selecting a home before they know how much they can afford. This can lead either to disappointment or surprise, but it almost never leads to ultimately purchasing the first home selected.

Mortgage lenders work within certain guidelines when deciding whether to approve a loan. They use terms such as income-to-debt ratio, principal, interest, amortization, mortgage insurance premium and FICO score to discuss what they can or cannot do for you, the home buyer. It seems logical, then, that you should become informed about these terms and about what the lender looks at when you apply for a loan. This is the information you need before you even begin to hunt for a home.

If you have done your homework and gathered all your records, set up a budget, evaluated your financial status and requested a credit report, you are prepared for the first step in learning how much you can borrow—which means understanding how lenders determine what you can afford to borrow and, therefore, how much you can afford to buy.

The following information will help you begin to explore what you can afford to buy. Because you need to understand the components of a mortgage and how it affects your buying power, you should review the overall process as you begin. As you proceed through the process and finally choose a home to buy, you will need to look at all of the financial alternatives in order to make a decision. See Chapter 13 for more information about your mortgage options. You can use this overview, however, to navigate through the first steps.

Prequalification and Preapproval

One easy way to find out how much you can afford is to get prequalified by a mortgage lender. This is a step you should take early in the process. Most lenders will be happy to tell you how large a mortgage they might offer you. Ask family, friends and your real estate agent to suggest a reputable lender.

At the prequalification stage, you do not need to commit yourself by paying an application fee and actually applying for the mortgage. Lender prequalification is an informal letter that allows you to see how much you may be able to borrow. It only offers general ballpark ranges of your buying power; it does not obligate the lender to approve your loan.

A better option is preapproval. This is a lender's actual commitment to lend you money. A preapproval letter shows what you can afford and demonstrates that you are serious about buying a home. While you can get prequalified over the phone without submitting paperwork that tells a lender your income, long-term debts and potential down payment, you can get preapproved only by submitting financial records and going through a preliminary approval process. The lender will want to see:

- pay stubs for the past few months
- proof of other income
- recent bank statements
- tax returns for the past 2 years
- information on long-term debt

The lender then runs a credit check and makes sure that everything you have submitted is accurate.

Getting preapproved for a loan tells you what your borrowing limit is and even how much you have to pay each month if you borrowed as much as you could. Once you know your upper limit, you can decide how much you want to borrow and how much you want to pay per month. This monthly figure plus your down payment will establish the upper price limit for homes you are looking at.

A preapproval does not mean that when you finally begin to look for a mortgage you are automatically approved. There may be a significant time lapse between the time you are preapproved and the time you actually find a house. People may change jobs or divorce or somehow change their financial status. In that case, the lender may do a second credit check to update your file or to see if you have changed your debt load or debt-to-income ratio. That is why most financial consultants advise potential home buyers not to make major purchases or add substantially to credit cards once they have been preapproved.

> **Tip**
>
> When you are ready to make an offer on a home, including a preapproval letter with your offer will strengthen your position. The preapproval shows that you are eligible for a mortgage.

The Mortgage Payment

A mortgage requires you to pledge your home as the lender's security for repayment of your loan. The lender agrees to hold the title to your home—or, in some states, to hold a lien on your title—until you have paid back your loan plus interest. If you do not repay your loan, the lender has the right to take possession of your home and sell it in order to satisfy the mortgage debt.

Principal and Interest

All mortgages have two features. The first feature is the mortgage principal, which is the actual amount of money you borrow. So, if you take out a $100,000 mortgage, your mortgage principal is $100,000.

The second feature is the mortgage interest, which is the money you pay for use of the money you borrow. The interest you pay on your mortgage can be deducted from your taxes, one of the benefits of homeownership.

Amortization

You will repay your mortgage gradually over time through regular monthly payments of principal and interest. The amounts of these payments are calculated to ensure that you own your home debt-free at the end of a predetermined period of time. During the first few years, most of your payments will be applied toward the interest you owe. During the final years of your loan, your payment will be applied almost exclusively to the remaining principal. This type of repayment method is called amortization.

When you sell you home, you will be required to repay any remaining principal balance due on your mortgage loan to your lender.

Factors Affecting Your Buying Power

There are four factors that may determine whether you can afford the home you want:

- the size of your down payment
- the amount of your mortgage principal
- your mortgage interest rate
- the repayment period of the mortgage

Your Down Payment

Your down payment will reduce the amount you need to borrow. Thus, the more cash you put down, the smaller the size of your loan. The smaller your loan, the smaller your mortgage payments will be each month.

Lenders often view mortgages with larger down payments as more secure because more of your own money is invested in the property. Saving for a down payment, however, is usually difficult, especially when house values are booming. That is why many lenders today require a smaller down payment than the traditional 20 percent required in the past. Now many lenders, including the Federal Housing

Administration (FHA), will offer you mortgage loans with as little as 5 percent down. Some may even accept 3 percent down.

Offering less than 20 percent down, however, often means you will be required to purchase private mortgage insurance (PMI). PMI protects the lender in case you fail to make your monthly mortgage payments. The cost of PMI will be added to your monthly mortgage payments and to your closing costs. However, despite the extra expense, remember that this insurance helps you buy your home years sooner than you otherwise would have been able.

There are some types of mortgages that do not require private mortgage insurance if you put less than 20 percent down. These include loans insured by the federal government, such as an FHA loan or Veterans Administration (VA) loan. Your state also may offer special mortgages for low- and moderate-income home buyers that use state-sponsored mortgage insurance programs.

Putting Together a Down Payment

Saving up enough for a down payment may not be feasible considering today's housing costs. However, there are other options you can explore. For FHA and some conventional mortgage programs that require only 3 percent down, you can negotiate with the seller to see if he or she will discount the selling price so that you can cover your down payment.

Some loans allow parents or close relatives to offer the home buyer a gift equal to the required down payment. Every individual can give up to $11,000 annually to another person without either donor or recipient being required to pay taxes or even notify the Internal Revenue Service (IRS). If the donor gives more than $11,000, he or she has to file a form with the IRS, but the amount over $11,000 is applied against a $1 million limit that the donor can give over a lifetime.

In a booming housing market, $11,000 does not seem like a lot of money. However, two parents can each give $11,000 to both a child and his or her spouse for a total of $44,000. The parents also can make a gift at the end of one year and then again at the beginning of the next year if they want to make a large gift within the proscribed limits.

Bear in mind, however, that some lenders put a limit on how large a gift you can use for a down payment. Many require that the home buyer contribute at least 5 percent. An exception is an FHA-insured loan, which permits the entire down payment to be a gift. In addition, lenders want to be certain that donors do not expect repayment of the gift; if the home buyer is repaying the down payment, it could interfere with paying the mortgage.

You also can use your Individual Retirement Account (IRA) or 401(k) plans to make up a down payment. You can withdraw funds from your IRA before you reach the age of 59½ without incurring a 10 percent early withdrawal penalty when you purchase a home for the first time.

The key term here is first-time buyer. The rules allow you to withdraw up to $10,000 once in a lifetime to buy a principal residence for yourself and a spouse, child, grandchild or your spouse's child or grandchild so long as the home is the residence of a first-time buyer, someone who has not owned a home within the previous 2 years. If the home buyer is married, the spouse cannot have owned a home within the past 2 years either. If both you and your spouse have IRAs, each of you can withdraw $10,000 to make up a $20,000 down payment, provided you are both first-time home buyers.

Other sources to borrow from include insurance policies, investments, credit unions or equity from another property. If you decide to borrow from these sources, keep in mind the long-range goals you and your family established. Think carefully before depleting savings and other assets for a down payment. Remember, you must be able to afford the home not only when you buy it but also throughout the term of the loan.

Letter of Credit

Some buyers may be able to use a letter of credit instead of a cash down payment. A person who obtains a letter of credit from a bank is promising to make a future payment; if that person does not make the payment, the bank that wrote the letter of credit is responsible. Some letters of credit may be secured by the person's assets. This type of down payment is a good option if you are buying a new house in a development that has not yet been built. In this case, a letter of credit allows you to sign for a house without tying up your cash while the house is being built.

Buying with No Down Payment

Although rare, there are some mortgage lenders who are willing to make loans without a down payment to qualified borrowers. Fannie Mae and Freddie Mac Foundations even offer programs loaning up to 103 percent of home purchase prices for well-qualified home buyers. Fannie Mae and Freddie Mac are investment corporations chartered by the U.S. Congress to provide low-cost funds to local lenders for home mortgages.

Naturally, there are extra costs, such as PMI, to insure the lender against loss if the lender loans more than 80 percent of the purchase price. However, if you work with a lender, you may be able to minimize these costs.

This will work only if your credit is excellent and your FICO score is high. You also will need preapproval in writing; do not settle for prequalification. You may not get the lowest interest rate, but your good credit, income and FICO score can get you a house with little or nothing down.

Qualifying for a Low or No Down Payment Loan

To be considered for a low or no down payment mortgage, you need to have:
- enough income to support the monthly mortgage payment;
- sufficient cash to cover the down payment, if any;
- a good credit report indicating your payment history and willingness to pay;
- a high FICO score;

- sufficient appraisal value showing that the house is at least equal to the purchase price; and

- a cash reserve equivalent to two monthly mortgage payments.

The Amount of Your Mortgage Principal

Mortgage lenders have established certain criteria to let first-time home buyers determine what should be their debt-to-income ratio based on how much income they have and how much can be spent on a home mortgage, housing expenses and other debt.

For conventional loans, a household should spend no more than 28 percent of its gross monthly income for monthly housing costs–mortgage principal and interest, taxes and insurance and no more than 36 percent of monthly income on other costs and debt–utilities, maintenance and credit card payments plus long-term debt, such as car or student loan payments, child support and alimony. For FHA loans, the ratio for qualifying for a mortgage is 29 percent toward housing costs and 41 percent toward expenses and debts.

This means that your monthly mortgage principal and interest payments, real estate taxes, insurance, maintenance, utilities, car loan, credit card payments and other long-term debts combined generally should not exceed 36 percent or 41 percent of your gross monthly income.

For example, if your income is $75,000 per year, as a first-time home buyer applying for an FHA loan, you can spend $21,750 of this year's income on mortgage payments (about $1,813 per month) and $30,750 (about $2,563 per month) on costs and other long-term debt. The remainder of your income goes to other spending and savings.

Mortgage lenders require you to make a 5 percent to 20 percent down payment, and you now should consider the amount you can borrow compared with the price or appraised value of the house you want to purchase. This is called the loan-to-value (LTV) ratio. Every loan has its own LTV limit.

In other words, with a 95 percent LTV loan on a home priced at $100,000, you can borrow up to $95,000–95 percent of $100,000–but must make a down payment of $5,000.

Most lenders, however, would prefer that you make a larger down payment and that they loan you money at a lower LTV. As protection against risk from a loan default when a small down payment has been made, the lender will require a PMI policy. When the equity in your new home reaches 20 percent, you may be allowed to cancel the PMI and save that money. However, canceling the PMI is often time-consuming and requires effort on your part, because lenders are reluctant to cancel the policy even when you are eligible to do so.

> **Tip**
>
> The lender is more interested in how much you want to borrow than in how much the house costs. The debt-to-income ratio figures apply to the total amount of the loan, not the total cost of the home.

The Mortgage Interest Rate

As with any loan, the lower your interest rate, the lower your monthly payments. To look at it another way, the lower your interest rate, the more buying power you will have when looking for a home. With lower rates, you can borrow more money for approximately the same monthly payment.

In addition, as a rule, the shorter the term of the loan, the lower the interest rate you may pay. Therefore, a 15-year fixed rate mortgage usually has a lower interest rate that a 30-year fixed rate mortgage.

Each type of mortgage may carry a different interest rate, and getting the best interest rate is an important part of your shopping for a mortgage. When you are ready to look for a mortgage that fits your needs, review the information about mortgages in Chapter 13.

The Term of the Mortgage

The length of your mortgage repayment period will affect your monthly mortgage payments directly. The shorter the repayment period the higher your monthly payment will be, but the total interest you pay over the life of the loan will be less. On the other hand, the longer your repayment period the lower your monthly payment will be, but the total interest you pay over the life of the loan will be more. Selecting a loan term involves finding a balance between how low you want your monthly payments to be versus how quickly you want and can afford to own your home debt-free.

Stated Income Loans

A stated income loan is a way to get a mortgage without proof of income provided that your credit is good enough. Lenders have learned over the past decade that credit scores are the best predictors of whether a borrower will pay back a loan. However, you will pay slightly higher interest rates for such loans.

Because of changing employment patterns and demographics, there is a growing number of people who do not have steady paychecks and cannot easily document their income but who are good candidates for stated income loans. This group includes small-business owners, commissioned salespeople, independent contractors and new immigrants who often pool their family's resources to buy a home.

In the past, stated income and similar loans carried high prepayment penalties or much higher rates. Today, however, penalties are less common, and rates often are not much higher than for a more standard loan.

To qualify for a stated income loan, you typically need to have FICO credit scores in the mid- to high-600 range. See Chapter 2 for more information on FICO scores. In addition, most stated income loans require that the borrower have a down payment or equity of at least 20 percent of the property's value.

Anticipating Other Costs

A move, whether across the street, across town or across the country, always means hidden costs. You are aware of closing costs and the need for homeowner insurance, but the extras may catch you by surprise. The movers take longer than estimated, and you are paying them by the hour. Your new home has no overhead lights in the bedrooms and you have no extra lamps. You forgot that your new commute to work includes a toll road.

These are all costs of moving into a new home, and as long as you have mortgage payments, interest rates and income-debt ratios on your mind, you may dismiss these additional expenses. Nevertheless, these are real needs, and you have to remember to put aside some money in a contingency fund for these extra expenses. While you are negotiating the purchase of a house, do not push yourself to the edge of your financial capability without a cushion for unexpected expenses.

Closing Costs

Closing costs should not be an unexpected surprise. Your lender should tell you what your closing costs will be and when it has to be paid. In fact, according to the Real Estate Settlement Procedures Act (RESPA) passed by the U.S. Congress in 1974, the lender must disclose all closing costs, lender servicing practices and relationships between closing service providers and other parties to the transaction.

You should receive a good faith estimate that lists all fees to be paid before closing. The lender must supply this within 3 days of your application so that you know what to expect and can compare lenders. But you should remember that a good faith estimate is just that, an estimate, not a commitment to a loan.

Closing costs vary but generally cover:

- attorney or escrow fees;
- property taxes for the remainder of taxes due during the tax period to date;
- interest paid from the closing date to 30 days before the first monthly payment;
- a loan origination fee covering the lender's administrative costs;
- deed recording fees;
- a survey fee;
- the first premium of the mortgage insurance;
- title insurance fee;
- loan discount points;
- the first payment to the escrow account for future real estate taxes and insurance;

- homeowner insurance policy, other insurance policy, such as flood or fire insurance, receipts; and
- miscellaneous fees, such as for documentation preparation.

> **Tip**
>
> Some closing costs may be waived by the closing agent before the actual closing, so shop around for closing agents who will provide the requested services at the lowest fee. Ask the agent to send you a listing of the fees he or she will charge. Some fees, however, such as the one for recoding the deed, cannot be waived.

Moving In Costs

When you are trying to determine how much you can afford, you have to evaluate the costs of living in a home. You may have calculated your down payment, your monthly mortgage costs and all the fees you must be prepared to pay when you close on a home—you have even set aside the money for the move itself. But that is not enough. You have to anticipate the expenses you will face after you move into a home.

Utilities

Consider, for example, your utilities: electricity, gas, cable and telephone. Some utility companies will charge you a deposit to establish an account in your name at your new home. After a certain length of time, the deposit may be refunded, but you have to be prepared to put down some money if you want lights, heat, water, cable and a telephone in your new home.

Take a look also at the monthly utility bills. Ask the previous owner if you can see some utility bills to get an idea of what to budget. If you are moving from a two-bedroom apartment where the heat is included in your monthly rent, will your budget be able to absorb a heating bill for a two-story home? Have you been paying a water bill? This may be an entirely new utility bill for you if you are moving from a rental into your own home.

Is your new home wired to accept cable? Will you need to install new wiring or upgrade to accommodate your appliances and electronic equipment? Does the home have central air conditioning, or will you have to rewire to accept window units?

Minor Repairs and Standard Maintenance

Most of the major repairs will have been handled by the seller before you close on the house; this is part of the negotiations when you make an offer. However, there are always some minor repairs that you will need to make, and once you have moved in, you will likely find that you want to make some changes or additions. The hall inside the back door is a perfect place to install coat hooks. New shelves in the bathroom help relieve the clutter in the linen closet. The kitchen sink needs a new washer. All of these situations can be resolved by a trip to a hardware or home improvement store, but you may be surprised at how much money that quick trip can cost. A coat of paint here, a new cabinet there, and you have spent money you had not counted on spending in your home purchase.

Everyday maintenance–furnace filters, cleaning supplies, yard tools–costs money. If you have been living in a rental unit, you may not have the necessary tools to care for a house. You may not even have a toolbox if you kept the obligatory screwdriver, pliers and hammer in a kitchen drawer. Basic tools can be an expensive investment, but you will need to have them to maintain and protect your biggest investment, your new home.

Summary

Even if you have budgeted for maintenance and repairs, you probably will find yourself making upgrades–anticipated or unanticipated–as you move in. What about those energy-efficiency improvements you decided to make when you inspected the house? Can you afford to make these upgrades before the winter heating bills arrive? That new, open great room or larger living room needs more furniture. The house has a laundry room but no washer or dryer. The backyard looks bare and muddy. Does your budget allow for new sod?

No matter how carefully you plan for closing expenses, fees and other immediate repairs, you will find yourself in danger of becoming overextended financially as you move in and try to set up your household in a new home. The temptation to buy new furniture or install a fireplace may not fit within your budget. That is why establishing and maintaining a financial discretionary fund is always a good idea before buying a home.

All of these potential expenses should be in the back of your mind. As you settle in, you will find even more costs that you had not anticipated. That is why you must establish a contingency fund early in the home buying process.

Tip
Many lenders advise that you have enough savings to live on for 6 months before even thinking about buying a home. This means not only housing expenses but also all living expenses.

What You Have Learned

- The advantages of getting prequalified or preapproved for a mortgage.
- What the mortgage principal is, the mortgage interest rate and the repayment term of a mortgage.
- What percentage of the home's cost you need to pay up front.
- The costs of closing and moving into a home.

4
. . . . . .
Preparing to Hunt
for a Home

In This Chapter

- Learn how to find a mortgage lender.
- Discover special home buying programs for first-time buyers.
- Find a real estate agent and real estate attorney.
- Determine what you need to do before you buy a home.

You have taken the preliminary steps toward getting ready to buy a home. You have analyzed your current income and budget and have made updates or corrections as needed. You have tried to anticipate the expenses of moving into and living in a new home. You have used these calculations to narrow your choices about what kind of home you can afford comfortably. You have learned the rudimentary facts about mortgages, interest rates and down payments, and you have looked into mortgage preapproval.

Before you start hunting for a home, however, you still have some research to do and decisions to make. You need to think about who is going to help you. Have you investigated lending institutions and their programs? Have you selected a real estate or property agent, or are you planning to work without an agent? Do you need an attorney?

These are your resource people, and you should decide if and how you want to use them. Each brings a different perspective to the process of buying a home, and you need to understand what each has to offer you. While these resources are discussed in greater detail in later chapters, take some time to explore your general options at this point in the process so that you will be prepared to make decisions later.

Mortgage Lenders

A good mortgage lender does more than just lend you money to buy a home. A good lender provides financial guidance and offers suggestions to help you make the most appropriate decisions for your individual circumstances.

For example, early in your home buying endeavor, you will want to contact a lender to obtain prequalification or preferably preapproval for a mortgage loan. Lender prequalification allows you to see how much the lender may let you borrow. However, preapproval is a statement from the lender stating how much the bank will let you borrow and what your borrowing limit is based on you financial situation. Being preapproved is better than being prequalified, if you are seriously considering buying a home. See Chapter 3 for more information about prequalification and preapproval.

The preapproval step may be your first encounter with a lender, so it is important to shop for lenders early in the home buying process.

Finding a Lender

You can finance a home with a loan from a bank, a savings and loan, a credit union, a private mortgage company or various state government lenders. Shopping for a loan is like shopping for any other important purchase: you can save money if you take the time to look for the best prices. Different lenders offer different interest rates and loan fees, which can make a big difference in how much home you can afford. Talk with several lenders before you choose one.

Look for a lender with financial stability and a reputation for customer service. Be sure to select a company that makes you feel comfortable and that is ready to offer helpful advice. A lender that has the authority to approve and process your loan locally is preferable, since it will be easier for you to monitor the status of your application and ask questions. In addition, it is beneficial if the lender knows home values and conditions in the local market.

Ask family, friends and co-workers who have bought a home recently if they liked their lender. Real estate agents are also good resources because they work with lenders on a regular basis. They are especially discriminating because their livelihoods depend on reputable lenders. You also can look in the local newspaper's real estate section; most newspapers list interest rates being offered by local lenders.

Once you have compiled a list of potential lenders, you are ready to compare them. First, devise a checklist for each institution. Include the company's name, contact information, type of mortgage, minimum down payment required, interest rates and points, closing costs and loan processing time.

You can speak with companies either by phone or in person. However, be certain to talk with every lender on the list on the same day, since interest rates can fluctuate daily. Although your primary purpose in talking with lenders is to compare them, you also are trying to find a lender with whom you feel comfortable working with and trust.

In addition to doing your own research, ask your real estate agent if he or she has access to a database of lender and mortgage options. Even though your agent may be affiliated with a particular lending institution, he or she also may be able to suggest a variety of different lender options to you.

Good Faith Estimate

Some borrowers use a good faith estimate to compare lenders. A good faith estimate lists all fees paid before closing, all closing costs and any escrow costs you will encounter when purchasing a home. By law, the lender must supply it within 3 days of your application so that you can make accurate judgments when shopping for a loan. It is a good idea to ask for good faith estimates from at least three lenders for comparison purposes. See Chapter 3 for more information about the closing costs fees and a good faith estimate.

Researching Special Home Buying Programs

There are many home buying programs available, some of which you may qualify for depending on your situation. The Department of Housing and Urban Development (HUD) offers some special home buying programs, and many local governments offer home buying programs to help low-income buyers. Visit **www.hud.gov** and contact your local, county or state offices of housing and community development for more information. If you cannot find what you are looking for, get in touch with the office of your mayor or county commissioner.

First-Time Buyer Programs

If you are a first-time buyer, you may be eligible for special programs that will help you buy a home. A neighborhood bank in Chicago, for example, has a program called HOME–Home Ownership Made Easy–that reaches out to first-time buyers in the area. "We think purchasing a home has always been an American dream, but lately it seems more like a pipe dream," says Laurene Rose Huffman, commercial real estate officer of Devon Bank. "We encourage first-time buyers by offering a plan that finances 97 percent of the purchase price or the appraised price, whichever is lower, with no points. That means the buyer has to save for only a 3 percent down payment. Plus, we try to make it fast and affordable."

This program applies to all residential property, including single family homes, condominiums, townhouses and two- to four-unit buildings; it is available in federally designated low- to moderate-income census tracts within the bank's service area. Huffman points out, however, that there is one mandatory stipulation for the applicants: "They must attend a class to learn what it means to buy and own a home. It is a Saturday class, lasting a few hours, and they learn about the responsibilities–including financial–of owning a home."

Your community also may offer opportunities for first-time buyers. For example, many urban communities that are encouraging housing development require a set-aside policy that obligates developers to sell a certain percentage of each new development below market rate in order to give first-time buyers an opportunity to own a home. These communities deem it essential that there be moderately priced homes so that the neighborhoods do not force out middle- and lower-income families. Contact your local ward or district representative to ask how to apply for these discounted properties.

When you begin your search for mortgage lenders, real estate agents or attorneys, ask your real estate agent about special programs for first-time buyers. They have more information than you do and are eager to help you buy your first home.

The Unscoreables

Some first-time buyers face a tough obstacle because they are what lenders call unscoreables; they lack a credit history because they do not use enough credit to develop a credit file. Many are young adults, minorities, immigrants or people who live by a cash-and-carry system and avoid conventional banking. Nevertheless, they earn a good income, pay their bills on time and would be considered good risks under the traditional credit system.

Because the U.S. Congress estimates that 35 to 50 million people in the United States may not have a full credit reporting history, a House of Representatives Financial Services subcommittee has looked into nontraditional scoring and evaluation systems that would enable first-time buyers to obtain loans without paying higher fees and interest rates. Massachusetts, for example, has begun to use a nontraditional credit scoring system called Anthem that analyzes utility bill payment data as a means of evaluating creditworthiness. Fair Isaac Corporation, the developer of the FICO score widely used to rate consumer credit as mentioned in Chapter 2, also is marketing a nontraditional expansion score. This system accesses private databases for information on payday loans, rental history and other financial transactions.

Another nontraditional scoring system is PRBC, a private national credit bureau; it uses a bill payment scorecard to rate consumers' performance based on rent, child support, student loan and utilities payments. See Chapter 2 for more information about this system.

All of these systems are available to mortgage lenders who want to offer home loans to creditworthy consumers whose low scores are the result of their invisibility to national credit bureaus.

Islamic Buyer Programs

Some buyers' religious beliefs prohibit certain features inherent in conventional banking transactions. Observers of Islam, for example, are prohibited from obtaining interest-based loans or mortgages, and therefore, many are unable to satisfy their dreams of owning their own homes. To remedy this, some banks have created programs specifically for Islamic customers. Chicago's Devon Bank offers non-interest-based financing plans that conform to the standards of the Shariah Supervisory Board of America as well as to the appropriate U.S. government regulations. There are two options available:

- **Murabaha**—A Murabaha transaction involves a purchase and deferred payment resale. The bank acquires and then resells the property to the customer for a fixed price, which is the purchase price that the bank pays plus a profit. The customer then pays this total price to the bank in an initial down payment and in fixed installments over an agreed-upon period of time at no interest.

- **Ijara**—An Ijara transaction is a type of rent to own program. The bank buys the property, and the customer then makes payments over time to purchase the property. While the customer is purchasing the property, he or she also is leasing it from the bank. The bank may adjust the rent at preset intervals, just like a traditional lease, based on an objectively measurable index. The bank transfers the ownership to the customer when the customer has paid the full purchase price. The customer reimburses the bank for all direct costs, such as appraisal and filing fees. There are no points charged in either transaction.

Both of these financing plans are compliant with both U.S. and Islamic legal requirements and are designed to be comparable to conventional plans so that customers can make comparisons.

Real Estate Agents

During this planning stage, you should think about whether or not you want to use a real estate agent. While you do not necessarily need an agent to buy a home, using one is an excellent idea.

All of the details involved in home buying can be overwhelming, particularly the legal and financial ones. A good real estate agent can guide you through the process and make the experience easier. A real estate agent will be well-informed about the neighborhood you are considering—the quality of the schools, the number of children, safety, traffic, parking, etc. The agent can help you determine the price range you can afford and search the ads and multiple listing services for homes that fit your needs.

Real estate agents have immediate access to homes going on the market, so they can save you time. When you are ready to make an offer, the real estate agent can help you structure the deal so that you save money. He or she will guide you through the intricacies of all the mortgage options, walk you through the paperwork and answer last-minute questions at the closing.

As the buyer, you do not have to pay the real estate agent; the home seller pays the agent. Many buyers hesitate to use an agent because they have the misconception that they will bear the expense.

Finding an Agent

There are many ways to choose an agent. Start by asking for recommendations from family and friends. Talk to an agent at a Sunday open house. Compile a list of possibilities and talk to each one after checking their references. Look for an agent who:

- listens to you and shows an interest in finding the type of home best suited to you and your needs;
- is familiar with the area you are considering and can point out a broad range of prices within that area;
- has a network of resources available;
- answers your questions completely and clearly; be certain that the agent is willing to clarify and redefine terms you do not understand; and
- is comfortable for you to work with.

For more information about selecting and working with a real estate agent, refer to Chapter 7.

Real Estate Attorneys

Whether or not you need a lawyer when buying a home depends on the state in which you live and the circumstances under which you are buying a home.

Most states do not require a lawyer when buying a home but do require the involvement of a qualified real estate professional, such as an escrow agent or a title company. However, some states require a lawyer to assist with some aspects of the sale, such as closing. Specifically, nine states—Alabama, Connecticut, Delaware, Georgia, Massachusetts, New York, South Carolina, Vermont and West Virginia—mandate that closing a mortgage is the practice of law and must be handled by an attorney to protect the consumer.

Even if you are not required to hire one, a lawyer can represent you in negotiating the contract or clarifying aspects of the deal. Hiring a lawyer to review the real estate sales contract, particularly if anything is even slightly out of the ordinary, also may be a wise decision. In addition, the lawyer will be familiar with the situation in the event that there is a dispute.

In certain circumstances, using an attorney can be very helpful. For example, people who buy condominiums or townhouses should read and understand the conditions, covenants and restrictions (CC&Rs) that pertain to their ownership interest. Reading a CC&R can be daunting, and turning to an attorney to explain the important elements of the document is the safest way to go. You do not want to discover later that your ownership rights are restricted in an unacceptable way. Also, many condominium associations are involved in pending litigation. You will want an attorney's opinion of the probable outcome of the litigation before you buy into an association that may have problems.

In general, having an attorney to call upon can be a prudent move. It is always best to err on the side of gathering too much information rather than not enough. You may want to ask an attorney to help prepare an offer, review the offer and/or counteroffer and represent you at the closing. Remember, however, that attorneys usually charge by the hour, so ask in advance how much you can expect to pay for a consultation.

Tip
If you prepare an offer using a standardized contract, add a contingency rider that requires the offer contract to be subject to review and approval by your attorney within 5 days of the seller's acceptance. Be sure the contingency clause is written in such a way that an unfavorable review by the attorney allows you to revoke the purchase offer. This contingency rider should be in addition to, not instead of, the home inspection contingency clause, which provides you a way out of the contract if the inspection reveals real problems.

Finding an Attorney

If you decide to use an attorney, be sure that you find someone who specializes in real estate. Again, friends and family are often good sources for names of real estate attorneys, but you also can ask your general attorney or real estate agent for a recommendation.

> **Tip**
>
> Visit **www.abanet.org/legalservices/findlegalhelp/home.cfm** for the American Bar Association Lawyer Referral Services locator.

Things to Do before Buying a Home

As you move from making the initial decision to buy to actually looking for a home, there are steps you can take to make the process easier, and there are missteps you should avoid to prevent obstacles along the way.

What to Do

- Develop a realistic budget.
- Save for a down payment and closing costs.
- Set up a contingency fund for unexpected expenses.
- Check your credit score and correct any errors.
- Pay down your credit cards but do not deplete your savings.
- Decide how much you are willing to pay for a home.
- Shop for a mortgage lender.
- Learn basic mortgage terminology.
- Compare interest rates and different types of mortgages.
- Determine if you qualify for special mortgage or down payment assistance.
- Get preapproved for a loan.
- Shop for a real estate agent.
- Work with the real estate agent to develop basic criteria for houses—price, size, features, neighborhoods, location, schools and safety.
- Shop for an attorney.
- Develop a strategy for house hunting.
- Plan the timing of your move—end of rental lease, end of school year, season.

What Not to Do

- Do not change jobs suddenly—lenders look at job stability.
- Do not make any major purchases.

- Do not move money around or manipulate funds—lenders require 2 to 3 months of bank statements and documentation of withdrawals and deposits on all financial accounts; they want to know the sources of down payment money and closing costs.
- Do not accept the first mortgage offered; shop and compare.
- Do not look at houses above your price range.
- Do not overlook the inspection process.
- Above all, do not rush into buying a home or buy the first home you visit; this is an enormous investment and must be undertaken carefully.

Summary

Once you have started looking for a home, it is important that you find a lneder, a real estate agent and a real estate attorney to help you throughout the home buying process. They will help you avoid costly mistakes and ensure that your first home buying experience is a success.

What You Have Learned

- When searching for a lender compare the loans, interest rates and fees.
- There are many special home buying programs for first-time buyers.
- How to find a real estate agent and attorney to help you during the home buying process.

Free Forms and Checklists

Visit **Socrates.com** and register to receive a variety of useful FREE forms, letters and checklists. See page iv for details on how to register (you will need the seven-digit registration code provided on the enclosed CD).

5

· · · · · ·

Developing House
Hunting Strategies

In This Chapter

- Learn about the buyers' and sellers' markets.
- Discover what resources you can use to find homes that are for sale before consulting an agent.
- Learn how to purchase a FSBO home.
- Find ways to avoid first-time buyer frustrations to make the home buying process a success.

Now that you have lined up your resource people and completed your initial planning phase, it is time to map out your house hunting strategies. It makes no sense to spend time and effort looking at homes without a strategic plan in place for beginning your search.

Do you understand the difference between a sellers' and a buyers' market? Do you know how to read and interpret the real estate ads? Should you start your search with the ads? Is the Internet a good resource? Have you considered a for sale by owner (FSBO) home? Exactly how do you plan to start your search? This overview will provide you with the necessary information to map out your house hunting strategies.

Understanding Sellers' and Buyers' Markets

No matter when you decide to buy a home, the market will be in some state of flux. Sometimes it is a sellers' market, which is advantageous to the owner trying to sell, and sometimes it is a buyers' market, which means the buyer has a better chance to negotiate a good deal.

The fluctuation of the market depends on economic factors, such as current interest rates, local employment and the national economy. Interest rates, in particular, affect what kind of market you may encounter: high rates can flatten demand because few buyers can afford to buy when rates are high. Conversely, low rates stimulate sales because most buyers find the lower cost of borrowing money more affordable.

When there is a relative balance of buyers and sellers in the market, home sales prices will be driven by economic factors. When there are few homes on the market to sell and many buyers who want to buy, it is a sellers' market: the seller can set a high price, and the buyer may have to act quickly to get the home. In this type of market, buyers should get prequalified and should not expect to submit a contract with a lot of contingencies.

In a sellers' market, houses are not on the market for long. In fact, sales are generally so good that many houses may sell before they are even listed. One woman, for example, prepared to list her home after the death of her husband. By the time she had finished the paperwork with the real estate agency, an agency employee had made an acceptable offer for the house. On the other hand, in a sellers' market, real estate agencies may not even become involved because many sellers will sell their homes themselves.

When there are many homes on the market and only a few buyers who can afford to buy, it is a buyers' market: the buyer has a large selection of homes to view, and sellers may be forced to lower their prices to make a sale.

The market will determine how much you will pay for a home. If you can wait for a buyers' market, you may get the home you want at a good price. However, if you must buy during a sellers' market, it likely will take more time to find an affordable home that you like.

Other Timing Considerations

As a rule, home sales increase when the economy is good and a high percentage of people are employed. Within this framework, the real estate market goes through certain cycles. Many buyers start looking, and many sellers put their houses on the market in the spring because the school year is about to end and job changes often occur. In fact, approximately 40 percent of home sales occur in the late spring and early summer.

In the fall and winter, home prices tend to be lower in many parts of the country because of uncertain weather and travel conditions as well as the time and financial commitments of the holidays. The worst selling week of the year is typically the week between December 25th and January 1st. In warm weather areas, however, the market is generally more active during the fall and winter when temperatures are lower and more people are visiting these areas while on vacation.

You may want to do your house hunting in the off-season. You might find a home at a lower price than if you bought it in the spring when everyone else is looking to buy. But remember, while there will be fewer shoppers to compete against, there also will be fewer homes on the market. Late summer may be the ideal time for a buyer to shop. The peak months of April, May and June are over, and bargains may appear while competition for homes may diminish. In addition, families who are timing their moves based on the school year may be eager to sell in August.

Another timing issue to consider is whether you will have more funds to buy a home during a certain time of year. In the spring, you may receive a large refund from your income taxes that can be used for a down payment. During the holidays, you may incur substantial expenses and have less money to spend on a house.

However, buying early in the year will allow you to get a full 12 months of interest payment deductions to offset your taxable income.

Buying a New Home in a New Development

Seasonal factors have little impact when you are considering a new home in a new development. Timing remains important but for different reasons.

Purchasing a new home during the preconstruction period has advantages:

- Preconstruction sales allow you to take advantage of the lowest prices. Builders will increase prices over time and may raise prices numerous times between the opening and closing of a development.

- The home will have built-in appreciation. For example, if the price of a certain home design goes up $10,000 from the time the builder sells the first one to the time the last one is sold, the market value of the first home presumably would increase by $10,000 from the raise in price alone.

- You may be in a position to select from the best home sites during the preconstruction phase. However, this is not always guaranteed, and at this stage, you may not know what ultimately will be the best choice.

However, buying a new home after the preconstruction stage also has advantages:

- You may be able to make a more informed decision about the site once all phases of the development are open and you can see exactly how the homes are situated.

- You can tour model homes and select the design that meets your needs rather than buy a home by looking at blueprints.

- You will move into a more established neighborhood with sidewalks, streetlights, parks and other facilities.

- You will miss the inconvenience of construction noise, dirt and traffic. The earlier you buy, the longer you have to tolerate it.

- During the final, or closeout, period of the development, the builder may offer substantial price savings to sell the remaining homes. To hasten the completion of the development, many builders also save the best sites for this sales push.

When buying in a new development, your timing is based entirely on your own preferences and needs. There are advantages and disadvantages to purchasing before, during and after the building stage. You have to decide how your situation coincides with the development's timetable.

Researching Sources

Other than driving around neighborhood after neighborhood in search of For Sale signs, how can you find out what is for sale and where? If you have decided to work with a real estate agent, he or she can help you find many homes that match your criteria using the agency's database. If, however, you want to do some background research on your own before consulting an agent, there are some steps you can take.

Real Estate Ads

Start reading the real estate section of your local newspaper. Many newspapers devote a full section of the Saturday or Sunday edition to the real estate market. In larger cities, the real estate sections also include information about suburbs and other outlying regions. There are articles about the local market, buying and selling tips and trends in housing as well as display and classified real estate ads.

Display ads are often very informative. For example, an ad for a new subdivision or a new condo building may include room layouts and photos of several different models. The ad may list notable amenities within each model—kitchen appliances or wood floors, for instance—and may point out the desirable ambience of the neighborhood. Reading the display ads for several weeks should give you an overall picture of the various neighborhoods and/or homes that may meet your needs. Refer to a local map if you are unfamiliar with the area.

Reading the classified ads also can be useful. In the weekly newspapers, they often are listed by real estate agency. If you are still in the beginning stages of selecting a real estate agent, these ads may help steer you. They usually include a phone number or Web site address so that you can contact the agency for additional information. If you are not quite ready to talk with an agent, you can go to the Web site to explore listings and other information. Some sites even include virtual tours of homes. See Chapter 6 for more information on how to use the Internet in your search for a home. However, reading the newspaper may provide additional information about the neighborhoods where you are looking to buy a home.

You can also get a feel for a neighborhood by driving around it. Attempting to view a neighborhood in a detached way can be enlightening. Are there many For Sale signs? If so, could this be a signal that the neighborhood is changing? Does the name of one real estate agency seem to predominate on the signs throughout the area? Could this affect how you are represented if you should choose to use this agency in your own search? Are there many FSBO signs? Does their number indicate a strong sellers' market in the neighborhood?

Stop at local stores to look for fliers and other information posted by home sellers and real estate agencies. Many grocery stores, for example, maintain bulletin board space near their entrances or exits where sellers can post brochures or fliers. You also may want to drop in at the local community center, chamber of commerce or other community agency for brochures containing information about the region.

While you are visiting, do not neglect to talk to people who live in the area. Strike up a conversation with shoppers in the stores or ask the employees at the community centers about their neighborhood. Most people are willing either to brag about their community or complain about its shortcomings.

Simply exploring a neighborhood can help you decide if you want to look at the area as a serious possibility. You also can gather contact information from fliers, brochures and signs so that you can make some follow-up phone calls before beginning to search in earnest.

> **Tip**
>
> Visit **www.bargain.com** for a database of foreclosures, HUD and Department of Vetrans Affiars (VA) homes, and FSBO homes.

Dealing with a FSBO Transaction

A FSBO transaction is different in many ways from buying a home with the help of a real estate agent. The biggest difference is that the buyer and seller do not have to factor in the 6 percent real estate agent sales commission when making a deal.

This can be an advantage for you, the buyer, because the seller can offer a more attractive price if he or she is not paying a sales commission. While the general rule is that seller pays the commission, in reality the buyer often ends up paying more for the home in order to cover the cost.

Another way a FSBO deal differs is how the paperwork associated with the transaction is drafted and processed. There is no agent to write up the purchase agreement, handle disclosures or arrange escrow accounts. Fortunately, however, most FSBO sellers arrange for a fee-for-service consultant or attorney to take care of these matters.

A buyer often wants to arrange for his or her own consultants to help negotiate the final sale too. For example, most buyers find that paying a fee to an attorney, an appraiser and an inspector is cheaper than the sales commission and provides them with the information they need to make an informed decision about a property.

In the past, buyers were hampered in their attempts to buy homes directly from sellers by the limited availability of information. There was a time when buyers could not get good information about available properties in an area, asking prices and comparative differences in neighborhoods without the help of an agent. This is no longer the case. The Internet is a vast source of information for both sellers advertising their property and buyers looking for the right home. Savvy buyers are using these information resources as well as the professional services of attorneys, appraisers and inspectors to guide them through this process. See Chapter 6 for more information about using the Internet.

This is not to say that all buyers are eager to work directly with a seller. Some buyers are unsure about the process. They may lack confidence in their ability to negotiate an offer or manage the necessary paperwork that goes with every sale. These buyers prefer to use a real estate agent to guide them through the process so that all the financial, legal and regulatory issues have been addressed.

Working with a FSBO Seller

If you decide that dealing with a FSBO seller directly is best for you, there are some steps you can take to ensure that the process moves forward smoothly:

- **Get prequalified**—You can go to a lender or even explore ways to do this on the Internet. A prequalification letter shows the owner that you have the wherewithal to buy the home. After all, you are asking the seller to turn over his or her biggest asset to an unknown person. A prequalification letter also allows you to conduct business without having to disclose any personal financial information to the owner.

- **Learn about the market values in the area in which the home is located**—If you are working solely with the owner, you need to know if he or she is asking too much or is offering a bargain. The only way to decide this is to find out what comparable homes in the area are selling for. The classified ads or the Web sites of other sellers or real estate agencies can give you a sense of the neighborhood market.

- **Decide if you really want to pursue the transaction**—There is no reason to waste your or the owner's time if the house is not what you need. If the owner has advertised on the Internet, visit the Web site and look at the description. A seller who is serious about selling will include photos and other information about the neighborhood on the site. You also can use the Internet to investigate schools and other neighborhood amenities. Drive by and study the home and its neighborhood. If the price is within your range, is comparably priced to other homes in the area and both the home and neighborhood look promising, call the owner for an appointment.

- **Set up a time to tour the home**—When you call, provide some information about yourself, including your name and phone number, as a courtesy to show that you are really interested. During the inspection, look at everything carefully. Do not allow the owner to make you feel rushed. You may want to come back two or three times. Each time you will learn more about the home and, equally important, about the owner. Establishing a rapport with the owner is desirable; before you make an offer, you will want answers to important questions about the home, and a cordial relationship with the owner will make that easier.

- **Finally, make an offer**—Negotiate the price and terms and determine how the paperwork will be handled. You may suggest that your attorney take care of these details, or the owner may have someone in place to manage the transaction.

Buying a home directly from the owner is not that difficult if you have done your homework and if you feel comfortable negotiating. You also can save a substantial amount of money.

> **Tip**
>
> One way to find out about market value and appreciation in an area is to check out the schools. Visit **www.houseappreciation.com**, which rates the top 32 percent of U.S. communities based on school quality and home appreciation. The ratings are derived from student performance on high school standardized tests since 1986.

Questions to Ask a FSBO Seller

One of the advantages of buying a home directly from the owner is the opportunity to ask the owner both general and specific questions about the property. In some ways, an informal chat with the owner can be as informative as a professional inspection. An owner who is eager to sell will answer your questions openly and honestly and will be willing to resolve any issues that may impede your closing a deal.

To elicit the most helpful answers, ask open-ended questions. Do not ask questions that can be answered with a yes or no; you will not learn what you need to know. Start with general questions and proceed to more specific ones:

- **Why are you selling this home?** The owner's reason may be obvious, but if not, you need to know his or her motivation for selling the home. This will help you devise negotiation strategies if you decide to make an offer later.

- **How much did you pay for the home?** It is also wise to ask if there is a mortgage balance, a second mortgage, a mechanic's lien or a home equity loan against the property. Answers to these questions give an indication of the play you have in negotiating a final price. For example, if the owner needs to meet outstanding loan or lien obligations or if he or she recently bought the home for only a few thousand dollars more than the current asking price, you probably will not be able to negotiate. If, however, the owner originally paid a price considerably lower than the current market value, he or she may be willing to negotiate price and terms.

- **What problems does this home have?** In general, an owner does not have to reveal problems that have been corrected. Nevertheless, it is important that you as the buyer be aware of any past problems.

Tip
FSBO sellers may disclose any known defect in writing yet refuse to pay for repairs because they are selling the house as is. This is legal when the defects are listed and the house is clearly being sold as is.

Buying a FSBO Condominium

Buying a condominium or condo directly from the owner means following the same procedure as you do when buying a home from the owner. However, there are a few additional factors you have to take into consideration.

Buying a condo means becoming part of the condo's homeowners association (HOA). Therefore, checking out the HOA is crucial. You should request and receive copies of the bylaws and the CC&Rs that govern the association. You also should ask for financial statements. Study all documents carefully. This is the time to talk to the seller about his or her impression of the HOA and the board. Ask to talk with board members to find out if there are any pending lawsuits that could affect your ability to get financing or might increase your assessments in the future.

Be alert for the following warning flags:

- lawsuits

- unusually strict rules about making changes to the condo unit

- building or repair problems, such as a cracked foundation, leaking roof or warped window frames, that could result in a big assessment later

- complaints about neighbors
- high fees because of poor financial management or lack of reserve funds

For additional information, go to the Resource section in Appendix A to find the FSBO Web sites.

Avoiding First-Time Buyer Frustrations

No matter how much information you acquire or how well you plan your house hunting strategies, you are going to encounter frustrations.

Some of the frustrations can be avoided with careful planning; others cannot. For example, you start out with the home of your dreams firmly in mind only to find that your financial condition simply cannot support it. This can be both frustrating and disappointing. That is why experienced buyers highly recommend obtaining a prequalification letter early in the search. If you know how much financing you can get, you can tailor your search to include those homes within your purchasing range.

Even when buyers take a more realistic approach to their selection, the remaining steps in the home buying process can still be an emotional roller coaster ride. Their spirits plummet when they actually see what they can afford. They become excited when they find a home that meets all of their needs and expectations. Negotiating the deal, however, is tedious and time-consuming; the buyers' enthusiasm wanes until the seller accepts the bid and again when the inspection reports arrive. Many buyers do not revive until after the closing when they finally walk into their own home for the first time and the ups and downs of the previous months are forgotten.

This experience is quite common for first-time buyers, even those who are well-informed, and today many first-time buyers are knowledgeable consumers. They look for free resources and are accustomed to using the Internet to gather information. They are interested in getting good value for their money but do not view the lowest interest rate as the only criterion for value. Even with all their research, they still can experience the same frustrations as less informed buyers.

Following are some preplanning steps that can smooth out the home buying process:

- Find a good real estate agent and ask questions.
- Set a ceiling on how much you are willing to pay. This can help prevent an impulse offer on a house.
- Look for a home within your price range that has a large feel to it. The actual square footage may not be much, but a house with high ceilings or a two-story entrance feels big. So does a home with a lot of natural light.
- Look for homes that have been on the market for a long time. In many cases, the home is still on the market because it was overpriced in the beginning. Eventually, the seller may be forced to lower the price, and you want to be ready to make a deal on the spot.

- Consider homes that need cosmetic work. This does not mean looking for a fixer-upper or a handyman's special that has structural problems. Rather, look at homes that have been neglected or poorly decorated. You may be able to save money on the purchase price and cover the cost of most or all of the necessary improvements.

- Do not buy a home on the rebound. If you lose a house you really like to another bidder, do not rush into a new deal without thinking it through.

- Look at enough properties to make a sensible comparison. Do not buy the first place you see, no matter how much you love it. Look at a minimum of six to 10 homes before making an offer.

- Be sure you understand local property values. This is important now and later when you resell.

- Always arrange an inspection of the property. Some buyers are afraid owners will back out of a deal if the home is inspected. In most cases, buyers are entitled to arrange a home inspection after their offer is signed by the seller. Do not eliminate this step. An inspection may reveal a potential problem that the seller is unaware of and thus did not include on the disclosure form.

- Try to reevaluate any negatives as positives, especially if you are buying directly from the owner. The owner may be too close to the home to see it from a buyer's perspective. For instance, a FSBO seller may be so proprietary about a feature of the home that he or she is unwilling to acknowledge that it could be changed or eliminated. What is a negative to the owner may be a positive to you.

- Protect yourself by making sure all contracts are properly worded and contain the necessary contingency clauses. If you are unsure about this part of the process, consider retaining an attorney to review the paperwork. All the other parties to the agreement may feel an attorney is unnecessary, but you may want to have at least one adviser who does not have a vested interest in seeing the deal close.

- Finally, do not ignore your own instincts about a transaction. If all conditions are acceptable but your intuition says this is a mistake, stop and analyze the situation. A home is too large an investment to ignore this feeling.

Summary

It is important to gather as much information as you can before beginning your search. Having this information will help you develop a house hunting strategy that will prepare you for the obstacles you may encounter during the searching process. Buying a home is a huge commitment that takes a substantial amount of time and may seem financially overwhelming, but if you have planned well, the outcome can be very satisfying and well worth the effort.

What You Have Learned

- The differences between a sellers' and buyers' market.
- How to research and find what homes are for sale without an agent.

Section Two

·····

Starting the Search

6

· · · · · ·

Using the Internet

In This Chapter

- Determine which home buying Web sites you should visit.
- Learn how to shop and compare loans using the Internet.
- Use tools and calculators to get estimates and evaluate your financial status.
- Learn how to shop for homes using the Internet.

Buying a home can seem a long, tedious undertaking. Setting up a budget, checking your credit rating, getting prequalified, calculating possible mortgage payments and finally looking for a home are daunting tasks. Driving through neighborhood after neighborhood and viewing home after home can be exhausting. However, there is a faster, easier way to do this.

Surfing the Internet for a few hours can eliminate a great deal of the legwork. By using the Internet, you can:

- become preapproved and prequalified;
- use online calculators to figure mortgage payments;
- find potential lenders;
- learn about your target location;
- check out target neighborhoods;
- investigate schools;
- evaluate homes and properties;
- take virtual tours of homes;
- research special government programs;
- download helpful forms, such as budget sheets or home buying checklists— visit **Socrates.com** for useful forms; and
- search for real estate agents.

Using the Internet is especially convenient when planning a long-distance move. You will be able to research the area to which you are moving before actually traveling there. You can learn about the housing market, schools, neighborhood amenities and other features of the area from the comfort of your computer chair.

You can find a moving company and save on airline tickets, accommodations and other moving needs.

Starting to Surf

Many people turn first to search engines when they start to explore a topic on the Internet. While this is a good way to begin, you may find it more productive to start with government Web sites. Not only are they comprehensive, but they also contain terms that you can use on search engines. In addition, the information on most government Web sites is available in Spanish as well as English.

Tip
Web research is perfect for busy people. You can surf the Internet at all hours of the day or night without conforming to a workday schedule or expending any energy on legwork.

HUD Web Site

The first Web site you should visit is the one maintained by HUD (**www.hud.gov**). This agency has an online guide to buying a HUD home, including listings, but it also provides a wealth of other general information about buying a home. There are articles for consumers about buying, selling, owning and improving homes as well as information about communities. You can find out how to understand and repair your credit report, how to buy a home and how to locate a housing counselor. You can read about specialized housing, such as Section 8 or home foreclosures. There is also a section outlining programs and grants administered by HUD.

In addition, the site has links for lenders, brokers, bankers, housing agencies, appraisers and others associated with the mortgage industry. The information within these sections can provide you with background knowledge about the housing industry's guidelines and regulations.

The HUD site conveniently directs you to the state of your choice and allows you to pursue those housing subjects that are under the jurisdiction or regulation of the individual states where you are interested in buying a home. This gives you an overall picture of the federal, state and local governments involvement in housing matters.

Homes for Sale

The HUD site contains a section entitled "Homes for Sale." Within this section you can visit single family homes for sale from various government agencies, including HUD, the Federal Deposit Insurance Corporation (FDIC), the IRS and the Department of Agriculture Rural Development. This part of the Web site directs you to the state in which you are interested in purchasing a home. From there, you can go to the site of the state agency involved or to outside sites to find agents to help you find a home.

The HUD site also includes a page entitled "FAQs about Buying HUD Homes" (**www.hud.gov/offices/hsg/sfh/reo/reobuyfaq.cfm**), which provides a brief overview about HUD homes. Basically, when someone with a HUD-insured mortgage cannot meet the payments, the lender forecloses on the home; HUD pays the lender what is owed and takes ownership of the home. HUD then puts the home on the market and sells it at market value as quickly as possible. However, this page also explains many caveats about HUD homes that you need to know—the fact that HUD homes are sold as is without warranty, for example.

Tip
Be wary about Web sites that charge a fee for listings of HUD homes. These listings are available for free on the Web sites of contractors that HUD has hired to sell foreclosed properties.

Webcasts

HUD offers live webcasts and previously aired segments of its "Homeownership for All" program (**www.hud.gov/webcasts/archives/homeforall.cfm**). The series provides easy-to-understand advice about the homeownership process. You can select all five of the programs or just the ones that fit your needs:

- "ABC's of Homebuying" (18 minutes)
- "Elevate Your Credit" (13 minutes)
- "Where to Find the Homeownership Money You Need" (10 minutes)
- "Ten Homeownership Facts That Will Save You Thousands" (12 minutes)
- "Easy to Understand Mortgage Programs" (14 minutes)

During a live webcast, you can call and talk with the panelists who are discussing the topic.

HUD's webcast resource allows you to visit the archives (**www.hud.gov/webcasts/archives/index.cfm**) if you have missed a live program or want to review a previously aired show. Webcasts are generally archived within 24 hours after a show ends. In addition to "Homeownership for All," you may want to view "Your Home—Yours to Keep," which was archived in June of 2005.

To take advantage of webcasts, you need a computer capable of playing sound, a connection to the Internet that is at least 56Kbps and a video player that you can download for free. Links to each webcast appear on the HUD Web site (**www.hud.gov/webcasts/index.cfm**) shortly before the program airs. The program will be stored in the archives within 24 hours of airing. If you need technical assistance with a webcast, call HUD at 202.708.6067.

Other Government Web Sites

The U.S. government maintains numerous Web sites that provide valuable information to home buyers, first-time or otherwise.

FirstGov

FirstGov (**www.firstgov.gov**) is the U.S. government's official Web portal where citizens can get easy-to-understand information and services. FirstGov pulls together more than 26 million state and local government pages. In addition, FirstGov administers the Web page **www.consumer.gov**, one of the primary federal government resources for consumers.

Two subsections of this site are particularly helpful to home buyers. One (**www.firstgov.gov/citizen/topics/family/homeowners.shtml**) offers articles on home buying and finance, including such topics as coverage of home loans, financing, home and community information by state, homeowners' insurance and fair housing regulations. The other (**www.firstgov.gov/shopping/ realestate/mortgages/mortgages.shtml**) has articles about federal mortgage programs that may help you buy a home. Titles include "Looking for the Best Mortgage," "Mortgage Calculator," "Rural Americans Housing Assistance" and "Federal Housing Administration (FHA) Loan Guarantees."

FDIC

The FDIC (**www.fdic.gov**) is an independent agency created by the U.S. Congress in 1933 to supervise banks, insure deposits up to $100,000 and help maintain a stable and sound banking system in the United States. The FDIC also sells properties from bank failures. Their Web site provides important financial information, such as how to avoid predatory home loans. It also can direct you to publications, other Web sites, staff and additional resources that can answer your questions and guide you to the state or federal agency that regulates a particular lender.

Federal Trade Commission (FTC)

The FTC (**www.ftc.gov**) works to prevent unfair business practices. You can visit their Web site to obtain brochures and information about procedures for filing a complaint against a lender that is not a bank. The FTC, along with the Federal Reserve Board (**www.federalreserve.gov**) also administers the laws pertaining to credit reports.

Federal Citizen Information Center (FCIC)

The FCIC (**www.pueblo.gsa.gov**) is a clearinghouse for free and low-cost booklets published by various federal agencies on topics such as getting a mortgage or home equity loan. Four examples of the many booklets and articles offered by the FCIC are:

- "Looking for the Best Mortgage," published by 11 federal agencies
- "Buying Your Home: Settlement Costs and Helpful Information"
- "Home Buyer's Vocabulary"
- "How to Buy a Home with a Low Down Payment"

House Price Index (HPI)

The HPI (**www.ofheo.gov**), administered by the Office of Federal Housing Enterprise Oversight (OFHEO), is a broad measure of the movement of single family home prices at various geographic levels. The HPI includes home price figures for the nine Census Bureau divisions as well as separate home price indexes for the 50 states, the District of Columbia and many metropolitan statistical areas (MSAs). This site may be of interest to you because it provides a means of gauging housing affordability in specific geographic areas. (See also Real Estate Web Sites later in this chapter.)

GovLoans

Govloans (**www.govloans.gov**) is a useful Web site for comparing government home loans. The site allows you to browse all types of government loans, including housing loans, which are described by program name, characteristics, terms and qualifying requirements. Some of the loan programs are veterans' loans, Native American veteran direct loans, adjustable rate mortgage insurance, basic FHA loans, condominium unit purchase loans, manufactured home loan insurance and rural housing loans.

> **Tip**
>
> Visit **www.searchsystems.net** for links to local government databases. This is a public records directory that includes sections on local home values, crime statistics and permit applications. Pay careful attention to the permit application listings to learn about recent upgrades or repairs on specific homes.

Shopping for Loans

The Internet hosts numerous sites that offer loan and mortgage options. The choices range from small lenders to large, all-inclusive lenders that feature prequalification and loan applications as well as various types of calculators and detailed comparison charts. Browsing through these sites is an excellent way to get a feel for available mortgage options before you actually begin the process for yourself.

National mortgage lenders manage some mortgage sites and direct queries to their local offices. Other mortgage lenders are Web-based and work only by telephone and e-mail. Still others use a combination of the two methods. For example, E-Loan's Web site (**www.eloan.com**) supplies a form that you can fill out to get prequalified and preapproved for a loan you can afford. Within minutes, you will be provided with a worksheet that specifies what you can qualify for as well as a breakdown of the proposed loan.

Many of these sites also offer the option of initiating a loan application. If you decide to do this, within a few hours you will receive a list of lenders' offers and terms, or you may be instructed to contact the lender directly. Other organizations assign a loan officer to you and handle all the paperwork.

Naturally, the lender will want to see a current, accurate credit report. (See Chapter 2 for information about obtaining and correcting your credit report.) There may be a fee for this, but do not agree to pay any fees in advance other than for the credit report; some unscrupulous companies may try to charge a large commitment or loan guarantee fee upfront. This often is called a predatory loan trap.

Comparing Loans on the Internet

When you are surfing the Internet to find Web sites that will help you learn about buying a home and arranging financing, look for sites that permit you to compare the available options. Many Web sites include loan comparison charts that allow you to view the numbers side by side.

If you are using the Internet to do some preliminary research before actually starting the home buying process, it is a good idea to compare mortgage terms, down payment requirements and interest rates. Look for extra information as well; for example, E-Loan's Web site lists interest rates you can get by paying up to three points; each point equals 1 percent of the loan amount. Also, look for lenders' good faith estimates, making a comparison can often point out the most advantageous deal.

Finding the Cheapest Loan

If you have decided to buy a home using an Internet lender you will appreciate the time savings and convenience of using the Internet to search for various lenders. After talking with a few lenders from various Web site listings and reviewing the good faith estimates each lender sent, select the one you fell most comfortable with. The loan representative will send you the necessary forms, which you will fill out and returned with paycheck stubs, bank statements and other required documents. You will then pay the associated fees and wait for the lender's response. In less than a month, the lender should complete the loan deal and send it to a local title company for closing.

The entire process will progress quickly and smoothly, and you will have saved approximately $1,500 in lender fees because you have excellent credit, good ratios and a 10 percent down payment.

Therefore, if you have good credit, good ratios and a good down payment, Web lenders can offer you a cheaper deal by simplifying the process and eliminating overhead. On the other hand, if you have credit problems that require an individualized loan package or if you want to use an FHA/VA loan, you probably will see no savings by using the Internet. Instead, you would be smart to work with a local lender who has contacts and the necessary experience to get you a loan.

Using Tools and Calculators

As you look at each Web site, you probably will find various tools, calculators and software you can use to evaluate your financial status as well as to explore your options. Do not hesitate to take advantage of these aids. The Web site developers have found that helping potential buyers learn as much as they can about the home buying process is a sound business practice. The more help a Web site provides the more likely it is that you will return to it to conduct business.

E-Loan.com and **HomeLoanSearch.com** are two examples of sites that provide useful tools to help you. **E-Loan.com** lists several calculator sheets, including "Monthly Payment Calculator," "Rent vs. Own Calculator," "Home Affordability Calculator" and "Amortization Calculator." In addition to the prequalification and preapproval sheets, there are forms to compute your credit score and determine the best mortgage for you. There is also a home inspection checklist and a property preference checklist as well as help guides, such as "Mortgage Basics," "Home-Buying: What to Expect" and "FAQs: Working with E-Loan."

HomeLoanSearch.com offers many of the same features as the **E-Loan.com** site, including a selection of calculators:

- "Prequalification Calculator"
- "Standard Mortgage Calculator"
- "How Much House Can You Afford Calculator"
- "How Much Can You Borrow Calculator"
- "How Much Down Payment Do You Need Calculator"
- "Amortization Schedule Calculator"

This site also has a feature that allows you to type in a question and then receive a personalized answer.

Shopping for Homes on the Internet

Shopping for a home on the Internet appeals both to shoppers who are planning to make a local move and to those who are contemplating long-distance relocation. The Internet is popular for local moves because it is up-to-date and allows a potential buyer to locate a new home when it first comes on the market. In a sellers' market, this is an advantage for the buyer. People relocating across the country find the Internet a good way to narrow down choices of neighborhoods and homes before traveling to the new location. Some sites even offer virtual tours of a home, which allows the buyer to further refine his or her search.

Real Estate Web Sites

Many real estate agencies have Web sites. If you can identify four or five agencies that work within your target neighborhood, you can check their sites periodically for homes. If you see one you like, you can call the agency to set up an appointment to tour it. Look for agency sites that offer e-mails of new listings or open houses so that you do not have to check the site constantly. More importantly, you will not miss out on an open house or a new listing because you did not go to the site for a few days.

If you are still in the research stage or if you want to try to buy a house on your own, visit a general Web site, such as **Realtor.com**® or House-for-Sale-Online (**www.house-for-sale-online.com**). In addition to listings, both of these sites provide information about schools in the target neighborhood as well as demographic and socioeconomic characteristics of the area.

Realtor.com is the official site of the National Association of Realtors (NAR), so you may find that many realtors in your target neighborhood list on this site. Likewise, **House-for-Sale-Online.com** is a network of independent real estate professionals, so you also will be dealing with agents if you select a home from this site. Both list homes all across the United States.

Because a real estate market is always in flux, some general sites may have outdated listings. If you find a house that looks interesting, be sure to call to see if it is still available.

FSBO Transactions

General and real estate agent Web sites do not have listings of homes that are FSBO. However, there are specific sites for FSBO sales, including **www.virtualfsbo.com**, **www.forsalebyowner.com** and **www.fsboadvertisingservice.com** to name a few. For a complete list of Web sites turn to the Resources section in Appendix A.

You also can use search engines to find other FSBO sites by typing in "for sale by owner" and the name of the state, or you can scout your potential neighborhood for free newspapers or fliers that include Web sites of individual FSBOs.

Online Newspaper Classified Ads

Many newspapers now have classified ads online. Visit **www.newspaperlinks.com** to access links to newspaper real estate sections in your state or city.

Homescape (**www.homescape.com**) is another Web site for newspaper listings. Homescape's network represents more than 150 local newspaper affiliates with nearly 1 million real estate listings throughout the country. This Web site also offers other information about home loans and local real estate news and resources. By filling out the appropriate forms on the site, you can become prequalified, obtain a mortgage quote, acquire real estate agent contact information or receive e-mail alerts about real estate news.

Tip
Some newspapers publish the sales prices of recently sold homes, which will give you a feel for the market prices of the area. Listings in weekly neighborhood or suburban papers can be especially helpful if you are trying to narrow down your choices of neighborhoods.

Property Values Information

Home Price Records (**www.homepricerecords.com**) offers a free service that helps you determine the market value of the homes in a neighborhood by making publicly available home price records accessible online. Likewise, Home Smart Reports (**www.homesmartreports.com**) provides home price estimates, area risk profiles and information about property values online. This particular service, however, charges a fee.

Caveat Emptor

The warning, caveat emptor, "Let the buyer beware," applies to Internet shopping as well as to other consumer shopping. While the Internet is a quick and efficient way to research your target neighborhood's recent sales, market prices, home types and community features, it does not include all the information you may need.

By dealing personally with a real estate agent, either on the phone or face to face, you can take advantage of the agent's experience and insight into the area and the neighborhoods. A real estate agent can give you referrals to local service providers, such as bankers, insurance agents or financial advisers. Plus, an agent can consider your particular needs and customize your home buying process.

Summary

If you are moving from out of town, the Internet will provide information about the area and even offer photos and tours of a property, but it may not reveal the true quality of the school system or public transportation. That is why you need to talk with a local agent in order to learn the inside information about an area. The Internet is a good beginning and a good supplement, but it cannot tell you everything you want to know about the quality of life in a neighborhood.

The best way to use the Internet is as a source of preliminary information, which will make you a better informed consumer when you are ready to buy. If you visit government and real estate agency sites, you can learn a great deal about the home buying process. You also can eliminate inappropriate homes and neighborhoods to narrow your search and take care of early transactions like prequalification. The Internet is just one of many tools you can use in your search for a home. For a list of useful Web sites to use when searching for a home, go to the Resource section.

What You Have Learned

- The Web sites to visit to search for home listings and FSBO transactions.
- Where to go to find the cheapest loans.
- How to use calculators and other online tools to research your financial status.
- What caveat emptor means and how using the Internet as a research tool may not offer enough information. You might consider contacting an agent.

Discounts on Other Socrates Products

In addition to a variety of free forms and checklists, you will find special offers on a variety of Socrates products. Visit **www.socrates. com/books/ReadyHouseActionPlan.aspx** for more information.

7

. . . . . .

Using a Real Estate Agent

In This Chapter

- Learn the differences between a buyers' and sellers' agent.
- Determine if you want to use a real estate agent or broker.
- Discover how a real estate agent's commission is factored into the purchasing cost of a home.
- Learn how to choose an agent that has your best interests in mind.

By this stage of the process, you probably have decided whether or not you want to use a real estate agent. The preceding chapters have shown that while more people are selling their homes themselves, a good real estate agent can guide you through the process and make the experience easier.

An agent can provide valuable information about the neighborhood you are considering—the schools, crime, shopping, etc. He or she can help you determine the price range you can afford and can find homes that fit within your parameters. Best of all, the seller typically pays the real estate commission.

Selecting an agency and an agent are important decisions, and you should study both before making a decision.

Note
Most real estate agencies use an MLS database that lists all of the homes currently for sale in a particular area. Your agent should have access to an MLS and be able to provide printouts of homes you may be interested in buying. Ask for comparable listings that show housing prices.

Buying on Your Own	Buying with an Agent
You can buy a FSBO home at a lower price.	You have a wider choice of homes, especially with an agency's multiple listing services (MLS).
You control the entire process.	You have the experience of an agent who is familiar with the market and the area.
You can negotiate your own deal.	You have an experienced negotiator.
You can select your own professionals–inspectors, closing agents and attorneys–to follow up and help you close.	You can choose professionals from a list of tried-and-true associates.
You are responsible for fulfilling all the legal requirements of buying a house, such as recording the deed and purchasing insurance.	You can rely on your agent to take care of final details and process the paperwork.

Types of Real Estate Agencies

Throughout the history of buying and selling real estate, the real estate agent's primary loyalty traditionally has been to the seller of the property. This was the case whether the agent was representing the seller or working with the buyer, and was often confusing to buyers who assumed that the agent who was showing them carefully selected homes was representing them. In truth, the agent was representing the owners of the homes the buyers saw and was obligated to tell the owners any information he or she discovered about the buyers.

In today's real estate industry, this type of relationship has changed. Instead, there are four types of real estate agents:

- listing agent
- seller's agent
- buyer's agent
- dual agent

The listing agent handles the listing of real property for sale. This person may or may not be involved in the actual selling of a home. The selling agent represents and conducts business on behalf of the seller; he or she seeks to obtain the best and/or highest price for the home in the shortest period of time. The buyer's agent provides services for the benefit of the buyer. The dual agent is an agent–or two agents–who works for the same broker and represents both the buyer and the seller in the transaction. A dual agent must disclose this relationship to both the seller and the buyer; he or she must not reveal privileged information–for example, the price that the seller will accept or that a buyer will pay–to either party without permission.

Seller's Agent

The seller's agent is an agent working for the firm that has the seller's listing. Unless otherwise stipulated, this is still the default situation. You should assume that any agent is a seller's agent unless you have signed a contract that changes the agent's status. In most states, a real estate agent is required to disclose which party he or she represents at the first contact with the buyer.

The seller's agent's loyalty is always to the seller. Therefore, you should not reveal any confidential information to the agent, such as the maximum amount of money you are willing to spend on a home. At the same time, the seller's agent cannot disclose personal information about the seller to the buyer, including the fact that the home is in foreclosure.

Furthermore, a seller's agent cannot reveal anything that may be detrimental to the seller or give the buyer an advantage, including the results of a comparable market analysis (CMA) of the prices that similar properties in an area have sold for during the past couple of months.

Nevertheless, a seller's agent can help you find a home and may provide some of the same services as a buyer's agent, including monitoring the process to its completion. However, a seller's agent has a responsibility to negotiate the best deal for the seller, so always assume that any information you give to the agent will be passed along to the buyer. It is important that you never forget that the agent is working for the seller and not for you.

Buyer's Agent

A buyer's agent signs a contract to represent the buyer in a home search and sales transaction. The buyer's agent is loyal to the buyer and should not reveal confidential information about the buyer to the seller or the seller's agent. On the other hand, a buyer's agent can reveal information about the seller to the buyer. For example, the agent may know the seller's reasons for selling, the seller's potential concessions and other facts that may be used to the buyer's advantage.

A buyer's agent will be knowledgeable about homes, neighborhoods, schools and other facts you may want to know. The agent also will handle the financial and legal details of the transaction through the closing. This includes recommending contract contingency clauses to protect your interests. The agent also can develop a CMA of selling prices in the area and will have other inside information. If you have done some preliminary homework on the Internet, you will be better equipped to evaluate what he or she tells you.

Having a spokesperson on your side can be crucial to your success in buying the right home. Remember, however, that a buyer's agent's contract is binding; you must understand all of its clauses before signing it.

You can sign either an exclusive contract or a nonexclusive contract with a buyer's agent. An exclusive contract commits you to using only one agent. In some cases, you may have to pay the agent a commission even if you switch to another agent.

A nonexclusive contact allows you to use multiple buyer agents without changing standard contracts, but some agents refuse to work under this condition.

Whichever contract you choose, the agreement should be in writing and should stipulate the expectations of both the buyer and the agent. The agreement may be open-ended or limited to a specific geographical area, and it should cover a specific time period that is agreeable to both parties. Many experts think that a buyer should not sign an exclusive contract for an agent's representation for longer than 30 days. The buyer's agreement also should address the agent's compensation. (See Understanding Real Estate Commissions in this chapter.)

Dual Agent

A dual agent is a real estate agent who has signed a buyer agency agreement with a buyer who wants to purchase a listing held by the agent's firm. A dual agent is required to be loyal to both the seller and the buyer, so if you find yourself using a dual agent, you should be clear about what you can expect as a buyer.

This situation must be disclosed to both the buyer and the seller, and privileged information cannot be revealed to one party without permission of the other party. In fact, dual agency usually must be agreed to in writing by all parties involved. Because dual agency regulations differ among states, check your state's real estate laws before entering into this type of agreement.

Note
As an agency rule of thumb, if you do not specify the kind of agent you want, your agent will automatically represent the seller in the transaction. If the agent does not represent the seller, he or she most likely will represent the buyer, especially if you seek out a buyer's agent. If the home you are interested in is listed by the broker that your agent works for, you automatically have a dual agency situation.

Real Estate Agent vs. Real Estate Broker

Real estate agents generally are licensed by the state in which they work and may be members of the NAR. They are usually independent salespeople who provide their services to real estate brokers.

Real estate brokers are independent businesspeople who manage their own offices for the purpose of selling real estate. While brokers and agents may have many of the same job duties, a broker essentially will supervise an agent working for his or her office. Brokers also may help find financing for a buyer, arrange title searches, rent or manage properties for a fee and perhaps sell insurance as part of their real estate business.

Depending on the customs in your area and each company's individual guidelines, agents usually receive a percentage commission on the sale of a home. If both the buyer's and seller's agents assist with the sale of a home, they generally split the commission. If a broker listed the home for sale, the broker also will receive a portion of the commission.

> **Tip**
>
> Real estate agents who have taken at least 90 hours of specialized real estate related courses from the Graduate REALTOR® Institute (GRI) are awarded the GRI designation by state associations of the NAR. As members of the NAR, GRI designees subscribe to its code of ethics.

Understanding Real Estate Commissions

Traditionally, the seller pays the standard real estate sales commission. The only time a buyer pays a commission is when the buyer's agent shows and sells a FSBO home and the FSBO owner refuses to pay the buyer's agent's commission. In that situation, the buyer's agent looks to the buyer to pay the sales commission in return for the agent's finding the FSBO home and negotiating the sale. Fortunately, however, many FSBO sellers will pay a buyer's agent up to 50 percent of the usual sales commission for helping with the sale. In more standard transactions, buyers' agents usually are paid a portion of the seller's commission at closing.

Most buyers and sellers do not know how home sales commissions are divided among everyone involved in a sale. There are usually four parties:

- the listing broker
- the listing agent who represents the broker
- the selling broker
- the selling agent who represents that broker

As a rule, when a sale closes, 50 percent of the sales commission goes to the listing brokerage and the other half to the selling brokerage. Of these amounts, the listing agent will receive one-half–or more, depending on the agent's commission deal with the broker–of the listing brokerage's share, and the selling agent will receive one-half of the selling brokerages' share. These amounts are then shared with the individual agents according to their commission agreements with their brokers. If the listing agent also finds a buyer–dual agency–the sales commission is split between the listing agent and the brokerage.

Real estate commissions are negotiable, but most agents are unwilling to negotiate lower commissions when selling modestly priced homes. There is more room for discussing lower rates if a house is selling for $500,000 or higher. Furthermore, figures show that most home sales involve both a listing agent from one brokerage and a selling agent from another brokerage, usually a result of the local MLS. A lower sales commission rate means less income for the agents. Understandably, they will be less motivated about showing a home if they have to split the commission with other brokerages and if they can show similar homes offering a full commission rate.

What this means to buyers–other than those involved in FSBO sales that may require them to pay a commission to an agent–is that their purchase offer should always take into account the amount of commission a seller will have to pay. If a buyer really wants a particular home, then he or she will have to consider making a high enough offer to enable the seller to pay the sales commission.

Finding an Agent

There are several ways you can find an agent. You can start by looking through newspaper and other classified ads for agents or brokers who specialize in buyer representation. While you are reading the classified ads, jot down times and places of open houses; you may meet an agent that you would like to consider at one of these gatherings.

Family, friends and co-workers also may have suggestions. If they recently have bought a home, they will have firsthand insight into the way their agents worked for them. Ask for names and whether or not they would work with a particular agent again. Do not be afraid to press for details about negative experiences; there is no reason you should repeat a friend's mistake when choosing an agent. For example, look for agents who are career real estate agents and not dabbling in real estate in temporary or part-time positions. You will receive better service from a professional real estate agent.

> **Warning**
>
> It is important to note, if you look for homes first and contact the agent who has a specific property listed, you will automatically get a seller's agent who will represent the seller, not you.

Once you have located an agent–either on your own or through recommendations–do a little research into the agent's background. Is he or she affiliated with a reputable agency? Does the agent seem interested in advancing his or her professional credentials? For example, does the agent have a GRI designation or professional affiliations? Is the agent familiar with the communities you are targeting as well as with houses in the price range you are looking at?

Try to check references for any agents you are considering. Ask for references of past and current clients and call them to determine the quality of the agent's services. You may ask previous clients if the agent was helpful, whether or not they would use that agent again and if they were satisfied with the price they paid.

Also check out whether or not an agent or agency receives a fee for recommending supplemental services. For example, an agency may work with a number of mortgage lenders, home inspectors, title companies, repair contractors or insurance companies, and you should know if the agency receives a referral fee when they recommend these service providers.

Many real estate consultants recommend that a buyer interview at least three agents who sell homes in the area, check their references from recent sellers and/ or buyers and then list with them for 30 to 60 days.

Broker Gretchen Brewster, GRI, of Prairie Shore Properties stresses the importance of looking for agents whose personalities are compatible with yours. "The most important thing buyers can do to help an agent is to be direct, clear and honest about what they want in a home," states Brewster, "and that can only happen if the buyer's and the agent's personalities mesh. This is very important because the buyer needs to feel comfortable enough with the agent to be forthright if there are changes in the buyer's needs. If, for example, the buyer changes his mind about what he is willing to pay, he must tell the agent immediately."

Consultants also warn against signing on with buyer agents who offer to reduce their commissions. For obvious reasons, buyers' agents often will not show listings on which they will receive a reduced commission. That is why you should list with at least three agents.

Tip

The National Association of Exclusive Buyer Agents (NAEBA) can help you find an agent in your area. Visit **www.naeba.org** for more information. Also visit **www.homegain.com**, an independent real estate Web site with no direct affiliation with real estate firms. The agents listed there are members of the NAR. Searching for an agent is done anonymously and with no obligation.

Questions to Ask a Potential Agent

Compile a list of specific questions to help you narrow your selection of agents:

- What are your educational qualifications and professional credentials?
- How long have you been a real estate agent?
- How long have you been with your current firm?
- Are you a full-time agent?
- Do you usually represent a seller or a buyer?
- How many buyers are you currently working with? How many sellers?
- How many of your clients' homes have closed in the last 6 to 12 months?
- What is the average price of the homes you sold last year?
- What three references can you give me?
- What services do you and your agency provide?
- Are you familiar with the area in which we want to look?
- How do you go about finding a home for your clients?

The answers to these questions plus your background check should enable you to select agents who will work with and for you. But before you sign a contract with your agents, take the time to:

- verify that the agents can work as buyers' agents and represent your interests;
- ask the agents to describe the services you can expect;
- request a blank copy of the buyer agency contract and study it before signing;
- review the contract with the agents and ask for deletions or alterations of those parts that concern you;
- discuss how dual agency is handled by the agency; and
- weigh all the information and decide if you want to sign.

> **Tip**
>
> Most reputable real estate agencies do not recommend a specific resource such as an attorney, inspector or lender. Rather, they provide a list of names and contact information from which to select a resource and, if asked, will put you in touch with someone who has used the resource.

When you sign a contract, tell your representatives exactly what you are looking for in a home, a neighborhood and a community. Be specific about such concerns as schools and commutes. You will save time and avoid misunderstanding if you are specific about your requirements in your early discussions with your agent.

Brewster sums up whether or not to use a real estate agent in a simple, yet compelling way: "Buying your first home or any home is highly emotional. After all, you are spending more money on one purchase than you have ever spent before. It is critical that you have someone–your agent–acting as your promoter and a buffer when it comes to negotiating the final sale. An agent can be objective and supportive, steering you through the negotiations to the final closing. This is a person you need on and at your side at this time."

Summary

Having a good real estate agent makes the home buying process less stressful. Agents can provide you with information about the neighborhood you are considering to buy in and help you determine which type of home is best for you in a price range you can afford. The agent can also help you through the negotiations and guide you through the entire buying process.

What You Have Learned

- How to identify a buyers' and sellers' agent.
- How to narrow your search and find an agent.
- How real estate commissions affect the price of a home.

Free Forms and Checklists

Visit **Socrates.com** and register to receive a variety of useful FREE forms, letters and checklists. See page iv for details on how to register (you will need the seven-digit registration code provided on the enclosed CD).

8
· · · · · ·
Choosing the Type of Home

In This Chapter

- Learn the differences between all the possible types of homes you could buy.
- Learn the advantages of buying an older home versus a new home.
- Evaluate what type of home is best suited for you.

Before you can look at individual homes or even neighborhoods you need to decide what kind of home is right for you and your family. Do you want a single family home, a multifamily home, a townhouse, a condo or a co-operative? What about a manufactured home, such as a mobile home or prefabricated home? Is an older home a better option than a new home in a new subdivision?

You want to buy a home that fits the way you live and meets your needs. Just because a home looks nice does not mean that it will accommodate you and your entire family. It should have spaces and features that work for all family members.

Consider the following factors when determining what type of home is best suited for you:

- Do I want a single family home?
    - I have seen homes that I can afford in a certain neighborhood and I like them.
    - This type of home offers more privacy than other types.
    - My family is growing and a smaller living space just is not big enough.
    - I have considered all of the yardwork and house maintenance.
- Would I prefer a townhouse?
    - I would have less maintenance and landscaping than I would in a single family home.
    - I would have no one living above or below me but I would have less privacy than I would in a single family home.
    - Neighbors on either side would make me feel more secure.
        - I might find a townhouse with such amenities as a pool or playgrounds.

- ○ I might have limited or no choices in how I could change the exterior of my townhouse.

- • Is a condo or co-operative right for me?

  - ○ I am single—or we have no children—so a smaller place would be best.

  - ○ I do not want to be responsible for yardwork or exterior maintenance.

  - ○ I feel safer living in a building with others.

  - ○ A condo may have amenities that a single family home does not have such as a pool or tennis court.

  - ○ I may have to pay monthly fees for use of the amenities for security or for common area maintenance.

  - ○ I will have to adhere to the rules and regulations of the building.

  - ○ The noise level between units can be annoying.

  - ○ I have considered that it can be difficult to sell a condo or co-operative later.

- • Do I want to live in a manufactured home?

  - ○ I will have a better initial estimate of what the home will cost.

  - ○ The manufacturer offers levels of customization.

  - ○ If I buy a prefabricated house I can get more house at a better quality in a shorter period of time for the same money.

  - ○ A prefabricated house is better protected from the weather during assembly because it arrives in prebuilt units and this will eliminate such problems as mold in the walls later.

  - ○ A mobile home costs less per square foot than a conventional home.

  - ○ A mobile home requires less maintenance.

  - ○ I understand that I may not own and may have to pay rent on the land on which a mobile home sits.

  - ○ There are lease-to-purchase plans available for mobile homes.

  - ○ I realize that building equity on a mobile home will be slower.

  - ○ Today's mobile homes cannot be moved easily.

- • Is an older or newer home best for me?

  - ○ I love the charm of an older home and am interested in maintaining its features.

  - ○ Older homes usually are located in established neighborhoods.

  - ○ The tax rate on an older home may be lower than that on a comparable new home.

  - ○ Newer homes often have fewer maintenance problems and my schedule is too busy to take on heavy maintenance duties.

  - ○ I dislike always having something that needs repair and therefore an older home is not what I want.

  - ○ I like the newer appliances and energy efficiency of newer homes.

As you answer these questions and consider others relating to your own special circumstances, you will begin to see what type of home suits you and your family best. To aid you in your decision making, you can read more in the following sections about the pros and cons of each type of home.

Single Family Home

The single family home is the most common type of housing in the United States. Basically, you are buying a plot of land on which sits a newly constructed or existing home. The home is not attached to any other home or property.

The biggest advantage of a single family home is the privacy and autonomy it provides its owner. You can do whatever you want with your own home, as long as it conforms to local ordinances and housing codes. You can add on more rooms or tear down sections of the house. You can paint it, side it or redecorate it without any restrictions except those imposed by local housing codes or neighborhood associations. Naturally, personal courtesy requires you to consider your neighbors when you select color schemes or landscape options. But, with few exceptions, you are the owner and have the final authority about what is done to and on your home.

Along with these privileges, however, comes responsibility. You not only have the sole authority about how your yard is landscaped but also the sole duty to maintain the landscaping. Furthermore, all repairs and ongoing maintenance fall to you. You cannot call the owner or landlord when a pipe bursts. You are the owner, and all emergencies are yours to resolve. Maintaining a property can be very time-consuming and expensive. This fact often is overlooked by prospective buyers who only see the advantages of owning their own homes.

By and large, the advantages of owning a single family home do outweigh the responsibilities. Privacy, space and tax breaks are strong incentives for owning a home. Perhaps even more important is the pride of ownership, which cannot be measured in tangible terms but which may be the most compelling incentive of all.

Single Family Home	
Advantages	**Disadvantages**
Privacy	Isolation from neighbors
Freedom to add on or remodel	Maintenance/repairs owner's responsibility
No management fees	Initial cost of property greater
Resale value higher than other housing types	No extras–pools, playgrounds, gyms– as found in other housing types
Customization of exterior possible	Lawn care and expense

Townhouse

A townhouse combines characteristics of both a single family home and a condominium. A townhouse is a home attached to one or more other homes on either side. The land under each individual townhouse, however, is the property of the owner of the townhouse, unlike the land under a condominium, which is owned by the condominium association. Most townhouses have two stories, although some may have three or more floors.

A townhouse offers some degree of privacy in that no one is living above or below you, but you may be aware of noise or activity on either side of you. In addition, any yard area is usually only as wide as your townhouse and is contiguous with the yards of neighbors on either side.

If you buy a townhouse in a small development, you probably will purchase the home and the land it is situated on as an individual owner. In a larger development, you may share ownership of the common areas as well as any extra facilities, such as pools or playgrounds, with other townhouse owners. In this case, you will have to budget for the homeowners association fees. If you consider buying a townhouse that requires you to join a homeowners association, be sure to get a copy of the association's agreement and rules before making a decision. It is also wise to ask for copies of minutes from the previous association meetings.

You are responsible for the exterior maintenance of your individual townhouse and the care of your yard. However, you may not be free to change the exterior of your townhouse or the appearance of the yard without conforming to the standards set by the homeowners association.

You also will want to read the homeowners association's requirements about insurance. While the association probably insures the common areas of the development, you may have to insure the roof and exterior walls of your own unit. Of course, you are responsible for insuring the interior space of your townhouse as well as your own possessions.

Townhouse	
Advantages	**Disadvantages**
Less exterior maintenance	Exterior changes may be regulated
Better security because of nearby neighbors	Less privacy than detached homes
Facilities such as pools, gyms and playgrounds on premises	Possible homeowners association fees to support common facilities
Less yardwork	Smaller yard with less privacy

Condo

A condo is a form of homeownership in which you hold the deed to a specific house, townhouse or apartment and share ownership of the development's common spaces and facilities with your neighbors and fellow owners. You own what is inside your walls, floors and ceilings. The common property consists of the land, which includes recreation areas, grounds and parking lots, and the shell of the building, which includes entries, lobbies, hallways, elevators and interior common spaces. The common property is maintained by the condo association, which stipulates rules that every condo owner must follow and charges a monthly fee to maintain the common areas.

In essence, you are purchasing a share in a privately held real estate company. While you own your own unit outright, you have business partners–other owners–who have an equal say in how the development is managed.

Condo and homeowners associations are legal entities created to maintain common areas such as swimming pools and green belts, to enforce private deed restrictions and to provide services such as recreational activities and security. Condo associations usually are governed by a volunteer board of directors consisting of owners in the development. Larger condo associations may have a professional management team to provide operational and financial services.

Living in a condo is much like living in a townhouse. You will enjoy some privacy, but unlike the townhouse, you may have someone living above or below you. All exterior maintenance and repairs are the responsibility of the condo association, although you will be paying for them either through your monthly association dues or a special assessment fee. In a small condo–perhaps made up of six units in a single building–the association may decide that individual owners should clean the interior common areas to reduce the monthly dues. Part of the monthly dues should be earmarked for a reserve fund, which is a cash fund on hand to take care of large repairs; be sure to check the status of the reserve fund when you look at a condo.

All interior maintenance in your condo is your responsibility, including appliance replacement. Be certain to read the condo rules and regulations to see if you are responsible for any interior maintenance or repairs beyond that of your own unit; ask about pipes in the wall that exclusively serve your unit, for example. In fact, ask for and carefully read the regulations, minutes of the past association meetings and any financial statements pertaining to the association.

Condo	
Advantages	**Disadvantages**
Initial cost more affordable	Resale more difficult
Stable property value or appreciation	Slow recovery from drop in value
Better security because of nearby neighbors	Less privacy than detached homes
Little or no exterior maintenance	Restrictions on decorating and landscaping
Consistent quality of appearance because of restrictions	Assessment fee in addition to property taxes
Facilities such as pools, gyms and playgrounds on premises	Potential for inadequate development of reserve fund to cover repairs and replacement

Challenges of Buying and Owning a Condo

Buying a condo presents unique challenges that you will not encounter when you buy single family houses or other detached homes. Therefore, you should arm yourself with as much information as you can find and be ready to ask questions before you make a financial commitment to this housing option. Here are some facts to consider and questions to ask when you look at condos.

Rules and Regulations

Obtain a copy of the rules and regulations early in your visit and determine if there are any restrictions that will affect the way you live. For example, some condos either do not allow pets or enforce pet size or weight restrictions. Others set limits on the activities of children, such as prohibiting skateboarding on the grounds. You also may want to ask if there are rules about:

- the colors of paint and trim you can use on your exterior;
- fencing or landscaping around your condo;
- alarm systems or security lights you can install;
- the size and type of parties or events you can host in your home or in the common areas;
- quiet hours or noise restrictions;
- long-term houseguests;
- garbage storage and pickup;
- regulations and hours of recreation facilities, like the pool, gym or basketball courts; and
- parking.

Parking and Pets

Parking and pets in a condo are two sensitive topics. No one wants either one to be restricted, yet many condo associations have established guidelines and restrictions about these matters

Parking

If at all possible, you want to buy a condo–or any type of home–with a space to park one or more cars. Even if you do not own a car and do not know how to drive, you will need a parking space if you ever want to sell your home.

There are many parking options available. Some condos include parking spaces or garages in the price of the home; other condos, particularly in city high-rises, require that you buy a parking space as an extra cost of living in the building. One option is called a deeded parking space and is usually a marked off rectangle in a parking garage. Because it is deeded, you have a percentage ownership of its common elements and pay an assessment on it. You also will receive a tax bill for it just as you do for your condo. Because it is deeded property, you can sell or rent it.

Another option is a parking space owned by the association that you have the exclusive rights to use. This often is referred to as a limited common element space. You do not pay taxes on it, and the association controls the use and transfer of the space. For this kind of parking space, the association has the authority to charge expenses related to the space back to you or to the entire membership. If the association chooses the latter method of reimbursement and you have no car or space, then your general assessments subsidize those who do have parking spaces.

Some condos offer a parking right service. In these cases, valets take your car when you drive in, park it somewhere–on-site, off-site, in parking lots, private garages, communal garages or on the street–and retrieve it when you are ready to leave again.

When you explore parking options, ask about fees and restrictions. For instance, your condo association may allow only one car or one guaranteed space per unit, so if you have more than one car, you may have to pay an extra fee to park it. Garage or space owners may have to contribute to a garage reserve fund. Any guests to your home may have to pay to park. You may not be allowed to use guest parking for one of your extra cars, and you may not be allowed to park overnight in your driveway or on the street. All of these rules and the fee structures should be spelled out clearly when you are considering a condo.

Pets

For many people, regulations or restrictions about pet ownership mean the difference between closing a deal and walking away. Some condos do not welcome pets at all. Others have stringent regulations about the numbers, types and sizes of pets. For example, many condo associations limit the size and weight of dogs. They also may regulate when and where you can walk a dog. Virtually all of them require adherence to local leash and cleanup laws.

Cats are often acceptable, particularly if they are inside cats. In general, condo associations consider cats to be quiet, unobtrusive pets that do not disturb other residents. For the same reasons, fish are welcome, but some associations limit the size of the aquarium. Large tanks full of water can cause a great deal of damage to attached units if the tanks leak or burst.

Few condos allow unconventional pets, such as large snakes, alligators or exotic spiders, which is understandable, considering that condo units often share air ducts, piping and walls. If a boa constrictor is part of your family, you may have a more difficult time finding a condo development that will allow you to move in to the building.

Finding a condo association that accepts pets may not be easy, but it can be done. Your real estate agent should know which condos accept pets. Visit pet stores in the neighborhood and ask about housing developments where there are pets. Look for dog walkers in parks and on the street. They often know which buildings are friendly to pets.

The Packet of Important Documents

Most states require that buyers or prospective buyers be given a packet of the governing documents of the condo. Unfortunately, many buyers do not read every document carefully. If you want to know exactly what you are signing on for, you must read the packet and compile a list of questions to clarify any information that is unclear.

Tip
Make your offer for a condo subject to approval of the association's documents. It may take a few days for the association management to assemble a packet, so be sure to allow enough time for this contingency to be satisfied.

The packet for your review should include:

- the association's governing documents, sometimes called the CC&Rs— covenants, conditions and restrictions;
- bylaws;
- budgets;
- balance sheets;
- profit and loss statements;
- reserve fund statement outlining amount of current assessment allotted to the fund and anticipated repairs;
- minutes from the last year's meetings; and
- insurance documents, including a copy of the certificate of insurance.

When reading the packet, you should determine if the association is financially sound and if any lawsuits are pending against it. You do not want to buy into an organization that might levy a large assessment against the homeowners to pay legal expenses. The association should have sufficient funds to maintain and repair common areas, to pay its staff and to have reserves. When a reserve fund is more than 70 percent funded, there is less chance that there will be a special assessment or that repairs will be deferred; the lower the funding, the higher the risk. Be sure to check out the reserve fund in a new condo. In some areas, the developer is not required to fund reserves for an association and only has to disclose in a prominent spot on a financial statement his or her decision not to fund a reserve amount. Low assessment fees may be a tip-off to this situation.

You also want to be sure you fully understand the insurance responsibilities. The association should insure the common areas, but you probably will need insurance for your own personal property in your unit as well for certain areas of the building that serve your unit. Also find out if the association subscribes to a hold harmless policy; for example, if a neighbor's dishwasher regularly leaks and damages your unit, you or your insurance–not the association–must pay for repairs. Also, ask if the association has a building ordinance clause in its policy, which means that its insurance company will cover the cost of bringing a building up to code.

In addition to the reserve fund and insurance coverage, these other financial matters deserve your careful attention:

- What is the owner occupancy percentage or, conversely, what is the renter percentage?
- What is the percentage of assessment slow pay or delinquencies?

Knowing this information offers you a thumbnail sketch of how a condo is managed.

Real estate experts recommend that prospective buyers look for a condo with an owner occupancy rate of more than 70 percent. This means that there are more owners to make certain the association is being managed properly. If more than half the units are rented, fewer residents have a truly vested interest in the property.

The percentage of delinquencies in assessment payments is a sign of how well the management is doing. If more than 10 percent of the homeowners are late 90 days or more with their assessments, the association may be poorly managed and underfunded. Fewer than 5 percent delinquencies is a sign of a well-run association.

Who is Responsible for What?	
Owner's Responsibility	**Condo Association's Responsibility**
Interior unit decorating	Landscape maintenance of common areas
Unit electrical fixtures	Interior maintenance of common areas
Insurance on unit contents and personal property	Snow removal on streets, walks, parking areas, recreation areas
Unit liability insurance	Insurance coverage on common areas
Unit security—locks on doors	Doorbell and intercom system
Unit plumbing—sinks, toilets, tubs, showers, laundry, dishwasher	Roads and parking areas within property boundaries
Unit appliances—stoves, refrigerators, disposals, dishwashers, washers and dryers, air conditioners	Clubhouse, pool, gym, tennis courts, golf course, other recreation areas
Kitchen and bathroom cupboards and counter tops	Main and/or cable TV system
Unit carpeting and window covering	Management according to CC&Rs
Windows and screens	Main line sewer systems

Tip
If you are buying a condo in a new development, ask about the real estate taxes estimate. Real estate taxes for a new condo may be estimated on the value of the land before development while later tax bills take into account the value of the improved land and property.

Co-operative

In contrast to buying a condo, in which you own a percentage of the building or development, buying a co-operative or co-op means that you buy shares in a corporation that owns the property. You do not own real estate; rather you lease your unit from the corporation, and the numbers of shares you own determine your monthly payment or assessment. The monthly fee includes the assessment, taxes and most utilities, and you also may receive a separate assessment invoice if revenues fall short of expenditures. As a shareholder, you have a vote, and most bylaws require two-thirds or three-fourths majority to change or enact a rule.

Because co-ops are corporations, a board of directors or a co-op board manages the property. The board sets policy, determines who is permitted to buy shares and decides what improvements you can make to your unit. This means that the board selects your neighbors and decides who gets to live in the building.

Many people find this advantageous since shareholders or neighbors can be controlled as opposed to a townhouse or condo, in which anyone with the financial wherewithal can move in to the building. However, that exclusivity also means that applicants are thoroughly scrutinized, and you may have to provide more personal information than you would to a mortgage lender. In addition, when you are ready to move out, the board's lengthy evaluation of a potential shareholder may delay your departure. Also, although it is illegal to discriminate on race, sex or religion, the board nevertheless can reject an application if its members feel the applicant will not fit in with the other neighbors.

If you are interested in a co-op, you need to be aware of three potential problems. First, in some areas, a seller does not have to provide a seller's disclosure form; the seller is selling stock not real estate, so a disclosure form is not required. In this case, you will have to schedule a professional inspection of the unit.

Second, some co-ops impose what is known as a flip tax or fee if you sell. The fee can be a percentage of the sale price, a specified cost per share or a portion of the profit from the sale. If you encounter this, research the history of the co-op and find out if the fee has caused problems with sales in the past.

Third, financing a co-op may be different from other types of housing. Many require 30 to 50 percent down payment; some allow you to finance the balance and some do not. Each board and each area is different, so be certain you are clear about this requirement upfront.

Visit **www.cooperator.com** for more information about buying co-ops.

Co-operative	
Advantages	**Disadvantages**
Selective acceptance of new buyers	Discriminatory exclusivity
Monthly fee for assessment, taxes and utilities	Special assessment if revenues fall short of expenditures
Owners voting shareholders	Two-thirds or three-fourths majority to change rule
Stable shareholders	More rigorous financing requirements
Good investment	Difficulty selling

Manufactured Homes

The manufactured home category encompasses two basic types of homes: prefabricated and mobile. Prefabricated homes can be modular, panel or precut kits; these three types of homes differ by how much of the construction is done at the factory and how much work is needed on-site. A mobile home is what used to be called a trailer but today can no longer be differentiated in many cases from a conventionally constructed home. In fact, once a mobile home is permanently anchored on its lot, it is no longer mobile.

Both types of homes have advantages and disadvantages compared to more conventional housing options. Competitive prices and the speed with which a prefabricated home can be erected are the two best selling points of these homes. The average cost of a manufactured home is approximately one-half the cost of a conventionally built house. Much of the savings derive from the fact that a manufactured house or even a custom-built home can be ready to move into in 4 to 6 weeks in any kind of weather. The reduced construction time and the assembly line efficiency lead to substantial cost savings.

Because all manufactured homes are built to conform to government code, you can obtain market financing easily and even buy with a low down payment. Furthermore, manufactured homes permanently anchored in a good neighborhood tend to hold their value and appreciate in value over time.

Of course, you have to shop around for the best financing deals, because your needs are different from someone buying a conventional house. You will need financing for the actual structure, and you also may need a temporary construction loan to pay contractors to assemble the components. But because your home will be completed in less than a month, the interest you pay on the loan will be less. This does not even take into consideration the savings in construction wages for building a home in 1 month versus the 6 or more months for a traditional or conventionally built home.

Manufactured Homes	
Advantages	**Disadvantages**
Lower total cost	Building equity slower
Lower down payment	Rental land site for some mobile homes
Fast construction	Resale difficult on rental site
Customization available	Mobile home no longer mobile
Less maintenance	Fewer trained assembly contractors
Recreational facilities in some developments	Association fees for some developments

Prefabricated Homes

Approximately 90 percent of modular or sectional homes are built at the factory in an assembly line process that incorporates high quality control standards. Many manufactured homes are actually better built than traditional housing. Finished components complete with windows and wiring are loaded from the assembly line to carriers, which transport them to the homesite. A crane at the site positions the sections onto the foundation where they are permanently anchored. Utility lines are connected, and within a week, the home is ready to move into. You even can arrange to have an excavation crew from the dealer dig a basement ahead of time before laying the foundation.

Panel homes are built in much the same way as modular homes, but they are shipped in panels instead of modular units. This can be a definite benefit because you can choose how much home you want to construct at the beginning. Once at the homesite, the panels are connected and the home enclosed. This can take 1 or 2 days. Within a week the interior work is finished, and the home is ready to move into.

A precut or kit house arrives as a kit, with all the parts precut at the factory and shipped ready to assemble. You can assemble the kit yourself or hire the dealer's workers to construct the final home. If you have construction experience, you can put the house together and save a great deal of money. Everything is precut, and all the hardware is included.

All of these homes can be customized so that they do not seem plain, which has been an objection to manufactured homes. With the advent of computer-aided design, home manufacturers can offer individualized styles that meet all of your specifications. In addition, manufacturers build these homes to federal HUD code—the Manufactured Home Construction and Safety Standards—and state building codes that usually follow the Uniform Building Code (UBC) or the newer International Building Code (IBC), both of which may exceed federal standards. This means that this type of housing can qualify for FHA/VA and conventional financing.

Mobile Homes

Mobile homes are built in a factory under quality control standards to meet federal and state codes. As a rule, the entire home is finished at the factory. Unlike modular or panel homes, mobile homes are built on a steel undercarriage, whose wheels serve as its transport to the homesite. There it is slid off the carriage onto the foundation and permanently anchored.

Like other manufactured homes, mobile homes can be customized to include your own decorating preferences as well as options such as garages and slide-outs. You can purchase a double-wide or triple-wide and end up with more than 2,000 square feet of living space in a home that looks like a single family dwelling.

There is one major difference between owning a mobile home and another type of home—you have to find a place to put it. Many manufactured home developments operate in much the same way as a condo development. You own the land on which your mobile home is anchored, and an association maintains the common areas and grounds. Some even have such amenities as golf courses, clubhouses and pools.

Other developments only rent out lots for manufactured homes. Thus, you have the disadvantage of not owning the land while owning the home: you pay a monthly rent on the land without building up any equity. If the landlord does not maintain the development, then your resale value drops. All in all, it is best to buy the pad on which you install your manufactured home.

Note
Some mobile home styles incorporate universal design principles in their homes. (See Chapter 10 for more information.) For example, entrances are only one to two steps off the ground, entry steps have a no-slip pattern on their surfaces, switches are waist-high, doorknobs are lever handles and there is an oversized shower stall. The lower entry level offers an additional benefit: the unit hugs the ground, thus preventing storm winds from circulating underneath the home and causing damage. The possibility of storm damage can be further diminished by tying the unit down every 6 to 8 feet.

See the Resources section to find the Web sites you can visit to obtain information about manufactured housing.

Older vs. New Home

If your idea of a home is a large, charming house nestled among tall, leafy trees in a beautiful, old-fashioned yard, you may want to consider an older home. Older homes have character, and they tend to be in well-established neighborhoods with tall trees and long-standing landscaping. Their neighborhoods often have a variety of architectural styles and exude a sense of stability. The interior of the house also may have extra touches such as built-in cabinets or bookcases and unusual mantels and woodwork.

Despite these pluses, you have to take a close look at both the neighborhood and the home. An older home in an established neighborhood might have older schools and other community features with track records that you can evaluate. It may also have older residents and fewer young children, which may be a disadvantage if you have young children. On the other hand, older neighborhoods tend to have larger yards.

Every house has some problems, and older homes may have more problems than newer ones. There always seems to be something to repair, update or improve. Bathrooms and kitchens in particular may have to be remodeled to fit your lifestyle. The first few years that you live in an older home, you may have to replace a water heater or a furnace. The roof may need repair. Safety and energy saving features may not be up-to-date, so you may pay more for utilities. Or you may discover immediately that your house's wiring will not accommodate all of your appliances and electronic equipment. You suddenly are faced with expenses you had not anticipated.

On the other hand, if you asked for a disclosure form, if you questioned the seller and the real estate agent carefully and if you arranged an inspection, you may be prepared to expect some of these expenses. In some cases, you can ask the seller to upgrade as a contingency to your making an offer. Doing your homework and preparing your home hunting strategies as discussed in earlier chapters will help you make a deal that you can financially manage.

Nevertheless, be careful that you do not allow the ambience of an older home to blind you to conditions that you may not like. In an older home, the rooms may be small and divided, thus interfering with the traffic flow. Closet space may be practically nonexistent and storage may not be convenient. Wiring is especially important if your household has the usual complement of timesaving devices, electronic equipment and electrical appliances. Do you really want to turn off the lights so that you can use the microwave oven? You may be prepared to remodel in order to create the home you need, but do not forget that if extensive remodeling makes your home the most expensive on the block, you may have difficulty selling it later.

Still, an older home may be the answer for you as a first-time buyer. The affordability of an older home may outweigh potential disadvantages. Many homebuyers have begun their homeownership by buying an older home, renovating it to a saleable level and then selling at a profit. During the interim, they had the pleasure of living in an older home. The decision depends on what you need, what you can afford and what your goal is for your first home.

Advantages of Older Home vs. New Home	
Older Home	New Home
Character, individuality	Customized by buyer
Established neighborhood	Neighborhood with age diversity
Generally less expensive per square foot and lower tax rate	Modern floor plans
Warranties for repairs and replacements available as part of purchase	Warranties for repairs or replacement included
Access to established shopping, restaurants	Access to playgrounds, parks
Schools with a track record	New schools
Better construction	Less maintenance
Larger yards	Better parking
No low-flow toilets	Modern wiring and plumbing
Charm	Efficiency

Summary

All types of homes have their own appeal and obstacles with regard to ownership, maintenance and financing. It is important to investigate and weigh out all the factors before you buy.

What You Have Learned

- Which type of home is right for you.
- The challenges of owning a condo.
- The benefits of buying an older home instead of a new home.

Discounts on Other Socrates Products

In addition to a variety of free forms and checklists, you will find special offers on a variety of Socrates products. Visit **www.socrates. com/books/ReadyHouseActionPlan.aspx** for more information.

9

. . . . . .

Choosing a Neighborhood

In This Chapter

- Learn about the community and neighborhood you want to live in.
- Understand why you need to take a tour of the area and evaluate what you see.
- Discover the fair housing laws and public services available in your community.

Once you have decided on the type of home you want, your next step is to choose a neighborhood where this type of home exists.

Choosing a neighborhood is as important a decision as choosing a home. In fact, you probably have heard it said that the most important criteria in determining property value is location. You can update, remodel or improve a home, but neighborhoods tend to remain the same over long periods of time.

A neighborhood largely determines how you will live, from the stores you shop at to the friends you make and people you meet. It is a refuge from your workday world. It even has an impact on the home you choose: the resale value of a home depends on its neighborhood. Is a home in a safe neighborhood where people want to live and raise their families? Are the schools good? Is it convenient to shopping and jobs? Are homes selling quickly? A rule of thumb you can follow is that if houses in a neighborhood stay on the market fewer than 3 months, consider that a desirable area; if houses take 6 or more months to sell, look somewhere else.

How do you go about choosing a neighborhood? This part of buying a home may seem overwhelming, especially if you are moving into a new area from out of town. Even if you are looking for a home in your hometown, you may find yourself exploring unknown neighborhoods where there are homes you can afford to buy.

The simplest way to start is to draw up two lists, one labeled Must Have and the other labeled Would Like. If it helps, you can rank them by importance to further define your priorities. In this way, you start your search with a good idea of what you would like and what you will not accept. From the beginning, this focuses your search. For your convenience, there is a checklist in Appendix A that will allow you to fill in your preferences. Before you do that, however, you may want to read the rest of the chapter to gain a clearer idea of what you really want to look for in a neighborhood.

Facts about a Community

One of the best ways to learn about a neighborhood is to speak with the local alderman or city council member who represents that neighborhood. According to Alderman Ann Rainey, a member of the city council or the local representative of a neighborhood can give you information that you cannot obtain from a real estate agent.

Alderman Rainey often speaks with home buyers looking for information about her ward. She provides details about her own neighborhood, facts about the city in general and the history of relationships with neighboring cities. While she steers prospective home buyers to the appropriate Web sites for information about property taxes, schools, crime and jurisdictional matters such as county and state roles, her primary help to potential residents is her knowledge of and insight into the neighborhood.

"The other day someone asked about a very nice home for sale on the east side of the ward," she said, "but when I found out the family has small children, I told them it was the wrong block for them. Most of the people on that street are older or have teenagers, so their kids would have no one to play with, and the neighborhood park is crowded in the evenings with teenagers playing ball. I just did not think they would be happy there. Instead, I told them to look a few blocks farther north at a street where there were more small kids and a couple of tot lot playgrounds with special equipment for little children. I know several families with young children on one block that I thought these people would enjoy having as neighbors. Plus, that part of the ward has some housing bargains and a history of housing appreciation."

Alderman Rainey maintains her own Web site message board on the city's main site, on which she answers residents' questions and responds to requests for help or action within the ward. Residents also send messages to each other or respond to queries about the neighborhood on the site.

Web sites for the city, county and state as well as any local sites are a good place to begin your Internet research. You can learn about the area, individual properties and the jurisdictional hierarchy. Visit the town or city site to gather information about the specific neighborhood and property, including the name of the city council member; the ward and precinct; the police beat; the local school; the polling place; the census tract; and even the garbage, trash and recycling pickup schedules. Then visit the county Web sites to learn about individual properties and their assessments, property taxes and tax history.

You also can visit **http://factfinder.census.gov**, a page on the Web site of the U.S. Census Bureau. By typing in the name of the city and state, you can call up a fact sheet that summarizes the demographic profile of the city. The fact sheet lists four categories of characteristics: general, social, economic and housing. The sheet breaks down the demographics by gender, age, race, education, language other than English, household and family size, housing units–owner-occupied and rental–per capita and family income, and mean travel time to work in minutes.

Based on the most current census statistics, these fact sheets provide a good overall picture of a community you may be considering.

Starting with the Basics

Putting aside those characteristics that fit the specific needs of what you want, what are the basic signs of a desirable neighborhood? In your research about a neighborhood, you should look for:

- **Value appreciation**—Homes in a good neighborhood will have a history of appreciating in value, which you can check by investigating resale prices.

- **Low crime**—Contact the local police department for crime statistics by neighborhood and by block.

- **Good schools**—Schools dictate the property taxes of an area, and quality schools indicate interest in educational values, which translates into a stable neighborhood, whether or not you have children in school.

- **Residential zoning that is consistently enforced**—You do not want to live near an industrial factory or a waste landfill.

- **Pride of homes and neighborhood**—Look for well-kept homes and lawns as well as a neighborhood watch program.

- **Clean streets and public parks and facilities**—This indicates a sense of community pride.

- **Homeowners associations**—They are watchdogs for neighborhood character and consistency.

You also may want to check out other factors, such as:

- **Ethnic makeup of the neighborhood**—Are you a member of an ethnic group and would like to live in a neighborhood where language, food and customs reflect your ethnic background?

- **Diversity of the local residents**—Do you want and do you want your children to live in an area where you will meet people of different backgrounds, cultures and ages?

- **Socioeconomic status of the inhabitants**—Will you feel more comfortable living among neighbors of the same socioeconomic status as yours?

- **Ages of families and children in the area**—Do you have children or plan to have children who will need playmates?

- **Cultural attractions, including libraries, restaurants and theaters**—Is going to the theater or eating out on a regular basis an important part of your lifestyle?

- **Shopping access**—Is it important that groceries, drugstores or hardware stores be nearby? Do you want to be able to walk to or send a child to the store for a bottle of milk?

- **Transportation availability**—Do you need convenient public transportation within the neighborhood? Do you have access to a car? Would you like to use your car less often?

- **Local politics and political/sociological values, which affect school and community issues**—Do you want to be certain that local politics and politicians exert a positive influence on the community and its institutions, such as schools, libraries and parks?

You can learn about many of these factors, including the positions of local politicians, by reading a local or regional newspaper–often a weekly–or searching for the town's chamber of commerce Web site. Some newspapers in large urban areas also may feature a weekly column about the towns and counties surrounding the city.

> **Tip**
>
> Arm yourself with a detailed map of the target neighborhood. The map should indicate schools, fire departments, parks, shopping centers and any other significant landmarks. Local drugstores or bookstores may sell such maps, or you can ask for one at city hall. Check the local or neighborhood phone directory as well; some city directories include a map at the beginning or end of the book.

Touring the Area

After narrowing down your choices to a few neighborhoods that meet your general standards, it is time to take a walk. If at all possible, allow enough time to take four walking and driving tours:

- one during the day
- one during a weekend day where you can talk to neighbors
- one at night
- one on a weekend night

Touring the neighborhood at four different times may seem like overkill, but you probably will learn something different about the neighborhood with each visit. During a weekday, you can determine the focal point, if any, of the neighborhood: is it a lake, a park, a hill, a shopping center or a school? You can observe the pattern of streets–whether they are quiet cul-de-sacs or busy thoroughfares–lot configurations and general layout of the area. You can note the types of homes and/or developments and the ways in which the homes are cared for. You will be able to pinpoint the location of schools, houses of worship, stores, bus stops and other services.

You also will see the daily activity, including traffic patterns, mail deliveries and number of children playing outside. A seemingly deserted neighborhood may mean that it is a community of working adults, known as a bedroom community. That is, many of the inhabitants work in a nearby city and only sleep in the community. If this fits your lifestyle, then you may want to consider this neighborhood. On the other hand, if you have a young family, you may prefer a more community-centered neighborhood.

Strolling through the neighborhood on a weekend day gives you an opportunity to talk to people living there. You can strike up conversations with residents working in their yards or on their cars. If you see a house with a For Sale sign, you can make arrangements to tour it. This is the time to ask everyone you meet about the neighborhood—its pluses and minuses, special advantages you would not necessarily know about, the schools, the traffic, etc. Most people who are happy in their neighborhood are more than willing to talk about it. If you find, however, that those you question are reluctant to talk, that tells you something about the neighborhood as well.

Nighttime tours can be eye-opening. Many home buyers move into what they think is a quiet neighborhood only to find out otherwise later. For example, their new home might be a block away from a music club that not only is noisy at night but also parks customers' cars on nearby side streets. Perhaps the beautiful park in the heart of the neighborhood becomes a picnic ground on summer nights with noisy ball games and music until 11 p.m. There may be a lot of traffic in the neighborhood in the evening because the neighborhood streets are shortcuts from the highway to the local shopping mall. Maybe the neighborhood is peaceful and quiet, but on your evening visit, you discover that there is little or no street lighting.

Interpreting What You See

As you walk or drive through a neighborhood, try to apply what you see to the way you live. Do you like to walk, and are stores and schools within walking distance? Do you want a compact neighborhood with a closely knit community, or would you rather live in a more impersonal place? Do you like hustle and bustle, or do you prefer quiet, serene surroundings? Find out as much as you can about the place–both concrete facts and ambience–before you consider buying there. Remember, you probably will be living in a home and a neighborhood for a long time, so be certain about the area before your commit.

What should you be looking for as you explore the neighborhood? Following are a few guidelines:

- Are yards well kept, or are they full of weeds and overgrown? Are there broken bikes or toys in the yards? Are there cars on blocks? These are signs of a careless attitude about property on the part of the owners and a lack of community concern about appearances.

- Do children play freely in the yards or streets? This may indicate that it is a safe neighborhood, but it also can mean that there are no parks or playgrounds in the area.

- Are there older people sitting on porches or in the yards as well as families and children working or playing outside? This tells you that there is a balance of ages and types of residents.

- Is the street traffic within the neighborhood heavy? Is there street parking? Think about traffic noise and pollution.

- Are there neighborhood stores, restaurants or service stations located conveniently nearby? Are these establishments scattered among residential homes, indicating mixed commercial and residential zoning?

- Is there a shopping mall or a large industrial complex close enough to have an impact on traffic and parking?

- Are there any manufacturing plants or municipal complexes nearby, such as chemical manufacturers or sewage treatment plants, that could affect air quality or noise levels? These plants may be within the proper zoning area but still have an impact on the neighborhood's quality of life.

- What about noise? Is the neighborhood close to a major highway, and can you hear the traffic from the road day and night? How far away is the airport? Here is a good reason to visit the area at night and on a weekend. People who live near large airports will tell you that the noise is unremitting on Sunday evenings as travelers arrive and leave after the weekend. Is the block you are interested in near a fire station? While this is good for you in the rare event of a fire at your home, do not forget that sirens and noise can occur in the middle of the night.

- Are there signs of visual pollution—radio and TV broadcasting towers, utility substations and transformers, car dealerships, salvage yards, storage facilities or overnight parking for taxi fleets?

- Does the neighborhood have many vacant lots, abandoned buildings, empty stores or a large number of for sale signs? Does it have a feeling of being run-down or unsafe? Are the sidewalks and streets in a state of disrepair? Is it generally noisy? Do there appear to be illegal transactions occurring on the streets?

- Do windows on lower floors of the homes in the neighborhood have iron bars?

Mini-Tours

You have toured the neighborhood on four different occasions by car and on foot. You have noted what is available, accessible and desirable about the area. Now it is time to take a few specific mini-tours.

Shop in a Neighborhood Store

Does the store carry items you normally buy? Do you feel comfortable shopping there? How are the prices? Are there extra services—for example, someone to carry out your purchases and help load your car? Is the staff friendly and helpful?

One woman who was moving from the East Coast to a Midwestern city decided to visit some local stores to get a sense of the neighborhood. She went to the local grocery to buy a few items and at the checkout proclaimed that the local sales tax seemed high. Immediately, the employee and a dozen or so customers chimed in and complained about the sales tax.

Before the newcomer left, she had the names of a pediatrician, car insurance agent, the closest driver's license facility location, a mechanic, a plumber and a hairdresser, plus the story hours schedule at the local library. This was enough to convince her that this particular Midwestern neighborhood was friendly and helpful, and she decided to concentrate her home search in that particular area.

Make the Commute

If you are looking at a particular neighborhood, figure out the best commute route to your job and then make the commute. If you are going to drive, make the actual drive during the time you normally would be making it. Also, try to make the commute on a Tuesday or a Friday, typically the heaviest traffic days. Note the time and traffic congestion. Look for alternate routes. Ask someone in the neighborhood if the commute time would be shorter if you left earlier or later.

Look carefully at newly developed fringe suburbs. Often the existing roads cannot handle the growing traffic congestion of an expanding area.

> **Tip**
>
> Traffic congestion in a newly developing area may be the first sign of a community whose local government services cannot keep up with the growth of the community. These communities also may have poor teacher to student ratios and inadequate emergency services.

If you are going to use public transportation, again make the commute. How far is the bus or train stop from your potential home? How far is the walk at the other end of the commute? How long does the commute take? Do you have to transfer lines or buses? Is the bus or train crowded? Is there a regular schedule? Does it make a difference at either end what time you leave? How much does it cost round trip every day for a year's worth of workdays? Can you buy passes at a savings? Is there more than one way to go?

Many people do not pay sufficient attention to commuting time or distance when they are looking for a home. It is a personal choice to decide that a long commute is worthwhile in order to buy a home you like at a price you can afford. Many people choose to endure a long commute–even up to 2 hours one way–to live in a home they like and can afford. What about the fact that the lower home price may be balanced by the expense of the commute? Some people think of their housing and commute costs as one expense, and as long as the total of these falls below what the total transportation and housing costs would be in a closer location, they feel they are truly saving.

> **Tip**
>
> Do not forget other commutes. Make the commute you will face to take your children to day care, to school, to the park, to church, to the dentist or to after-school jobs. How far is a store where you can pick up milk or a prescription—can you stop on your way home from work, or do you have to drive out of your way either from work or from home? Are you involved in church or volunteer activities that require a commute? Try to find out if a target neighborhood is going to be convenient or if you will spend much of your time getting someplace else.

Go to School

If you have children, stop by the local school and ask for a tour and a visit with the principal. Look at the condition of the school—is it clean, quiet and neat? Ask about teacher-to-student ratio, special classes, enrichment classes, facilities—library, lunchroom, gymnasium, study halls, auditorium, playground. Are there special services like speech therapy, tutoring or special reading programs? Request a daily schedule, a list of school holidays and requirements for admission—immunizations, dental checkups, previous records, etc. Ask about busing and after-school activities. Does the school offer sports teams, art or music? Tell the principal about your children's special talents or needs and ask if the school can meet those needs. Finally, find out if you can attend a PTA meeting or an all-school event.

Attend City Council

On one of your tours of the neighborhood, stop in at a city council meeting. Try to arrive when the meeting begins because that is often the time period set aside for citizen comment. Learn the name of the alderman from the neighborhood you are investigating and pay attention to how that representative interacts with citizens, staff and other officials. Ask for minutes of an earlier meeting and any other handouts that you are entitled to have. In particular, look for information about taxes, zoning, infrastructure and projected uses for undeveloped land in the area:

- What is the property tax rate? Is a general tax increase expected?
- Are any special assessments anticipated on such infrastructure elements as sewers, water supply, paving or repaving, drainage improvements, sidewalks, schools or parks?
- Are zoning changes planned?
- Is new development anticipated that will change zoning codes, impose infrastructure assessments, overstrain utilities or parking capacity or impede traffic flow?

Visit Your Preferred Place of Worship

Go to a service to see if this neighborhood institution is a fit for you and your family. Do you feel comfortable among the worshippers, and is there a place for everyone in your family? Visit the children's religious education program and, if possible, stay for the social hour after the service.

Fair Housing Laws

While discrimination is unacceptable in any form, it does exist, and housing transactions are not immune. Some people believe that there are mortgage lenders and insurance companies that redline certain neighborhoods—that is, they draw an imaginary red line around the area on a map and refuse to extend loans or insurance to people in those areas because they regard the residents as having a high rate of default or the neighborhoods as deteriorating. Others think that minorities are denied loans because the mortgages are typically less profitable or smaller. Whatever the reason, this can lead to discrimination.

If you feel unwelcome in a neighborhood or have difficulty obtaining a mortgage or insurance in a neighborhood, remember that there are fair housing laws that prohibit discrimination. The Fair Housing Act covers most housing and prohibits discrimination in the sale, rental, and financing of dwellings and in other housing-related transactions, based on race, color, national origin, religion, sex, familial status (including people under the age of 18 living with parents or legal custodians, pregnant women, and people securing custody of children under the age of 18), and handicap (disability).

Contact your local HUD office or visit **www.hud.gov** for more information about violations or to file a complaint.

Getting Down to Specifics

If you like what you see on the walking and mini-tours, it is time to investigate your specific requirements.

Housing Stock

If you have selected the type of house you want—single family, townhouse, condo or some variation (see Chapter 8 for more information—scout out neighborhoods that have homes within your category. Look for more than just a cluster of homes that you like. You want a defined area with boundaries and a physical sense of community. In the 1970s and 1980s, some city planners and developers adopted a mixed-use concept of neighborhood development called planned unit developments (PUDs). These plans offered a variety of housing types in community layouts that incorporated open space to tie housing, retail and commercial uses together. Schools, religious houses and shopping centers also were located within the development. This type of planning has been expanded to neighborhood unit developments that incorporate mixed uses and encourage neighborhood cohesiveness.

This may appeal to you because of the housing choices as well as the planned sense of neighborhood. However, think carefully about your own preferences. You may not enjoy living in a single family home next to a five-story condo whose inhabitants can look down into your bedroom windows.

While you are still in the early stages of selecting a neighborhood, you should learn all you can about housing codes, zoning laws and homeowners association restrictions for each of your targeted neighborhoods. For example, some communities will not permit you to store your boat or park your recreational vehicle in your driveway. Other communities limit the number of nonrelated residents living in your home.

Finally, look at the age of the neighborhood and the housing stock. Is it an older, stable area with mature trees and well maintained homes, or is it just old? Is there undeveloped land that could be used for new homes that would clash with their surroundings? Is the area so new that it looks raw and has no amenities yet? A new cluster of townhouses sitting on open land far away from public transportation and shopping can feel like a series of motels surrounded by constant traffic.

> **Tip**
>
> Always keep resale in the back of your mind. The traditional advice is to buy the most modest house on a more expensive street. This house will maintain its value, and it will be easy to resell because there will always be buyers eager to buy into the prestige of the neighborhood. You even can remodel or improve it because alterations will not move it out of the price range for that street. Conversely, the fanciest house on that street will never earn back the money the owner invests, because buyers always will aspire to buy in another, even fancier neighborhood.

Schools

A good neighborhood with good schools equals rapid and higher home appreciation.

This applies whether or not you have children in the schools. If you approach buying a home with the terms resale and home equity value in mind, you will look for a home in a desirable school district. If you have children, you are getting a double advantage.

> **Tip**
>
> One way to pinpoint a good school system is to see if real estate agents advertise that their listings are within a certain school district. An area with a reputation for good schools will attract serious buyers.

To learn about the schools, start with the mini-tour as described above and make a personal visit. If the school appears to be satisfactory, then investigate a little more deeply. You can talk to a real estate agent, but he or she may not have detailed information or may choose not to divulge negatives. Instead, try searching the Internet for Web sites that publish statistical information from which you can draw conclusions about a school system.

The last and most important step in your school evaluation is to talk to parents in the neighborhood. On your neighborhood mini-tours to stores, schools, religious institutions and even bus stops, actively seek out parents and ask their opinions of the schools. This is also an opportunity to ask about day care and preschools. If you can attend a school function or PTA meeting, linger behind and ask some questions. As a side benefit, you probably also will find out about pediatricians, playgrounds, library programs and day care in the area.

Many school sponsored Web sites provide you with information about individual schools in a particular neighborhood. Turn to the Resources section in Appendix A for a list of Web sites.

Parking

Assuming you have done a practice commute, is there anything else you should investigate about transportation? Parking is especially important, and you need to look into it even if you do not own a car. In a congested urban area, parking is an important factor in the resale of a home. Plus, even without a car, you may invite guests who will need to park.

You may be looking at a single family home with its own garage, carport or driveway, but what about extra family cars? What about guests? Can you take deliveries or receive packages?

Be certain to find out about any restrictions. Some towns ban street parking between 2 a.m. and 6 a.m. Others regulate parking based on rush hours. Will you have to move your car every other Wednesday for street cleaning? Do local authorities tow cars to remove snow? Is the street dotted with driveways, curb cuts and restricted spots that reduce parking space? Does the local homeowners association or block group require parking permit stickers? If so, what do you do when you have guests who need to park?

In many urban neighborhoods, parking controls the residents' lives. They hurry home to get a parking space before 6 p.m., or they do not go out at night for fear of losing their parking space. Be sure you are willing to live that way before committing to a home with potential parking problems.

Tip
Beware of new developments being planned or built without adequate parking. Check out local zoning ordinances to find out if new construction must allow for parking for each unit. If not, then your street parking may become even scarcer once the new housing development is finished.

Public Services

Public services are those community services that often are taken for granted until they are not available. In any new neighborhood, find out all you can about the following:

- **Police and fire protection**—Are police, fire and emergency services readily available and adequate for the size of the community? Is there 911 or another emergency service number? Do police patrol beats either on foot or in squad cars? Is the fire department a municipal division or volunteer? Is there a neighborhood watch program in effect?

- **Hospitals and medical services**—Is there a nearby hospital? Does it operate an emergency room, or has it been closed due to budgetary constraints? Does the community have a medical clinic, dentists, medical specialists and a conveniently located pharmacy?

- **Street and road maintenance**—Are streets and roads in good repair? Do local or county crews remove snow and keep roads open in the winter? Are homeowners responsible for cleaning or maintaining any sidewalks or roads adjacent to their property? Some homes in more remote locations, including some suburbs, are in unincorporated areas that do not provide the usual public services. If you are looking at such a piece of property, be sure to find out which public services are available and whether or not you have to pay a fee to access their use.

- **Water supply**—Is the neighborhood part of a municipal water service, or will you have to have a well? Are there restrictions on water usage, especially in dry months? What about sewers? Is the area on a sewer line, or will you have to have a septic tank? Bear in mind that a newly constructed development may have more up-to-date utilities, whereas an older neighborhood may have infrastructure deterioration that could mean a special assessment later on. Ask the current owner of the home you are interested in if there have been any problems with tree roots clogging sewer and water lines.

- **Garbage collection**—What is the typical arrangement for trash removal? Is this a city or municipal service provided at no fee, or will you have to pay a fee? Are trash cans or trash bins provided? How often are the pickups? Will you have to haul away and dispose of your own garbage? Is the disposal site nearby?

Consider these questions when you look at a neighborhood. You may have other concerns such as the quality of TV reception, the location of the nearest post office and the availability of telephone, cable and satellite services. These are issues you should ask about when you talk to residents in the neighborhood. A cable company will extol its performance in its sales pitch, but the homeowner working in his or her yard will tell you the true quality of the service.

Neighborhood Pros and Cons

If you have found a neighborhood that you would like to consider, make a list of positives and negatives. Evaluate those areas where there are more negatives than positives. Some of your negatives may be pertinent to your specific situation and may not reflect on the neighborhood in general. But if you have found neighborhoods that do not look safe or may be detrimental to maintaining the value of your home, you may want to rule them out.

Crime

One of the most important pieces of information you need to know is whether or not the neighborhood is safe. Can your children walk to school or play outside safely? Can you leave your car parked on the street without fear of vandalism? Can anyone in your family come home late from work without worrying about assault or harassment? Visit the local police precinct or the city's Web site and look for the police blotter. Check out records of robberies, break-ins, vandalism, assault or illegal drug transactions. Try to determine where the highest concentration of crime occurs and whether or not the authorities are in control.

Overcrowding

Does it seem as if there are too many people on the street, in the stores or at the parks? Are there more cars than there are parking spaces? Do some single family homes appear to be rooming houses or broken into several units? Do you have a sense of being crowded or restricted?

Traffic

Heavy traffic, commercial trucks and roaring motorcycles generate noise and pollution. The steady roar of automobile traffic from a nearby expressway or the ceaseless whine of jet airplane engines approaching an airport is not conducive to a quiet, peaceful home setting. Check out the neighborhood for traffic sounds and sources.

Early Blight

Early signs of a neighborhood going downhill may not be obvious but still may exist. Does the area seem somewhat shabby? Do broken sidewalks and holes in the street indicate reduced municipal services? Do yards look presentable but not really cared for—grass is mowed but there are no flowers or extra touches. Are there no children playing outside?

All of these may be signals that a neighborhood is in the early stages of neglect. While you may find a housing bargain here, your property value will not hold up, and you may have trouble later when you try to resell.

Neighborhood Checklist

Below is a checklist to use when you are looking at neighborhoods. As you progress in your search, you may want to add items to either list to help in making your decision.

Must Have	Would Like
Safe community	Neighborhood watch
Good schools	Good library, park, recreation areas
Residential zoning	No commercial areas
Diverse community	Area with children
Trees, landscaping	Mature trees
Public transportation	Walking distance to stores, library, parks
Street parking	Low traffic
Accessible public and health services—police and fire, hospital emergency room, medical professionals	Municipal sewer and water services
Garbage collection	Street repair and maintenance—snow removal, pavement repair
Good resale value of property	Continued appreciation of property
Other:	Other:

Summary

Choosing a neighborhood is as important as choosing a home. There are many factors to consider like schools, crime rate, diversity of local residents, shopping and transportation availability. When touring a specific neighborhood it is important to make a list of your ideal neighborhood to help you prioritize your needs. This will help you narrow your search so you can find a home in a neighborhood that you enjoy.

What You Have Learned

- How to evaluate a neighborhood to see if it meets your needs.
- The time of day to tour the neighborhood.
- What public servies are available in the community.

Free Forms and Checklists

Visit **Socrates.com** and register to receive a variety of useful FREE forms, letters and checklists. See page iv for details on how to register (you will need the seven-digit registration code provided on the enclosed CD).

10

· · · · · ·

Looking for a Home

In This Chapter

- Learn what to look for when looking at homes.
- Understand what a universal home is and determine if it is right for you.
- Consider the future plans when choosing a home.
- Discover if you are a good candidate for a fixer-upper home.

Looking for a house has been your primary goal all along. Despite your eagerness to begin the search, you have taken the time to learn how much home you can afford, what type of home you want and the neighborhood you want to live in. This preliminary homework may have seemed tedious, but as you begin to look, your search will be focused and productive.

You probably have a good idea of what you would like in a home, and as you have toured through neighborhoods, you have seen homes that have some appealing features. All of these ideas are the beginning entries in your home checklist of Must Have and Would Like items—similar to the one you used while shopping for neighborhoods. This gives you a good idea of what you would like and what you will not accept.

You can use this checklist to describe to your real estate agent what you are looking for or to begin your own search in an organized fashion. Do not be surprised if your list changes as you look at homes. You may find that it is not possible to get what you want in the price range you can afford. More likely, after looking at a few homes, you will revise your opinions about what is really necessary in your new home.

Tip
Do not forget the adage that the top criteria for selecting a home is location. If you cannot afford a home in the location you want, give up some of your requirements for the home rather than giving up the location.

There are also checklists at the end of this chapter to guide you as you look at homes. These include your general wish list, a structural list that prompts you to look for current maintenance or repair needs and a fixtures inventory checklist, on which you can note what fixtures come with the house, such as the dining room chandelier. You can use a fresh set for each home so that you have a consistent review of everything you see and can compare homes using the same criteria. Before you make up your checklist packet, however, you may want to read the rest of the chapter to clarify what you really want to look for in a home.

Beginning with the Basics

As soon as you have made up your checklists, give them to your real estate agent. Be sure to include your short lists of absolutes. Also give your agent your mortgage preapproval information so that he or she knows the price range for which you qualify. Provide the agent with as much information as you can so that neither of you wastes time looking at homes you cannot afford or do not like.

At the same time, allow your agent some leeway to prescreen homes for you. After all, the agent knows the market and may suggest a home that he or she thinks you might like even if it does not meet all of your criteria. Many buyers surprise even themselves when they like a house that does not fit their prestated requirements.

To help your agent be a little more flexible in prescreening properties, you should sit down as a family and determine acceptable trade-offs. Would you rather have a bigger kitchen or a fourth bedroom? Do you need an enclosed garage, or will a carport do? Is an eat-in kitchen acceptable, or do you want a formal dining room—or both? Would you trade a mudroom at the back door for a screened front porch? The final selection of a home generally requires compromise.

You must communicate all of your preferences and trade-offs to your agent and then allow him or her to select some homes for you to look at. Do not underestimate the agent's analysis of a neighborhood or area. A good real estate agent is able to sense a shift in the real estate market of a given area, and his or her access to market data as well as sense of the market are invaluable tools when matching a property to a buyer. Take advantage of these assets.

As the buyer, you have some responsibility as well. As you look at each home, be honest with your agent; do not hesitate to convey any negative reactions. The agent needs straightforward feedback about what you like and do not like. This will help both you and your agent to refine your list of requirements and find a match. Feedback is especially important if you find yourself changing your mind about certain preferences.

If your agent does not pick up on your reactions, then you should think about using a different agent. Looking for a home is too time-consuming and important to waste your energy on homes that do not fit your predetermined criteria. Fortunately, most real estate agents are quite attuned to a client's reactions; after all, meeting their client's needs means making a sale.

Looking at Potential Homes

Here are some general tips for house hunting:

- **Wear comfortable clothing and good walking shoes**—You will be amazed at how many miles you walk while touring houses and neighborhoods. Also, try to find a backpack or shoulder bag to carry your checklists, maps and other reference materials. Do not forget to toss in a tape measure. If at all possible, use the bag only when house hunting; that way, you will keep all the pertinent materials together and ready for each new house tour.

- **Allow time to look at homes**—You will need approximately 1 to 2 hours to check out a home inside and outside on the first visit.

- **Do not schedule too many visits in one outing**—This is a recipe for fatigue and forgetfulness. All the features of all the home will merge together in your mind, and you will not remember which ones, if any, you want to revisit.

- **Do not take your children on the first visit**—You want to devote your full attention to the home and not to your children's behavior or their reactions. If you like the home and are thinking about making an offer, take the children on the second or third visit.

- **Have the agent check the sales on comparable properties in the neighborhood**—This gives you a basis to evaluate the neighborhood and to make a realistic offer if you like a home.

- **Ask the agent how long the home has been on the market**—This may be a clue to the asking price or to problems with the home.

- **Ask why the home is on the market**—This may help you understand the sellers reason for putting the home on the market and his or her motivation to sell it.

- **Try to establish some rapport with the seller**—This may help later when you are ready to make an offer.

- **Ask what comes with the home, such as fixtures, appliances or built-ins**—Use your fixtures inventory checklist.

- **Use your structural checklist to note problems with the structure of the home**—Be sure to view the home in daylight so that you can detect any problems. You can return at night to complete your overall impression of the property.

- **If you like the home, ask the agent to schedule a second tour**—Be prepared to make an offer if everything seems to be in order.

- **Be patient**—Many people spend at least 1 year looking for a home. Granted, if you are involved in a job transfer and need to find a place to live immediately, you do not have a year to visit homes. On the other hand, if you are not at all familiar with the area into which you are moving, you may want to rent first and take a year to learn about the area and look for a home. Whatever you do, do not make an offer just because you are tired of searching. Try to allow enough time to find the right home without making hasty decisions.

Thinking about What You Want in a Home

As you begin to construct your individual checklists and look at homes, think about what you want or need overall. Ask the following questions:

- **Is the home large enough?** Can it expand as your family expands? Are there unfinished rooms or an unfinished basement that can be converted into living space later? Be sure to look at the lot. If the house sits on a hillside, you may not be able to add rooms.

- **Are the rooms large enough to accommodate your furniture?** Will the layout of the floor plan fit your lifestyle? Is there a sense of openness, or are the rooms distinctly separate from each other?

- **Is the storage space ample or merely adequate?** Do not look just at the closets. Look at storage space in the kitchen—pantry, broom closet, cupboards; garage—overhead loft, built-in shelving; basement—built-in shelving, cabinets, crawl space; or attic. Ask about the availability of extra storage space in multiple family units, such as condos, co-ops or townhouses.

Special Feature: The Storage Entry

Is there space at the entrance foyers or at the back door or the door from an attached garage to create a storage entry? This is a place where family members can stow belongings as they come home. You might include a table for mail, a key rack, shelves for backpacks and sports equipment, a coat rack or closet and a bench. This type of entry prevents family members from shedding coats, packs, books and other paraphernalia throughout the main living areas of the home. Plus, everyone knows where they left their belongings. Some homes have mudrooms that can be converted to an entry storage room, or you may find a house with an appropriate space to create one.

- **Where will you be eating?** Is there a formal dining room or an eat-in kitchen? What about a breakfast area? Could the breakfast area be better used as a family room or a home office? Will the eating space allow you to entertain or serve at parties?

- **Is the kitchen well-equipped?** Does it have a workable layout? Is it a walking kitchen—that is, do you have to walk back and forth considerably to prepare meals—or is everything reasonably within reach? Is there enough storage for food, cooking equipment and dishes? Is cleanup efficient? Can you supervise homework or talk with guests while working in the kitchen? It does not matter how modern or attractive a kitchen is if you cannot work comfortably in the room.

- **Do the kitchen and other rooms have sight lines into other areas of the home?** Can you watch the children while working in the kitchen or home office, or are rooms isolated from the rest of the house's living area?

- **Where are the laundry fixtures?** In the basement? Next to the kitchen? Near the bedrooms and bathrooms? Many people prefer that the laundry facilities be located near the areas where the dirty laundry is generated—bedrooms, bathrooms or kitchen.

- **Are there enough bathrooms?** Are there enough showers and tubs? Some bathrooms have only shower stalls and others have only tubs, which may mean waiting in line no matter how many bathrooms there are in the home.

- **Are there enough bedrooms, and is there space for guests?** Does the house have a den, family room or other multipurpose room that can be used for extra sleeping space for guests or visiting family members?

- **How large is the garage?** Will it hold more than one car? If you are looking at an older home, does its garage have enough space for a sport utility vehicle? Does the garage have storage space for bicycles, mowers and garden supplies in addition to adequate space for vehicles? Does the garage have an attic that can be converted to another room? Finishing off or remodeling a garage attic can add space without changing the layout or proportions of the home.

- **What kind of light does the home have?** Are there large windows that let in natural light? Does it have a southern or western exposure that provides daylight for most of the day, or is the structure flesh up against a taller building or a wall that blocks light? Are there ceiling fixtures or recessed lighting, and are they adequate? Is there ample and directed lighting in the kitchen and other work areas, or do you stand in your own light? This is one of the reasons why you want to visit a home at night.

- **Does the home afford cross ventilation?** This may seem minor, but a home without sufficient ventilation can trap cooking odors or stale air, and you may find that heating and air conditioning are less efficient. If you live in a colder climate, will you be able to open the windows and air out the home in the spring?

- **What kind of heating and/or air conditioning systems does the home have?** Are there radiators or air vents? Do not forget to look for return air vents; an inadequate number or poor placement of these can affect the efficiency and cost of your heating and cooling systems. Can you control the temperature room by room, or does one thermostat control the entire home? What fuels the systems: electricity, gas or oil? An all-electric home may be efficient, but your electric bill will be very high. Everyone understands that electric heat and air conditioning are expensive to operate, but many people forget about the hot water heater or electric clothes dryer. People who live in electric homes often turn off the hot water heater if they are going out of town because they know they will see substantial savings on the electric bill. Ask the seller about the utility bills by season.

- **Is the wiring sufficient for your needs?** If you are considering new construction, the wiring is more than likely adequate for your appliances, lights and home entertainment equipment. If you are looking at older homes, however, you may be surprised at how minimal the wiring is. Some older homes were built before the advent of many household appliances. If you like to operate your microwave and run your dishwasher at the same time or blow dry your hair while the air conditioner is on, you may have to rewire or add circuits. Talk to the seller about the state of the electrical system; you want it to be both adequate and safe.

- **Is a cable hookup available?** Can you get both cable television and cable Internet service? What other utility services are available? Can you use gas for heating and cooking, or are you limited to electric furnaces and stoves? What about sewers and water services? In rural or outlying areas, you may have to use a septic tank and dig a well. You need to talk to your agent or the seller to learn what is available in that area.

- **Is the water pressure satisfactory?** Ask to turn on faucets to gauge the pressure. Is the flow full and steady, or does it trickle out? Try out every faucet; some may have been replaced while others are occluded with mineral buildup.

- **Is there a fireplace?** Ask the seller if the chimney draws well. Is there a place to store wood in the garage or yard?

- **What are your flooring options?** A new development may offer wall-to-wall carpet, wood floors or tile. Consider how you will use the home; you may want the look of wood or you may want the sound muffling benefit of carpeting. Older homes may come as they are, so you should be sure to check the condition of the floors or carpet. This could become a bargaining element in price negotiations.

- **Is a view important to you?** Do you want to be able to see a vista, or would you rather confine your view to the privacy of your own yard? If the latter is the case, can you build a fence or landscape to create your own view?

- **Does the outside of the house look well maintained?** Do you want low-maintenance siding, or are you willing to paint? Does the home need a paint job? Does it appear to have been painted recently in a haphazard way in order to spruce up the place for selling? Do you see signs of damage, leaks, cracks, poorly fitting windows or the need for tuck-pointing? Are storm windows and screens in good repair? Walk around the entire home and look at it from all angles. Do not forget to drive by the home at night. You may discover that a powerful streetlight illuminates the entire home and shines into all the bedroom windows, for example, or that your ideal location at the end of a dead-end street means that the headlights of every car driving down it beam into your windows.

- **Do you like the lot?** Is it the right size for the yard you envision or are willing to maintain? Does it suit the home, or does the size of the home overwhelm it? Is the lot average size for the neighborhood? This provides a sense of consistency and proportion to the neighborhood, which is important in the resale of a home. Is the lot shaped so that you can add rooms or another building, such as a garage or garden shed? What about drainage? Is the land sufficiently sloped and is the soil capable of absorbing water? Low areas that hold water can become problems, producing mud, damp or wet basements, foundation damage or breeding spots for mosquitoes. Is the home on a rise of land or in a low area? Does the lot slope away from the home on all sides? Do the contours of the lot affect the soil, which, in turn, can have an impact on the way the home settles? Ask the real estate agent and the seller about these potential problems, but do some homework as well. Find out if the home is in a flood-prone area or if there is any history of soil contamination from previous uses of the land. A mortgage lender can answer some of these questions and also put you in touch with commercial insurance agents who can sell you federal flood insurance.

Tip

Windows need more than a cursory glance. New homes often have thermopane glass windows with two panes of glass rather than one. This eliminates the annual spring and fall chores of putting up screens and storm windows. An older home may have standard windows, but in many cases, newer windows can be installed. Many new double-hung windows are one unit; the thermopanes and the screens slide up and down within the frame so that you can adjust them depending on the weather. Some of these even allow you to pop the window panes out and wash them inside the home. All of these features may eliminate the need to teeter on a tall ladder twice a year.

You also should check on the type of glass in the windows, including any sliding glass doors. A sliding glass door should contain glass that is a good insulator. The ideal is called low E glass, which, although expensive, has about twice as high the insulation value as regular glass. You can recoup the initial expense of installing new insulating windows in lower heating and cooling costs. For this reason, you may want to consider investing in new windows as your first improvement to a new home. Visit **www.efficientwindows.org** for more information.

As you start to look at homes, you will discover more questions that you want answered. If you are looking at rural sites, you will have different needs from those who are buying in an urban area. Your age, stage of life, family situation and personal preferences factor into what you want in a home. As new questions arise, you can add them to your checklists so that you are fully informed when you are ready to select a home and make an offer.

A Universal Home

A universal home is one that accommodates its inhabitants throughout their lifetime. Built using the principles of universal design, these homes are usable for people of different abilities and different ages.

Although these homes are accessible for people with disabilities, they offer much more. People who are very different can live comfortably in the same home. More importantly, its inhabitants can remain in their home even when their needs change. An elderly woman, for example, will not have to move out of the family home when she is no longer as active or agile as she was in her younger years. Young people also enjoy the comfort and convenience of a universal home; it is so much easier to open doors with lever door handles or turn on lights using rocker switches when your arms are full of grocery bags or small children. If you are temporarily incapacitated–because of a broken leg or a lingering illness, for example–universal design allows you to recover in comfort at home.

What features make a home a universal home? Following is a list of the more common ones:

- a stepless entry—without a ramp—onto a covered porch for easy access
- one-level living with eating areas, bedrooms, bathrooms and control panels located on a one-floor barrier-free level
- doorways at least 34 to 36 inches wide that allow wheelchairs and large baby strollers to pass through and permit residents to move large furniture or appliances in and out of the house
- thresholds flush with the floor to allow wheelchair access and to prevent tripping
- lever door handles
- wide hallways, preferably at least 42 inches wide
- extra floor space to allow wheelchair users to turn more easily and lend an air of spaciousness to the home
- well-planned lighting
- rocker light switches
- nonskid surfaces on floors
- handrails on steps and grab bars in bathrooms
- low entry door to showers
- easy-to-reach controls such as lighting, heating and cooling switches as well as electrical outlets at least 18 inches above the floor
- large closets with adjustable clothing rods and hooks that allow access for those in wheelchairs or for children, and that can be moved as needed to fit changing needs of the occupant
- front-loading washers and dryers
- kitchen sink base with leg room for someone who is seated

If you like the concept of the universal home, ask your real estate agent if there are listings for this type of home in your target neighborhood. If you are looking at conventional homes, you may be able to spot ways to convert a home to a more universal design. Many manufacturers realize the appeal of the universal home; they offer attractive and convenient appliances, cabinets and fixtures for the kitchen and bathroom that can be added to any home. Naturally, it is more cost-effective to build a new universal home—according to experts, it adds approximately 5 percent to the cost of construction—but you can adapt some of the ideas to an existing home if this type of design appeals to you.

Note

The idea of a universal home appeals to the federal and local governments as well; they are requiring that new federal housing or new housing built with public money be constructed with visitability features. This means that the home must be accessible enough for a visitor to get inside and use a bathroom. This type of legislation gradually may make universal design truly universal.

Looking to the Future

When you begin the process of buying a home, you are understandably focused on immediate tasks—finding a down payment, getting preapproved, finding a real estate agent. Nevertheless, take some time to look to the future. Although you may think you want to live in your new home for the rest of your life, you can change your mind or outgrow the house or condo or find yourself in different circumstances. That is why you must choose a home that can either change or grow with you or can be easily and profitably resold. Despite how you feel today, you may want a bigger and better home in the future, and you will use the proceeds from the sale of one home to buy the next. Resale value thus becomes a crucial part of a long-range plan.

Planning for Family Changes

As you pull together a list of features that you are looking for in a home, try to anticipate any potential changes in your circumstances. Is your family complete, or are you planning to have children? Do you have any older relatives who may need a place to live or at least some help in the future? Are there boomerang kids in your future—young adults who return to their parents' house after living on their own for awhile? Is there a possibility that you will start your own business and work out of your home or perhaps telecommute in your present job? Do you expect to be doing more business entertaining in your home?

Keep your future needs in the back of your mind when you are looking at homes. You may want to expand or remodel to accommodate family or work changes. Do not forget to check zoning laws in your preferred communities to see if there are restrictions about building onto existing homes or adding buildings to a lot.

If you plan on welcoming a new baby, you need to look at bedroom space; in fact, you should evaluate every space in the home. Babies and small children have a lot of equipment that consumes space. The narrow, efficient Pullman kitchen may appeal to the cook in the family, but it will not accommodate a highchair. The small rooms with intimate conversation areas and a state-of-the-art entertainment center soon become buried under toys, books, baby blankets and clothes.

The older generation has special needs as well. Privacy and quiet may be important, or a spot in the middle of the household's activity where they can observe as well as be observed may be necessary. A private bedroom and bath may be ideal.

Surprisingly, boomerang children often cannot return to living under the same conditions as before they left home. They–or you–may want their own private baths or areas. This may be the time to look into converting the garage attic into a small living unit.

The right home can be adapted to meet these changing needs, but you have to plan ahead when you select a home. If you are considering new construction, you might be able to find a universal design home that is geared to meet everyone's needs. If you are shopping for an older home, then you will want to determine if the lot and the home can accommodate additions or structural modifications. It may be years before you need to make these types of alterations, but you will at least have the comfort of knowing that you will not have to move if family changes occur.

A New Old Trend

Many years ago, second housing units called granny cottages were popular solutions to having family members nearby, but not too close. More recently, these types of housing units were zoned out of existence because many felt they lowered property values. Today in some areas, granny cottages are making a comeback, primarily because there is a socioeconomic trend toward reviving the extended family and because families need somewhere to put their boomerang children. The advantage is privacy both for the occupant of the cottage and the owner of the property. At the same time, both are able to help each other: grandma often baby-sits and the parents reciprocate by taking grandma on her errands, or the returning adult children take over exterior maintenance chores.

The concept of granny cottages makes financial sense because the homeowner owns the land on which the cottage sits. Plus, many modular home manufacturers offer a wide choice of cost-effective prefabricated models that can be erected in a short period of time. A common scenario involves a widowed elderly parent selling the old homestead and using the proceeds to buy a larger home for the son or daughter and adding a granny cottage to the property. Everybody wins.

Planning for Resale

There are two rules about reselling a home:

1. Look at properties where you can plan to live for at least 3 years, which is the time it usually takes to build equity that will exceed the costs of the transaction to sell. An important corollary to this is that first-time buyers should not engage in real estate speculation.

2. Focus your efforts on finding either a traditional single family detached home with three bedrooms, 2.5 baths and a two-car garage or a condo/co-op/townhouse with three bedrooms, two baths and a desirable location. These are typically the homes with the best salability potential should you have to move quickly.

Popular features that improve salability differ from region to region but there are a few standard guidelines that you should remember when you are looking at homes.

Location

Selecting the right neighborhood is essential. (See Chapter 9 for more information.) Try to determine if growth is moving in one direction. Are there good services–schools, shopping, public safety–in the area? Do the residents like living there?

Style

Home styles change, and homes that were once trendy may appear out-of-date. In some areas, split-level, split-entry or ranch houses were the style of choice at one time. Now, however, those styles of homes are no longer being built, which lowers their resale value. Likewise, interior decorating goes through fads; shag carpeting or avocado appliances may deter some buyers. Most will want to replace the outdated features, and their offers will reflect those anticipated remodeling expenses. The best plan is to buy a home that is more classic and less trendy so that you can resell it more easily.

Lot and Landscaping

As discussed earlier, you want to find a lot that is a standard shape and size for the neighborhood and shows no signs of flooding or drainage problems. For resale purposes, you want moderately sized front and back yards that allow flexibility in landscaping. Avoid constructing a showplace garden if you are trying to resell; many people will be unwilling to pay more for a stylish garden and, in fact, may shy away from the property.

Home Size

You want a home that fits its lot proportionately but is not the biggest or fanciest home in the neighborhood. The sizes of the homes next to yours are important when determining market value, and if they are all smaller than yours, they may lower your home's value. Of course, if you buy a smaller home than those of your neighbors, their larger homes can increase your value. In this situation, buying what you need in a good neighborhood is better financially than buying what you want in a less desirable neighborhood.

Interior Features

Most home buyers prefer three or four bedrooms, so a home with that many bedrooms will attract potential buyers when you are ready to resell. Two bathrooms are the minimum, and an additional half bath on a different floor for guests is preferred. A separate bath for the master bedroom is ideal.

Inadequate storage is a drawback. Buyers want plenty of closet space and prefer walk-in closets in the master bedroom. Linen closets in or near each bathroom are pluses, and pantries and ample storage facilities in basements and garages are good selling points. Ideally, condos should have extra storage space in common areas.

Laundry facilities, including work space and storage, should be conveniently located near the kitchen or bedrooms and baths in order to avoid carrying heavy loads of laundry up and down stairs.

As the center of family activity, the kitchen can be the most important room in the home. Buyers look for larger kitchens, modern appliances, plenty of counter space and a workable floor plan. There should be easy access to the outside for barbecuing and outdoor entertaining. An eating area in the kitchen appeals to most buyers, even if there is a formal dining room adjacent to the kitchen.

Garage and Parking

If there is a garage, it should be a two-car garage. In regions where traveling by automobile is mandatory, a three-car garage is important. The garage should have storage space and should be close to the home entrance so that carrying in groceries or other items is not a problem. Condos and other multiple family units should have two parking spaces per unit.

View

If you live in a scenic area, having a view will help sell the home.

Tip
Swimming pools do not add as much value as they once did. Safety and maintenance issues discourage many buyers. Therefore, having a pool may actually discourage potential buyers. If you want a pool for your own pleasure, however, buy a home that already has one. Installing a pool is costly, and you will never receive a good return on your investment when you sell the property.

Maintaining Perspective

Buying a home is both a financial investment and a personal adventure. It is important to resist emphasizing one aspect over the other. If you spend so much time and energy looking for a home you can resell, you will miss the emotional pleasure of owning and enjoying your home. On the other hand, ignoring the long-term effects of buying a home is tantamount to wasting money. Keep both the long-range financial costs and the personal fulfillment factor in mind when you look for a home.

Safe Rooms

Many homeowners and home developers are considering the idea of incorporating safe rooms or shelters into homes to protect families from the extremes of weather or storms. In fact, one condo developer in Iowa has included a 4-foot by 8-foot room in each unit that can withstand winds of up to 250 mph and more than 80,000 pounds of weight. Accommodating 10 people, the shelter room is lined with cedar walls, reinforced with Kevlar®–the material in bulletproof vests and tank armor–and bolted into a 4-inch concrete slab. The rooms can double as walk-in closets or safety deposit vaults.

The Federal Emergency Management Agency (FEMA) has developed a booklet on construction of residential safe rooms entitled "FEMA 320." The planning guide includes sections on understanding the hazards–hurricanes, tornadoes, wind–designing the room, complete with drawings, and building the shelter. Visit **www.fema.gov/mit/saferoom** for more information.

Housing Every Last Person (HELP) is the brainstorm of an architect and builder who have designed an emergency housing shelter that can operate in a self-sufficient manner using a gravity-fed water system, composting toilet and solar power. Easily transportable, the building has a living space with table, chairs, beds, shower and toilet. When the unit is no longer needed, it can be dismantled or used as a guest home or storage shed. Visit **www.helpishere.us** for more information.

Fixer-Upper Homes

Certain homes may be labeled handyman's specials or fixer-uppers. A fixer-upper often is defined as a home below neighborhood standards. These homes likely will be sold as is, meaning that all repairs will be at the expense of the buyer with no recourse against the seller for problems discovered later. If you have the experience or the skills to do extensive home repair, you may find the fixer-upper to be a very profitable undertaking.

Many fixer-uppers may be a good buy. They may require only minor work, such as a thorough cleaning, a new paint job, some landscaping, new carpets or minor repairs. Sellers of these homes often may not want the inconvenience of sprucing up the home and would rather sell it quickly at a lower price. Others may have inherited a neglected property and wish to sell the home and settle the estate. There are also elderly owners who have been happily living in an outdated home but now have to move for health reasons. You may be able to buy these homes and fix them up with minimal work and expense.

Properties needing extensive structural repairs or upgrades, however, may be unprofitable in the long run. You may be willing and able to repair the foundation, update the wiring and install new plumbing, but you will not recover your full investment because improvements that do not show do not add market value.

If this type of home is of interest to you, have an inspector go through the home carefully and list all problems. You also may want to hire an appraiser to estimate the home's current market value and its potential value after you make improvements to determine if buying this home is a worthwhile investment.

If you decide to buy a fixer-upper, be sure to look into HUD's 203K Home Rehabilitation Financing Program. The program allows the buyer to finance the acquisition cost of the home and the cost of repairs and improvements as one package based on the projected value of the home once the rehabilitation work is completed. A home must need at least $5,000 in repairs to be eligible for this program, which means you may be able to negotiate a lower purchase price and down payment because of the work needed. Furthermore, if you are a first-time home buyer, you will not need a down payment when assuming a 203K loan.

Finally, in terms of resale, the IRS Code 121 allows you to earn up to $250,000 in profits tax-free when you sell the house. The only stipulation is that you must have lived in the house as your primary residence 24 months of the 60 months before the sale. A married couple can qualify for up to $500,000 tax-free capital gains if both spouses meet the residency stipulation.

Checklists

Constructing your checklists may seem overwhelming at first—you have thousands of ideas about what you want. Perhaps the easiest way to begin is to make a very short list of what you absolutely must have and cannot live without. Some people want air conditioning in their new home; others want a fireplace. Some want an indoor parking space; others require accessible public transportation. You may want a basement that can be finished into a family room or workshop. What about a washer and dryer near the bedrooms and bathrooms to avoid toting laundry up and down stairs? The list should be short; these are the absolute requirements that will appear on all of your checklists. The first item on every list–and in some cases, perhaps the only item–is resale value.

Your second short list should be an itemization of what you do not want—what you absolutely cannot live with. Some people cannot consider a two-story house because a family member has difficulty climbing stairs. Those families with teenagers or young children, on the other hand, cannot imagine everyone living in a one-level home; they want a two-story house to separate the children's noise and the teens' privacy from the common areas of the household. Gardeners cannot live without a yard, and people with demanding jobs do not want a home that requires a great deal of regular maintenance. This short list also must include the one crucial feature that you cannot live with—poor resale value.

> **Tip**
>
> Think about specific features when you consider resale value. What may appeal to you–for example, a swimming pool–may be a negative to future buyers. What does not bother you at all, such as noise from a nearby airport, may hurt resale later.

Once you have pulled together the short lists, you can begin to expand them into workable checklists to use while house hunting. You can find sample checklists in the Resources section of Appendix A.

Summary

By now you have a good idea of what you would like in a home, as you have toured through neighborhoods. To further focus your search it is a good idea to make a checklist, similar to the one you used while shopping for neighborhoods, to help you figure the features and amenities you want and in the price range you can afford. Make sure when you are looking at homes you evaluate everything from the inside out and consider not only what your nees are today, but what your plans are for the future.

What You Have Learned

- The general tips for house hunting and a list of questions you should ask yourself when looking around the property.
- You now understand what a universal home is and whether it is right for you.
- When shopping, consider the future and resale plans for your home.
- The benefits of purchasing a fixer-upper home.

Discounts on Other Socrates Products

In addition to a variety of free forms and checklists, you will find special offers on a variety of Socrates products. Visit **www.socrates. com/books/ReadyHouseActionPlan.aspx** for more information.

Section Three

.....

Finding the Right Home

11

· · · · · ·

Making Home Inspections

In This Chapter

- How to do a thorough home inspection on your own.
- Learn who you need to contact for a professional inspection.
- What to expect after the inspection is complete.

After you have visited the available homes on your list, you must begin to narrow the choices. You have evaluated your finances, decided on the type of home you want and selected a neighborhood. After weighing your choices against your criteria, you settle on a final list. Now is the time to think about a home inspection.

The term home inspection sounds so official, but you already have begun the process by filling out the home ratings checklist while you toured homes. The first inspections are your own, from the one you conduct on your first visit to the one you should do as one of your last tasks before making an offer on a home.

In addition to your own inspections, you should arrange for a whole-house inspection by a professional inspector. If you are financing a home through a government loan, FHA or VA, there will be another inspection at the time of the appraisal.

Although the professional inspection occurs after you make an offer, you should still be concerned about it before you make the offer. A contingency clause in the offer contract stipulates that an inspection will be subject to a time limit–often 7 to 10 days–during which it must be completed. If you wait until the offer is made to find and schedule a professional inspector, you face the possibility of running out of time to research and schedule the inspector or of missing the deadline. Since you want to make any offer contingent on a satisfactory professional inspection report, you do not want to miss the inspection deadline. If that happens, you eliminate any chance of having the seller make any necessary repairs.

Therefore, you should start looking for an inspector as soon as you begin to focus on your final choice.

> **Tip**
>
> Most states mandate a written home defect disclosure form before a home can be sold. This is to prevent future lawsuits by buyers; if a home seller discloses a defect, then the buyer cannot file a misrepresentation lawsuit after a sale closes. If, on the other hand, the seller fails to reveal a defect, the buyer may have cause for a lawsuit if he or she can prove that the seller knew about it.
>
> Disclosure laws vary from state to state. Check your state and local ordinances to find out what type of information a seller must disclose at the time of the offer. As a rule, sellers are not exempt from the disclosure laws just because they are selling a property FSBO. In some areas there may be an exception for sellers who have never actually lived in the house—perhaps they inherited it through an estate or bought it but did not move in. This may change, however, if a locality is experiencing a surge of land or house speculation. It is important to obtain the most current disclosure requirements for the area you are considering.

Your Own Basic Inspections

If you have used the home ratings checklist from the Resources section in Appendix A, you already have noted your general impressions of the property: good condition, average condition or poor condition—unacceptable. If a home passes your general evaluation, ask for a second showing so that you can spend more time looking at the home carefully. This may be an opportunity to see a home without furnishings or other decorating that may be distracting or hide problems. Try to schedule this walk-through during the day when the best light is available and when you can walk around the outside of the home. This time look for specifics. Use the following checklist as you inspect the home.

Final Personal Inspection Checklist

Address:_____

Municipality:_____School district:_____

Asking price:_____Property taxes:_____

Square feet:_____Style:_____

Number of bedrooms:_____Number of baths:_____

Area	Yes	No	Notes
Exterior needs paint, repairs, cleaning			
Siding in good condition			
Foundation cracked or shifted			
Lot flat, good drainage			
Lot flexibility to add to house			
Tree branches or roots threatening roof or foundation			
Sidewalks in good condition			
Landscaping appropriate			
Decks/patios/porches in good condition			
Garage in good condition			
Driveway/carport in good condition			
Outbuildings in good condition			
House roof in good condition			
Eaves in good condition			
Chimney plumb and in good condition			
Evidence of roof leaks inside and/or outside			
Double glazed windows			
Window frames tight and in good condition			
Evidence of leaks around windows			
Exterior doors in good condition			
Attic ceiling in good condition			
Attic cold			
Attic warm			
Attic insulation at least 12 inches			
Attic ventilation good			
Attic suitable for storage			
Basement damp			

Area	Yes	No	Notes
Basement insulated			
Basement walls cracked or stained			
Mildew odor in basement			
Insect damage in basement			
Sump pump in basement			
Dehumidifier in basement			
Basement suitable for storage			
Basement finished			
Electrical wiring in good condition			
Wiring adequate and meets current code			
Amperage			
Voltage			
Number and location of outlets			
Outlets three-prong			
Cable installed			
Dead end or exposed wiring			
Electrical service overhead or underground			
Plumbing in good condition			
Water pressure good			
Water supply pipes meet code			
Hot water heater electric or gas			
Source of water: municipal or well			
Sewers or septic tank			
Heating/cooling in good condition			
Heating system functioning and energy efficient			
System fuel: gas, electric, oil			
Heat sources: radiators, baseboards, registers			

Area	Yes	No	Notes
Heat source in each room			
Fireplaces in good condition			
Flues functional			
AC functioning and energy efficient			
Appliances in good condition and energy efficient			
AC sources: central, window/wall units			
AC source in each room			
Dishwasher working			
Stove working			
Refrigerator working			
Laundry appliances working			
Interior needs paint, repairs, cleaning			
Wood floors			
Tile floors			
Wall-to-wall carpeting			
Floors and carpet in good condition			
Walls in good condition			
Ceilings in good condition			
Evidence of water damage on floors or ceilings			
Window hardware included			
Ceiling or light fixtures included			
Built-in furniture			
Interior doors in good condition			

> **Tip**
>
> A well-insulated attic should be cold. A large, uninsulated attic space is a source of heat loss, which is evident if snow on the roof melts and creates runoff that refreezes as icicles dangling from eaves. A warm attic can increase heating bills, and frozen runoff can damage the roof.

Test While You Inspect

Your second inspection is the time to test the home that you are examining. Walk around the lot to check sight lines and adjoining lots—is there a large doghouse in the yard next door, or will car headlights shine directly into your windows at night? If the roof looks old or has missing or curled shingles, ask if a roof inspector has looked at the house recently and request a copy of the report. Look at exterior and interior walls carefully and feel for dampness. Measure the insulation in the attic. Turn on the water in more than one place to see if water pressure drops—when you run the shower while the kitchen sink faucet is on, for example. Flip on lights, including exterior lights and lights in the garage or other outbuildings. Find out if all the appliances work. Check the insulation gasket on the refrigerator doors. Note the location of heating or air conditioning vents and the placement of the thermostat. Is there cross ventilation?

Will the floor plan work for your family? Walk through a typical meal preparation in the kitchen area. Is this a compact, efficient kitchen, or do you have to walk from the pantry to the refrigerator to the stove to the cupboards? Is there sufficient counter space? Do the same for the laundry facilities. Are the washer and dryer located in a convenient spot? Will you have to carry loads of laundry up and down narrow stairs? Is there a laundry chute? Does the laundry area have adequate work space for sorting and folding laundry?

In short, during this inspection, mentally live through a typical day for you and your family. Imagine how you will manage your daily activities in this particular home. If you have children, evaluate the play areas and the storage space. Look at the front and back doors: are there both convenient and safe ways to get into and out of the home? In fact, throughout the inspection, keep safety in mind, not only in regard to wiring and smoke alarm systems but also to traffic patterns and family routines.

> **Tip**
>
> If you see the home after the seller has moved out, take this opportunity to make sure that everything that is supposed to be included with the home is there, such as draperies or window hardware, appliances or fixtures.

Energy Efficiency

In an age of environmental awareness, not to mention high energy prices, it is smart to look for energy-efficient features in a home. Many new homes meet energy efficiency requirements, but an older home can be a concern. Although you may have investigated energy-efficient features when you first visited the home, this may be the time to evaluate them more thoroughly and look for ways to upgrade or install more.

Focus on the home's envelope–the roof, walls, foundation and windows–that shields your living space from wind, rain, heat and cold. This approach often is referred to as whole system design, integrated design or green design. The idea is to identify and work with the interconnections between the building, the inhabitants and the environment to find solutions for shelter, indoor environmental quality and cost savings issues.

Approximately 45 percent of a home's total energy bill goes to heating and cooling indoor spaces within the building's envelope. This adds up to several hundred dollars each year. Making envelope improvements, such as sealing air leaks, adding insulation and upgrading windows, can reduce this figure by almost half. Try this before you think about installing more efficient heating and cooling systems.

Therefore, in your second basic inspection, look for:

- wall and ceiling insulation—do not forget to check the attic and look at the studs throughout the home to see if more insulation can be added;
- tightfitting windows;
- insulated pipes that do not leak;
- house orientation—living space that requires heating, cooling or lighting ideally should be positioned so that the longest walls and largest windows face south and storage spaces, utility rooms and garages face north, which takes advantage of solar heat gain and light as the sun travels daily from east to west—in the winter, south-facing windows receive the most sun, and in the summer, awnings or leafy trees can reduce overheating;
- color of the roof—in warm weather, traditional dark roofs can reach temperatures of 250°F to 190°F, which makes your cooling system work harder, whereas houses with light-colored, reflective roof materials need 40 percent less energy to cool the interior; and
- appropriate equipment size—heating/cooling systems should meet actual use needs; systems that are too large for the demand will be expensive to run and inefficient since they are designed to operate at full capacity.

In addition, look for smaller energy saving devices, such as programmable thermostats, tankless instant hot water heaters and ceiling fans with built-in heaters.

You may be concerned that whole system or green design building can be expensive. In many cases, the savings offset the costs of installation. In addition, you can enjoy the benefits of good indoor air quality, natural light and fewer drafts. If you discover during your inspection tour that the building envelope allows for energy efficiency, you can add the prospect of improved resale value to your list of pluses for the home.

If an energy-efficient house is a priority, be sure to look into the possibility of an energy efficient mortgage (EEM) to buy an efficient home or to remodel. A participating lender may grant an EEM after a certified home energy rater completes a home energy rating systems (HERS) report. The rater looks at the amount of insulation, types of appliances and windows, and local climate to estimate energy costs. An EEM qualification usually requires a score of 3 or better on a scale of 1 to 5 or a rating of 85 or better on a scale of 0 to 100. The report costs between $100 and $300, and the buyer, the seller, the lender or a real estate agent can pay for the report.

An EEM most often works by increasing the amount you can borrow against your house because of reduced operating costs or allowing point reductions on mortgage interest when you buy an energy-efficient home or make energy-efficient improvements to a home. Visit the Residential Energy Services Network at **www.natresnet.org** for more information about this program and its availability in your area. The Resources section of Appendix A also includes additional energy Web sites you can visit.

A Professional Home Inspection

Many first-time buyers question the value of a professional home inspection. Many wonder if the cost of an inspection is really justified. Others think that the seller's disclosure form will tell them all they need to know.

If you are debating the need for a full inspection, remember that buying a home is one of the largest purchases you will ever make. Are you willing to lay out thousands of dollars for a purchase you have not examined carefully? Furthermore, the seller's disclosure form is not sufficient. There may be hidden problems that the seller is unaware of, and these would not appear on the disclosure form.

An inspection report will describe the home and identify areas that are or may become problems. If the inspector finds any problems, he or she can refer you to an appropriate specialist for further evaluation. More importantly, the inspector can alert you to the need for any major repairs before you make an offer so that you do not encounter an unpleasant surprise after you have moved in. In addition, if the offer contract is contingent on an acceptable inspection, the seller must repair any defects or reflect the problems in a lowered sale price. This gives you the option to cancel the offer if you are not satisfied with the condition of the house.

The inspection report also will discuss the positive aspects of a house and give you an idea of the maintenance required to keep the house in good condition. All of this information will give you a clearer picture of the property for which you are about to spend thousands of dollars.

Do not allow the cost of an inspection to be a deterrent in deciding to hire an inspector. Although inspections fees vary by regions and neighborhoods, you can expect to pay between $300 and $500 for a typical 2,000 square foot house. The inspection will take about 3 hours, and you should expect a detailed written report.

Do You Need to Inspect a New Home?

Many buyers of new construction assume that the ongoing inspection processes mandated by the local zoning board are sufficient to ensure a sound building.

However, you should arrange a professional inspection–in fact, maybe even several inspections as the building progresses–in a new home as well. A code inspector is trying to ensure that the new home complies with local codes or zoning standards. You need an independent inspector to look for problems that affect livability as well as the value of a home.

Do not consider the model home to be an accurate reflection of your new home. Builders and developers take special care in constructing the model because they use it as a marketing tool. You also should visit empty models and make arrangements to tour your own building project as it moves toward completion. Ask for a list of specifications and building materials that the builder plans to use on your unit so your inspector can determine if the builder substitutes cheaper materials as the project goes along.

Ideally, you should have a professional inspect your site at various stages of construction. However, this can become costly. To defray expenses, you might want to think about arranging with some other new home buyers to hire an inspector who will act as a site supervisor for each of you. Do not forget to visit the site yourself periodically to see how the construction is progressing.

As with any home buying process, do not sign off on a final contract until all issues have been remedied.

Do You Need to Inspect Historic Homes and Mobile Homes?

Inspecting a historic, antique or restored home is crucial in that some of the elements the inspectors are looking for affect safety. Many home restorers have taken care to retain the architectural and structural features of the original house while upgrading internal systems, such as heating and electricity. If you are considering an antique house, you need to employ an inspector who is qualified to check converted heating systems, improved plumbing and upgraded electrical systems to be sure that they are not only working properly but are also safe. A general inspection of the structural integrity of the building also is recommended.

A mobile home also requires a thorough inspection. In addition to conducting the customary inspection of the exterior and interior of the home, an inspector should remove the skirt, go under the home and examine the systems and components in the crawl space. The inspector also should make certain that the structure is securely anchored.

Reasons Why You Need a Professional Home Inspection

- You will learn about any problems or potential problems–including approximately how much it will cost to fix them–before you make a final offer.
- You may be able to negotiate a lower sale price if the inspector points out problems that may cost you money in the future.
- You will find out the maintenance requirements to keep the home in top condition.
- An inspector can detect home repairs or remodeling that have been done by the homeowner and that may not be to code.

- An inspector has the tools to detect lead, asbestos and radon in a home.
- An inspection fee of a few hundred dollars may protect an investment of several hundred thousand dollars.

Professional Inspections

The function of a professional inspection is to reveal defects or problems in a home that could affect safety, livability or even resale value. A professional inspector is not looking for cosmetic or superficial problems, such as scuffed floors or dated wallpaper.

Professional inspectors understand all the components of home construction as well as their installation and maintenance. Because of their experience, inspectors know how a home's systems and elements are supposed to function together and why they may fail. Most importantly, inspectors can determine what elements or systems have exceeded their life span or are unsafe.

How to Find an Inspector

You can look for a professional inspector by asking friends or relatives for recommendations. You also can go to the Yellow Pages in your local directory and look for listings under "Home Inspection Services." You should still be ready to evaluate the inspectors before you arrange the inspection.

The following list will enable to you to select an inspector who is right for you:

- **Experience**—How much inspection experience do potential inspectors have? How many inspections do they do annually? Are they full-time inspectors or are they doing this as a sideline?
- **Training**—Have the inspectors been though any specific training in home inspection? Do they have additional experience related to the housing industry, such as background in construction? Is it necessary that they be professional engineers?
- **Professional affiliation**—Are the inspectors members of a professional association? Have they been certified by a professional association? Inspectors affiliated with professional organizations are generally well-informed about new developments in their profession as well as changes in local building and zoning codes.
- **Liability insurance**—Do the inspectors carry professional liability insurance, also called errors and omissions insurance? The inspectors' insurance policy will pay on any legal claim you may face in the future should the inspectors miss a problem.
- **Specifics of the inspection procedure**—What do the inspections include? How much will they cost? How long will they take? Can you accompany the inspectors? What about additional services, such as radon, asbestos, lead, water and termite testing? Will specials tests cost more?
- **Report**—What will be included in the final report? Will the report suggest possible remedies for problems?

- **Questions**—Are the inspectors available and willing to answer questions after submitting their reports?

Once you have selected an inspector who meets your needs, you are ready to finalize your offer, secure in the knowledge that you can have the home inspected within the time period allotted in the contract.

Inspector Examination

The inspector will examine the condition of the exterior of the home from the roof to the foundation as well as the attic, the basement, the home's heating and cooling systems, interior plumbing and electrical systems, ventilation, insulation, walls, ceilings, floors, windows and doors.

In a condo, the inspector will inspect the interior of the unit as well as the common areas. You should provide access to any heating or cooling, electrical and plumbing systems that may service the building or your wing. Even if the condo association is responsible for the exterior of the building, you should ask the inspector to look at the roof and the outside of the building. After all, your condo assessments are related directly to the condition of the building, and before you move in, you should know if there are potential problems that may increase your fees.

For safety and insurance reasons, the inspector is not required to climb up onto a roof, but many will attempt to inspect it as closely as possible. Remember that if there is snow or ice on the roof, the inspector may not be able to scrutinize it as closely as you might like. However, if the inspector suspects problems, he or she may recommend an additional evaluation.

An inspector must have WETT (Wood Energy Technology Training) certification to inspect a wood-burning stove or a fireplace. A WETT inspection is not part of the standard inspection unless you request it, and it will add 1 hour to the inspection time. In addition, the chimney must be cleaned before it can be inspected.

You also may want to arrange a professional inspection to test for lead from lead-based paint, asbestos, radon levels–radon is a cancer-causing radioactive gas that may exist in a home or in the surrounding soil–and for chemicals in the home's water supply. This may require hiring an inspector with specialized training and certification because inhaling lead dust can cause brain or other organ damage, the federal government requires that sellers or real estate agents provide information to home buyers about lead-based paint and lead-based paint hazards in a home built before 1978. Home buyers will then have 10 days to conduct a lead-based paint inspection or risk assessment at their own expense. However, the law does not require testing or removal of lead-based paint by sellers, nor does it invalidate sales contracts. Therefore, it is your responsibility to make arrangement for these inspections.

Tip
The U.S. Environmental Protection Agency (EPA) recommends that you test for radon. If you decide to do this, be certain that there is a clause in your sales contract that the sale of the home depends on your satisfaction with the results.

Just as you should know what an inspection includes, you also should understand what an inspection does not include. An inspection does not include quotes for repairs, nor does it include warranties or guarantees. A home inspection is done to help you make an informed decision about the purchase of a home.

> **Note**
>
> Do not forget to ask the professional inspector to test for conditions that are hard to see, such as asbestos, radon, lead-based paint, insect damage, aluminum wiring, old lead pipes, moisture in plaster or wallboard, bathroom tile leaks, shower pan condition, defective furnace heat exchanger, carbon monoxide emissions, and integrity of underground electrical lines, oil storage tanks and septic tanks.

Observing the Inspection

You do not have to accompany the inspector, but most professionals recommend it. Following and observing the inspector will give you a better picture of the home you are considering. By asking questions during the inspection, you can learn how various systems work, either separately or together with other components, and you can get an idea of what it will take to maintain the home and its systems. Furthermore, if you follow the inspector while he or she performs the inspection, you will understand the written report better. Looking at a potential home through a professional's eyes helps you make a more informed decision about buying a home.

What to Expect After an Inspection

At the end of a professional inspection, you should expect:

- a detailed written report in language that is easy to understand
- an opportunity to ask the inspector any questions about the report or the house
- the assurance that the inspector will answer any future questions you may have

You should not expect the inspector to offer to repair for a fee any defects or problems uncovered. This is definitely a conflict of interest, and it makes the inspector's findings suspect.

For a list of Web sites that provide useful information about home inspections, turn to the Resources section in Appendix A.

> **Tip**
>
> An inspection is not the same as an appraisal. An appraiser is interested in the total value of the home as compared to others that have sold recently in the neighborhood. The appraiser only wants to determine that the house is worth what the bank loans on it—that the market value coincides with the sales price—and does not look for specific defects or problems with the property. The appraiser's job is to protect the bank's investment.

Summary

When you have finally found a home, it is in your best interests to have a professional inspector evaluate it. During this process an inspector will walk around the interior and exterior to determine the condition of the home and identify any areas that are or may cause future problems.

What You Have Learned

- How to conduct an inspection and test what you are examining.
- Use a checklist to evaluate what you see.
- The reasons why you need a professional home inspection and what the inspector will do.
- How to find an inspector.

Free Forms and Checklists

Visit **Socrates.com** and register to receive a variety of useful FREE forms, letters and checklists. See page iv for details on how to register (you will need the seven-digit registration code provided on the enclosed CD).

12

. . . . . .

Making an Offer

In This Chapter

- Learn how to make an offer based on several factors.
- How to find an appraiser and why it is important to have an appraiser look at the property.
- Learn how to negotiate a real estate contract once your offer has been accepted.
- Learn the importance of disclosure forms.

You have been looking at homes for weeks, and you have visited neighborhoods at all times of the day and night. You have investigated schools and timed your work commute. Finally, you have selected a home that fits your needs. It is now time to make an offer.

Where do you start? What exactly do you have to do? What kind of legal commitment are you making? Can you negotiate price and terms?

If you have done your homework up to this point, making an offer is the culmination of all your background research. Yet there are steps you can take to ensure that this part of the process moves along smoothly and protects your interests.

The First Steps

You probably already have taken the very first steps toward making an offer. You already should have done some preliminary shopping for a mortgage and become preapproved. The preapproval letter has given you the price range within which you have looked for a home and financial options for buying one. As recommended in Chapter 2, you have obtained your credit report and determined if it is accurate and up-to-date.

If you have not already done so, find a real estate agent. (See Chapter 7 for more information.) You want to select a buyer's agent who will work exclusively for your interests as opposed to a seller's agent whose job is to get the best deal for the seller. As you prepare to make an offer, your agent can be extremely helpful, so it is important to select one with whom you can work and who has access to all the information you need to make the offer.

Learning the Market

When you are ready to make an offer, you should do some advance preparation. Gathering as much information as you can about the home, the neighborhood and the seller will help you later in your negotiating. It is especially helpful to find out why the seller is selling. Does the seller have to sell–he or she is moving out of town or has suffered financial setbacks–or does the seller want to sell for other reasons—a new baby requires a larger home, or the seller is downsizing because the kids have left home. If your agent is a buyer's agent, he or she may be able to get this information for you, depending on what the seller and the seller's agent want you to know. If you are working with an agent who represents the seller or who is a dual agent, he or she cannot reveal this type of information without the permission of the seller.

> **Tip**
>
> Part of your preliminary preparation also should be taking a realistic look at your own situation. You may have moved into the home you are looking at emotionally, but are you able to take on the financial requirements? Set a realistic limit on how much you are prepared to spend on a home, and do not allow your emotions to overrule your common sense. Brace yourself to stay within your means and be ready to turn away from a home if you cannot manage the financial responsibility comfortably. You do not want to regret your decision every time you write a check for the mortgage payment.

Comparative Market Analysis (CMA)

Before you make a purchase offer, you have to know how much to offer. This is where an agent is critically important: real estate agents have access to the information on a comparative market analysis. Ask your agent for a written CMA to help you determine the fair value of the home. The CMA will list the prices for which homes in the neighborhood have sold recently as well as the asking prices of comparable listings in the area.

The CMA also should provide information about the homes that are being compared: the square footage, the number of bedrooms and baths, the listing price and the selling price. Be certain that your agent investigates homes that are similar to the one you want to buy. Comparing a three-bedroom, two-bath house to your four-bedroom, three-bath selection is of little value, as is a CMA that includes properties from a neighborhood three miles away. The CMA must list the sales of similar homes in the immediate neighborhood within the last year. Naturally, the more current the information the more helpful the CMA will be in determining the offer you should make. Ideally, you should look at homes that have sold in the neighborhood over the last few months.

> **Tip**
>
> Only real estate agents who are buyers' representatives have access to the CMA. If you are working with a seller's agent, you will not be able to obtain this information.

The CMA is a valuable piece of information because it is based on fact rather than on opinion. To get the most value from a CMA, you should concentrate on what a home sold for rather than the listing price. The listing price and the selling price can be very different from each other. By looking at the selling prices, you may avoid offering too much. After you make an offer, the real estate agent also can use the CMA to show the seller why your offer is fair and within the market price of the neighborhood.

Other Market Information

Gather information about factors other than the selling price of comparable homes. Look at the homes that have sold in the neighborhood. What kind of condition are they in? Compare their condition to the house you are considering. Does your home appear to be in better shape than the others? Look beyond the size and number of rooms. This kind of information can make a difference in how much you are willing to offer.

Also, does your home have some extras? For example, does your home have an addition that includes another bathroom or an expanded kitchen? Is there a swimming pool or an extra-large garage? Is the landscaping part of its charm? Expanded living space can influence the final price, but be careful not to overestimate cosmetic additions, such as a pool or a beautiful yard. The swimming pool may be a deciding factor for you, but it actually may be a disadvantage if you try to sell the house later. A pool that cost $30,000 does not add $30,000 to the value of the home.

Tip
You can go to public records to learn about the sale price of a house in the neighborhood, but the public record tends to run 6 to 8 weeks behind, so the information is not as current as the CMA data.

Determining What to Offer

Your offer is an important step in the home buying process, and you should give a great deal of thought to determining what is fair. If your agent is a buyer's agent, discuss the offer price with him or her; the agent can point out features that make the sale more or less attractive to you and help you adjust your price. If your agent is a seller's agent, request that any discussions you have about the offer remain confidential.

To determine a fair offer, consider the following:

- the prices of the homes that have recently sold in the neighborhood—refer to the CMA;
- the highlights and problems with the home, such as major items that need replacing within the next year or so;
- the time the home has been on the market—a home that has been on the market for a while places the buyer in a stronger position;
- the market—whether it is a sellers' or a buyers' market and whether or not homes are selling quickly or slowly;

- the financing of the purchase;
- the seller's situation, such as a job transfer that has required the seller move immediately, a divorce or financial difficulties; and
- the time of year—for example, home sales are generally slower during the holidays or the winter months.

In addition, think about any household items you want to include in the offer. Do the furnishings in one of the rooms fit the room perfectly? Is there portable shelving in the garage or basement that you would like? Does the yard have children's play equipment you want to keep? This is the time to ask the seller about including some of these items in your purchase for an additional amount of money. The seller may not plan to move the play equipment or may have plans to buy new furniture and would welcome the extra cash. Be sure to figure these items in before making the offer.

Surf the Internet for Pricing Information

Visit **www.homeprice.net** for information about properties and neighborhoods. For a nominal fee, the site's HomePrice Report provides detailed property information by specific address; facts about up to 30 comparable sales; a local street map; and details about the neighborhood demographics, schools and local businesses.

Elements of the Offer

When you are ready to make an offer, your agent can help you with all the paperwork. Here is where all of your previous preparation and documentation will be helpful, since the offer will require the following:

- a legal description of the property;
- a statement of the total purchase price and the amount due upon signing the real estate sales contract;
- a provision that the sale is dependent on a clear title;
- the amount of earnest money;
- the contingencies of the sale—inspection, appraisal;
- your down payment and financing details, including a fixed rate or adjustable rate mortgage (ARM), conventional financing or FHA or VA loan, or even cash—be sure you can document that you have the cash funds available;
- a provision for the time period in which the buyer must:
  - obtain a mortgage;
  - conduct the home inspection; and
  - close on the home;
- the length of time the offer is open;
- the proposed closing and moving in dates; and
- names of real estate agents and commission to be paid.

If you are very eager to purchase a particular home, you can try to make the offer more attractive by:

- offering more than the listing price;
- agreeing to pay some of the seller's expenses such as title or appraisal fees;
- increasing the amount of the earnest money;
- showing documented proof of mortgage preapproval;
- being flexible about the closing date; and
- limiting contingencies.

It is a good idea, however, to propose these incentives only when it is a sellers' market, there seems to be tight competition for the home or you have other reasons for wanting to close the deal quickly.

Earnest Money

Earnest money is money put down to demonstrate how serious you are about buying a home. It must be substantial enough to demonstrate good faith and is usually between 1 percent and 5 percent of the purchase price—although the amount may vary depending on local customs and conditions.

A 5 percent to 10 percent deposit shows that you are really serious, although many buyers do not like to tie up that much money. If your offer is accepted, the earnest money becomes part of your down payment or your closing costs. If the offer is rejected, your money is returned to you. However, if you back out of the deal, you may forfeit the entire amount.

Contingency Clauses

Even though your offer should be as simple and straightforward as possible, you should always insist on at least two contingency clauses. The first one, a professional inspection, allows you to hire a professional inspector to evaluate the property at your expense. You and your real estate agent should accompany the inspector; while the inspector will prepare a written report about any defects, the report will not be as revealing as the conversation you will have with the inspector while he or she is touring the house. If the home inspector finds undisclosed problems or defects, you can cancel the offer and ask for a refund of your earnest money, negotiate repairs with the seller or buy the home with the defects. See Chapter 11 for more detailed information about finding a professional inspector and arranging the inspection.

The second contingency clause is a professional appraisal. An appraiser is interested in the total value of the home as compared to others that have sold recently in the neighborhood. The appraiser wants to determine that the home is worth what the bank loans on it—that is, the market value coincides with the sales price.

Because the appraiser's job is to protect the lender's investment, the lender will arrange for an appraisal, but you want to include an appraisal of your own in the event that the lender's appraiser does not value the home as high as your purchase offer. If your appraiser determines that the home is not valued as high as the price you are offering and that the seller has accepted, you can renegotiate the price, cancel the offer or add the difference to your down payment.

It is also wise to obtain your own appraisal so that you can compare it with the appraisal presented by a loan officer whose commission depends on the appraised value of a home. Your own appraisal will not be influenced by the size of the loan officer's commission.

Some buyers like to add contingency clauses that stipulate that the sale is subject to the approval of an attorney or another person who may withhold approval if a significant problem is discovered.

> **Tip**
>
> Include in your offer specific information about which companies will conduct the inspections and appraisal, who will pay for these services and what will happen if the home does not pass the inspection or if the appraisal is lower than anticipated.

Common Questions about Appraisers

What does the appraiser do?

An appraiser's job is to provide an objective, impartial opinion about the value of a property. Appraisers determine a property's value by looking at recent sales of comparable properties, the cost of replacing the building and the earning power or resale value of the property. This helps a buyer make informed decisions.

What kind of report does an appraiser submit?

Most appraisers submit a written report, although, if requested, they can give an oral presentation. The report usually contains a description of the property and its location, an analysis of sales of comparable properties as geographically close to the property in question as possible and information about current real estate or market trends in the area.

What credentials does a professional appraiser need?

All states in the United States require that an appraiser be state licensed or certified to provide appraisals to federally regulated lenders. Most professional appraisers, however, acquire credentials beyond these minimum state requirements. Many have fulfilled stringent educational requirements and maintain a continuing education program. They also adhere to a rigorous code of professional ethics.

What should a buyer ask when hiring an appraiser?

Anyone employing an appraiser should ask the following questions:

- Are you licensed and certified in this state?
- Are you a member of a professional organization?
- How long have you been an appraiser?
- What types of clients do you have?
- Are you familiar with properties in this neighborhood?

How do you find an appraiser?

You can ask your real estate agent for suggestions or talk to a bank or lending institution about a recommendation. You also can visit the Appraisal Institute® at **www.appraisalinstitute.org** for more information, including a list of their members. The following is an example of an Appraisal Request Form.

Appraisal Request Form

Client/Lender: _____

Client/Lender Contact: _____

Client/Lender Address: _____

_____

_____

Client/Lender Phone: _____   Fax: _____

Lender File #: _____

Invoice and Mail Appraisal to: _____

Client/Lender

E-Mail Appraisal to: _____

Property Address: _____

_____

_____

Borrower: _____

Contact for entrance to property: _____

Home Phone: _____   Cell: _____   Work: _____

Type of Property: ❏ Single Family   ❏ Multi-Family   # of Units _____
                         ❏ Vacant Land   ❏ Commercial

Owners Name: _____

Occupant: _____

Listing Broker: _____

Appraisal Form: ❏ URAR   ❏ 2055 Form   ❏ Drive-by
                       Other: _____

Number of Requested Copies: _____ E-MAIL Address: _____

Photographs Requested: Exterior _____   Interior _____

Additional Instructions: _____

Thank you for your order. We will contact you with a confirmation of your order and approximate time for completion

The Real Estate Contract

Once you make an offer, the seller has a stated period of time—usually 24 hours—to accept or reject it. This can be a stressful wait. Be prepared to continue house hunting or make a second offer if your first offer is rejected.

If you make an offer on a home and then find another home you like better, you should give written notice to the seller's agent immediately that you are withdrawing your offer. In most cases, if the seller has not accepted your offer by signing the purchase contract, you can withdraw. If the seller has signed but your agent has not received the contract in hand, you still may be able to withdraw. However, if the seller has signed and your agent has received the contract, you are obligated to purchase the home or face legal consequences, including losing all or part of your earnest money.

If your offer is accepted, you still must negotiate a satisfactory real estate sales contract covering all of the details of the sale based on the offer. An accepted offer takes the property off the market.

A real estate contract should contain all the provisions necessary to protect your rights and cover all aspects of the sale. The contract should include:

- the address of the property;
- a legal description of the property;
- the purchase price;
- the earnest money amount;
- the amount of the down payment;
- mortgage information, including the interest rate;
- a list of contingency clauses stating that the contract is subject to inspections and appraisal satisfactory to the buyer or is subject to the approval of a person appointed by the buyer—for example, an attorney;
- acceptable outcome of well and/or septic tank inspection, if applicable;
- acceptable outcome of pest inspection, if applicable;
- a list of all that is included in the purchase price, such as any appliances and furniture that stay in the home, certain fixtures like a dining room chandelier, drapery rods and window coverings, and any yard or outdoor play equipment;
- a list of all appliances and/or systems that should be in working order;
- property disclosures;
- closing costs and fees;
- the agent's sales commission;
- a statement that all utility, insurance and tax bills are prorated to the time of settlement;
- the closing date; and
- the date the contract expires—generally between 30 and 90 days.

The following is an example of an Offer to Purchase Real Estate form.

Offer to Purchase Real Estate

BE IT KNOWN, the undersigned, _____ (Buyer), offers
to purchase from _____ (Owner), real estate
known as _____, located in the City/Town of _____,
County of _____, State of _____, said
property more particularly described as: _____
_____
_____

and containing _____ square feet of land, more or less.
The purchase price offered is _____ Dollars ($_____).

Earnest money herewith paid	$_____
Further deposit upon signing sales agreement	$_____
Balance at closing	$_____

Total: $_____

This offer is conditional upon the following terms:

1. This offer is subject to Buyer obtaining a real estate mortgage for no less than _____
Dollars ($_____) payable over _____ years with interest not to exceed _____
percent (_____%) at customary terms with a firm commitment thereto _____ days from date
hereof.

2. This offer is further subject to Buyer obtaining a satisfactory home inspection report and termite/pest report within
_____ days from date hereof.

3. Owner shall pay _____ (Broker), a commission of _____
_____ Dollars ($_____) upon closing.

4. Said property is to be sold free and clear of all encumbrances, by good and marketable title, with full possession to
said property available to Buyer at date of closing.

5. Owner shall include in the purchase price and transfer, free and clear of encumbrances, all fixtures on the property
on the date of this offer. The terms of this offer, detailed in the standard purchase and sales agreement to be
executed, will determine what items are included/excluded as fixtures.

6. The parties agree to execute a standard purchase and sales agreement according to the terms of this agreement
within _____ days of acceptance of this offer.

7. The closing shall occur on or before _____, 20____, at the public recording office,
unless such other time and place shall be agreed upon.

8. Other terms: _____
_____
_____

Disclosures

It is in your interest to find out as much as you can about a home from its seller. Often, one-on-one informal conversations are very informative and can be as valuable as professional inspections. If you ask questions that require more than a yes or no answer and refrain from interrupting, you may learn a great deal.

Ask about any structural damage to the home or the roof. Is there a history of termite infestation? Is the basement dry? Are the heating and air conditioning systems adequate for the house? You also might ask whether or not the home has ever been tested for radon.

In addition to talking with the seller informally, you should make sure you receive disclosure forms that are mandated by regulatory agencies. In most states, sellers are required to disclose material defects that cannot reasonably be discovered by a buyer. However, when a defect is open and obvious, the seller is not under this disclosure obligation. Material defects may include asbestos, urea formaldehyde insulation, remodeling or alterations that do not comply with building codes, crimes that occurred in the home or other defects that materially affect the market value of the home.

In most states, the seller is not obligated to make any guarantees about the future condition of the roof, heating and cooling and other systems.

If a defect is disclosed, you must consider your options. First, any problems or undisclosed material defects should be pointed out to the seller immediately. The seller may then correct these problems. However, if the seller does not make corrections, your payment on settlement day may be reduced. You may want to consult your attorney regarding continuing with the purchase and the costs of canceling the sale.

In addition to the material defects disclosure form, a seller of a residence built before 1978 must disclose any knowledge of lead-based paint in the home and provide the buyer with an information booklet about lead-based paint. These are the terms of the Residential Lead-Based Paint Hazard Reduction Act (RLPHRA). Lead-based paint was banned in 1978 because exposure to lead in dust, soil or paint can cause health problems, especially in young children. In 1992, the RLPHRA was enacted to protect home buyers from inadvertent exposure to lead by giving them a 10-day opportunity to obtain a lead-based paint inspection. The law, however, does not require sellers to remove lead-based paint.

Ask your real estate agent about any other disclosures you should request. For example, you may want to ask the seller for a personal property report from the Comprehensive Loss Underwriting Exchange (CLUE), which lists insurance claims filed on the property during the previous 5 years. Insurance carriers are often reluctant to write or renew insurance on property that shows recent claims activity, so you may have trouble obtaining home insurance on your new purchase if the seller has made several claims in the past. The CLUE report is available only to the property owner, so you will have to ask the seller for a copy or make your purchase contingent on a clean CLUE report. Visit **www.choicetrust.com** for more information.

Homeowner's Association Disclosure

Purchaser(s) should not execute a real estate sale or purchase contract until receiving and reading this disclosure summary.

1. This is a disclosure summary for _____ (name of community).

2. As Purchaser of property in this community, you will be obligated to be a member of a homeowner's association.

3. There have been, or will be recorded, restrictive covenants governing the use and occupancy of properties in this community.

4. You ❑ will ❑ will not be obligated to pay assessments to the association, which assessments are subject to periodic change. If applicable, the current amount is _____ Dollars ($_____) per _____.

5. Your failure to pay these assessments could result in a lien on your property.

6. There [check only one] ❑ is ❑ is not an obligation to pay rent or land use fees for recreational or other commonly used facilities as an obligation of membership in the homeowner's association. (If such obligation exists, then the amount of the current obligation is _____ _____ Dollars ($_____).

7. The restrictive covenants [check only one] ❑ can ❑ cannot be amended without the approval of the association membership.

8. The statements contained in this disclosure form are only summary in nature, and, as a prospective Purchaser, you should refer to the covenants and the association governing documents.

_____   _____
Date   Purchaser

_____   _____
Date   Purchaser

This disclosure must be supplied by the developer, or by the parcel owner if the sale is by an owner that is not the developer.

Negotiating Tactics

While you are deciding what to offer and how to write the sales contract, you also want to weigh bargaining strategies. The following information may provide some guidelines for negotiating:

- The asking price for a house is usually 5 percent to 10 percent above what the seller really expects to receive. Take this into consideration, but also bear in mind that making an offer of less than 90 percent of the asking price may be interpreted as insulting or cause the seller to be reluctant to negotiate with you.

- If your agent informs you that the price is firm or that the price already has been reduced and will not go any lower, you still may try to bargain for help with closing costs, payment for repairs or new appliances.

- If a property has been on the market for a long time, it may be that there are problems with the home, it is overpriced or the seller is unrealistic. Consider these possibilities when you are negotiating.

- If the seller is relocating, retiring, divorcing or out of work and wants to move as soon as possible, he or she may consider lowering the price for a faster sale or may be flexible about when you can move in. This is why you want to learn the seller's motivation for the sale.

- The seller may have another buyer or may state that there is another buyer ready to make an offer for the full asking price. Depending on your situation, you may want to counter the bluff and say that there is a similar home in the area at a lower price or that you can wait until a better-priced home goes on sale.

Buyer's Lament

The seller has accepted the offer. The paperwork is underway. It is time to celebrate. However, you suddenly are afflicted with buyer's lament. Have you made an enormous mistake? Did you offer too much money? Is this the right time? What if your income drops? Is there enough money to replace the roof if a tornado strikes? What were you thinking?

This is a natural reaction to the culmination of months of research and legwork in looking for a home. This kind of investment is bound to cause you second thoughts and worries. If you stop to weigh all the advantages against the disadvantages, however, you will find that your preliminary work and diligence has paid off. The advantages obviously outweigh any potential problems. It is time to move on and begin the process of obtaining a mortgage.

Summary

Your offer is an important step in the home buying process. As you prepare to make an offer, an agent can be extremely helpful in determining how much your offer should be based on the sale of similar properties in the neighborhood and help arrange and prepare all the documentation. Be prepared to negotiate the offer, for it is commong for the seller to decline your first offer. There may be some back and forth negotiating before the deal is finally complete.

What You Have Learned

- What price you should offer based on the CMA.
- The necessary paperwork needed and the steps you need to take to make an offer.
- How to negotiate your offer and real estate contract with the seller so you get the best price.
- What an appraiser does and why you need to hire one before making an offer.

13
. . . . . .
Finding the Right Mortgage

In This Chapter

- Discover the types of mortgages available and find one that best suits your needs.
- Learn about other mortgage options.
- Find out how to finance condos, manufactured or mobile homes.
- Learn what steps you need to take to apply for a loan.

You have found the home, you have made the offer and now you have to find a way to pay for it. Mortgage and lender shopping is a crucial part of the home buying process. Take the time to evaluate the different types and terms of the available mortgages and to locate a lender with whom you can work. A new home is an enormous, long-term investment, so be thorough when investigating your options. Remember, diligent shopping, comparing and negotiating may trim your monthly mortgage payment and save you thousands of dollars in interest over the life of your mortgage.

To begin your search for mortgage information, turn to your real estate agent, the real estate sections of the local newspaper, a mortgage lending institution, a credit union or a commercial bank. Gather as much information as you can so that you can be certain you are selecting the best lender and getting the best price.

As you begin the search for the type of mortgage you want and the lender you want to use, be sure you have completed the preliminary work, such as:

- preparing a budget
- determining how much down payment and mortgage payment you can afford
- checking your credit status
- deciding what portion of your income you can afford to apply to household expenses

A mortgage lender will consider your net worth–your total assets minus your total liabilities–when evaluating your mortgage application. A low net worth may subject you to high interest rates and may require a larger down payment or a smaller mortgage loan. Review Chapters 3 and 4 to be certain that you are ready to apply for a mortgage.

Types of Mortgages

Each mortgage is different, and you must find one that you qualify for and that meets your needs. Mortgages vary in qualifying conditions, interest rates, whether the rate is fixed or variable, points to pay, down payments required and monthly payment amounts.

Conventional Mortgage

The features of a conventional mortgage are its fixed interest rate and fixed monthly payment, typically over a 30-year period. You can decrease the payment period to 15 or 20 years, thereby significantly decreasing the total amount of interest paid, but your monthly payment will increase.

Some lenders offer the option of a 40-year mortgage. The primary advantage of this mortgage is lower monthly payments without adding to rates or fees. Added purchasing power is another advantage; buyers can afford a more expensive home than they could with a 30-year mortgage.

On the other hand, you pay more interest on a 40-year mortgage. Nevertheless, it may be a good option for young and first-time buyers who otherwise cannot meet the monthly payments of a 30-year mortgage. In addition, you can take an increased mortgage interest tax deduction on the extra interest you will be paying.

Adjustable Rate Mortgage (ARM)

An ARM allows you to obtain and begin paying the mortgage at a lower interest rate than a conventional mortgage. However, because the rate is usually tied to a rise or fall of the market interest rates, it changes annually or even monthly—sometimes in your favor but often at a higher rate—making this type of mortgage unpredictable. Often it is a trade-off: you get a lower rate in exchange for assuming the risk that your income or real estate values will increase.

ARMs may offer payment-option mortgages that allow you to select how you want to pay. Payment-option mortgages generally have 30-year terms but permit up to 5 years of reduced rates as one of several payment-option plans. There may be as many as four other payment options each month:

- a minimum payment;
- interest-only payment;
- traditional payment based on a 30-year term; or
- an accelerated payment based on a 15-year term.

One drawback to this is that home buyers paying the minimal amount may not cover all of the interest due in a given month. Any shortfall is then added to the loan balance, which means that the owner ends up owing a larger principal amount. This is known as negative amortization.

ARMs can be especially appealing to home buyers who expect to be moving in just a few years. These buyers may benefit by paying the lower interest rates on an adjustable rate loan before it readjusts. People whose monthly income may fluctuate–the self-employed, for example–can own a home under the payment-option mortgages.

> **Tip**
>
> If you select an ARM, find one that contains an interest rate cap that limits rate increases to 2 percentage points per year and 5 to 6 percentage points over the life of the mortgage. Bargain for an option to lock in a fixed rate or refinance at a certain time.

Interest-Only Loans

One form of ARM is the interest-only loan. Interest-only loans require no payment of the principal of the loan until the end of a specified time, usually 3, 5 or 7 years. Some lenders recommend starting with this type of loan and then refinancing before the specified time period ends. The advantage to this type of loan is that your monthly payments are low at the beginning. However, there are significant disadvantages. First, by paying only interest, you are not working down the principle and thus are not building equity in your home. Second, when the principal payments are scheduled to begin, your monthly payments may skyrocket. The favorable terms that allow you to buy a house for lower initial monthly payments eventually may lead to your defaulting on the loan when the monthly payments jump.

You can opt to pay down principal–up to 20 percent annually without penalty– during the interest-only years. If you do not or if you do not refinance with a traditional mortgage, you can face much higher monthly payments when the interest-only period ends because the loan must be spread out over a shorter period—for example, 20 to 25 years rather than 30 years. If interest rates go up at the same time, you may face an overwhelming financial outlay at the end of the interest-only period.

Therefore, despite their advantages for certain types of home buyers, interest-only loans can be exceedingly risky. In your haste to buy a home, take care not to become embroiled in a mortgage plan that will jeopardize your financial and credit standing, not to mention your home, later.

Unconventional Loans

In addition to interest-only mortgages, some lenders offer other nontraditional loan options to prospective home buyers.

80-10-10 or Combination Loan

The lender offers a first mortgage for 80 percent of the property value and a second mortgage–in essence, a home equity loan–for 10 percent. The final 10 percent is your down payment. If you do not have a 10 percent down payment, you may be able to arrange a loan in which the lender again extends a loan for 80 percent and then piggybacks a second loan for the remaining 20 percent. This is especially popular with home buyers who want to avoid paying private mortgage insurance (PMI) because they do not have a 20 percent down payment. In effect, the second mortgage lender is assuming the risk.

Jumbo Loan

This is a loan for a substantial amount of money based on the prevailing home sale values. Because the loan is so high, lenders generally charge a higher interest rate. In order to avoid paying the higher rate on the full amount, many buyers take out two separate loans, the second of which is at a higher interest rate. However, the second loan is usually for a smaller amount and a shorter term, so in the long run, piggybacking the two loans reduces the interest costs paid by the borrower.

Government Program Mortgages

A mortgage may be obtained through a state or federal program. For example, the Federal National Mortgage Association, also known as Fannie Mae, provides guaranteed mortgage loans with lower down payments to families with lower incomes. Visit **www.fanniemae.com** for more information.

In addition, HUD helps home buyers by administering a variety of programs that develop and support affordable housing. Specifically, HUD makes loans available for lower- and moderate-income families through its FHA mortgage insurance program and its HUD Homes program.

FHA loans require lower down payments and often accept a more lenient loan-to-debt ratio, which determines how much mortgage payment you can afford, than conventional mortgages. FHA also allows an approved lender to add extra funds for making repairs to bring a home up to minimum property standards after the closing. FHA also offers a hybrid adjustable rate mortgage that allows first-time buyers to lock in a relatively low fixed rate for the first 5 years. HUD owns homes in many communities throughout the United States and offers them for sale at attractive prices and economical terms. Visit **www.hud.gov** for more information.

VA Loans

The VA guarantees repayments of loans to the lender if the borrower defaults. As a rule, VA loans are available only to qualified members of the military. Depending on the individual circumstances, a veteran can use a VA loan to buy a house with no money down. Furthermore, the benefit can be used over and over, so long as the first or previous home has been sold. Visit **www.homeloans.va.gov** for more information.

Rural Housing Service

This government agency under the U.S. Department of Agriculture guarantees the mortgages of rural buyers who are just entering the housing market or are first-time buyers. Rural Housing Direct Loans are directly funded by the government and are available to help low- and very low-income households attain homeownership. Applicants may obtain 100 percent financing to purchase an existing dwelling, purchase a site and construct a dwelling or purchase newly constructed dwellings located in rural areas. Mortgage payments are based on the household's adjusted income. These loans are commonly referred to as Section 502 Direct Loans. Visit **www.rurdev.usda.gov/rhs** for more information.

Teacher/Officer Next Door

To achieve its goal of making American communities stronger, HUD has designed the Teacher Next Door (TND) program to encourage teachers to buy homes in low- and moderate-income neighborhoods. With the same goal in mind and because the department understands that public safety improves when police officers live in a neighborhood, HUD also offers the Officer Next Door (OND) program to make homeownership easier to attain and more affordable for law enforcement officers. These programs have been so successful that they will be expanded to include community fire and rescue workers.

The TND program is open to any person employed full-time by a public school, private school, or federal, state, county or municipal educational agency as a state-certified classroom teacher or administrator in grades K-12. Participants must certify that they are employed by an educational agency that serves the school district/jurisdiction in which the home they are purchasing is located.

Your employer must certify that you are a full-time teacher or school administrator and are in good standing with your employer. You do not have to be a first-time home buyer to participate, and you must agree to live in the HUD home as your only residence for 3 years after you move into it.

The OND program is open to any sworn law enforcement officer who is employed full-time by a federal, state, county or municipal government; or a public or private college or university. You must be sworn to uphold, and make arrests for violations of, federal, state, county or municipal law. Your employer must certify that you are a full-time police officer with the general power of arrest. You do not have to be a first-time home buyer to participate, and you must agree to live in the HUD home as your only residence for 3 years after you move into it.

Both TND and OND properties are listed and sold exclusively over the Internet, and available properties are marked with a special button. Properties are usually single family homes located in revitalization areas. Your bid must equal the amount of the list price, and you may submit it directly or use the services of a real estate broker. A computer randomly selects the winning bid, which is posted each week on the Web site.

You also may buy a home from a government agency or a nonprofit organization that bought the home from HUD. When an agency or nonprofit organization buys the home, HUD expects the full discount to be passed on to you.

In all cases, HUD requires that you sign a second mortgage and note for the discount amount. No interest or payments are required on this silent second provided you fulfill the 3-year occupancy requirement.

There are significant benefits to these programs. The selected bidder may purchase the property at a 50 percent discount from the list price. For example, if a HUD home is listed for $100,000, a teacher or officer can buy it for $50,000. To make a

HUD home even more affordable, you can apply for an FHA-insured mortgage with a down payment of only $100 and finance all closing costs.

If the home you want to purchase needs repairs, you may use FHA's 203(k) mortgage program. This program allows you to finance both the purchase of the home and the cost of needed repairs. You have the benefit of one loan for both costs and one monthly payment.

Because homes sold through the TND and OND programs are located in revitalization areas, there may be additional assistance from state or local government sources. Local or state governments want to encourage families and businesses to move into revitalization area neighborhoods. Contact your state government housing office or local municipal government and request information on assistance for home buyers.

Contact a TND/OND program coordinator at your local HUD Homeownership Center, call 800.569.4287 or visit **www.hud.gov/office/hsg/sfh/reo/tnd/tnd. cfm** or **www.hud.gov/office/hsg/sfh/reo/ond/ond.cfm** for more information.

Indian Home Loan Guarantee Program

In 1994, Congress established the Section 184 Indian Housing Loan Guarantee Program. This program is designed to offer homeownership, property rehabilitation and new construction opportunities for eligible tribes, Indian Housing Authorities and Native American individuals and families wanting to own a home on their native lands. Visit **www.hud.gov/offices/pih/ih/codetalk/** for more information.

Balloon Payment Mortgage

This type of mortgage requires the payment of a large lump sum at fixed intervals in addition to regular monthly payments. The benefit of this type of mortgage is that is considerably decreases the life of the mortgage. On the on the other hand, the balloon payment may be difficult to meet.

Graduated Payment Mortgage (GPM)

This type of mortgage features initial low monthly payments that increase over the life of the mortgage. If you anticipate that you will have a lot more income in the future, this type of mortgage may allow you to buy a more expensive home than you could obtain under a conventional mortgage. However, the danger with this type of mortgage is that if your income does not increase and you cannot make the higher monthly payments, you will not have significant equity in your home even after making regular payments for years. A forced sale will result in little or no investment return.

Shared Appreciation Mortgage (SAM)

The lender of this type of mortgage obtains an ownership interest in the property according to the conditions of the mortgage and on a specific date. In return for a lower rate of interest, the lender then receives a portion of the future increase in the value of the mortgaged property when it is sold.

Options Other than a Traditional Mortgage

If your circumstances do not fit with any of the other mortgage types, you might consider these options. Because these are less conventional types of loans for homeownership, higher fees may be charged. Determine and compare the fees.

Co-Signed Mortgage

A family member or relative may be wiling to co-sign or guarantee your mortgage loan. Banks often find this acceptable. This may or may not entail the co-signer having a part of the title ownership in the home. A reason a co-signer may be reluctant to participate is that if you default on your mortgage, the co-signer becomes responsible for the mortgage payments. Also, if you default, the co-signer may sue to become the sole title owner of the home.

Lease with Option to Purchase

If you do not have enough money for a sufficient down payment, one option is to enter into an agreement with a seller to lease the home until you can purchase it, usually 6 months to 2 years. The contract should be written so that all lease or rent payments are credited to the purchase price. This credit becomes a down payment.

Be certain that a final sales price is determined in advance and that an independent appraisal on the property is performed. Discuss the number of months you will pay rent before the final purchase and the mortgage rate if the seller is financing the mortgage. You may want to have an attorney review the contract for clauses that permit the seller to back out.

This also may be an option for people living in a rental building that is converted to a condominium. You can suggest to the developer that you would like to buy your unit over a period of several months using a portion of your rent as a down payment. This type of plan will help the developer reduce the carrying costs of unsold units.

Warning
If the contract does not contain a provision crediting all rent to the purchase price at the end of the option term, the seller may be able to evict you and keep the down payment if you do not qualify for a mortgage.

Equity Sharing

In equity sharing, you and an investor buy the home. The investor may make the down payment while you agree to make all of the mortgage payments. When the home is sold, both you and the investor share in the proceeds of the sale. This arrangement can be complex, so you should confer with an attorney during the process.

Seller Financing

Also known as purchase money mortgage or owner financing, this option may be desirable if you are a first-time home buyer, are self-employed or have a poor credit history. The buyer borrows funds from the seller instead of, or in addition to, from a bank or mortgage lender. The seller allows the buyer to use the equity in the home to finance the purchase.

This option, however, has its risks. The seller, not the buyer, holds title to the home. The buyer makes payments to the seller, not a bank or mortgage company. If you cannot make your payments, the seller can foreclose on the home, even though you have made consistent payments for a considerable length of time.

Foreclosure Purchase

Buying a property in foreclosure is not an easy process. After a homeowner has been in default on his or her mortgage payments for a specified length of time, the lender usually starts the foreclosure process by recording a notice of default or suing the borrower. At this point, the borrower usually has an opportunity to reinstate the mortgage. However, the owner may choose to sell the property, often at a bargain price. An advantage to buying during this reinstatement period is that you can inspect the property. A disadvantage is that you are subject to the existing mortgage, which you must reinstate or refinance.

You also can buy a property at the foreclosure auction, when most liens against the property are eliminated except unpaid property taxes and IRS requirements. The disadvantages to waiting until an auction are that you will not be able to inspect the interior of the property and you must have cash or a cashier's check ready.

Your final opportunity to buy a foreclosed property is after the auction when the lender is eager to dispose of the home. You are likely to get a better deal if you buy before the lender lists the property for sale with a real estate agent.

If you want to investigate this kind of purchase, start by locating your city or county's listing of foreclosed properties. You also can visit **www.foreclosures.com** for more information on how to buy foreclosed properties or visit **www.foreclosureworld.net or www.all-foreclosure.com** for lists of properties in default.

Other Loan Sources

Evaluate your pension plan, profit-sharing plan, union membership and life insurance. These may be sources from which you can obtain a loan to buy a home.

Financing Condos and Manufactured or Mobile Homes

Although many of the same stipulations of single home financing pertain to condominiums and manufactured homes, there are some differences.

Condo

A condo has separate property and common property. The separate property is the individual unit owned by an individual owner. The common property is the shell of the building and the common areas, such as hallways, elevators and parking lots. The common property is managed by the condo association, which charges monthly fees to maintain it.

A lender will include condo assessment fees when evaluating the borrower's permissible monthly housing expense. This conceivably could reduce the loan amount the borrower can afford. The lender also may want to look at any past or future special assessments as well as any pending judgments against the association. In addition, a lender often has an attorney review the condo's bylaws and regulations to see if there is any rule that could impinge on the lender's security. This may create an additional loan application fee for the borrower.

Manufactured or Mobile Home

A loan for a manufactured or mobile home is considered more of a risk than one for a typical single family home. Thus, the interest rate is a little higher, the term is shorter–a 7-year term is standard, and the outer limit is 20 years–and the qualification process is more demanding than those for conventional financing. However, the home itself is usually much more inexpensive—typically between $80,000 and $90,000.

Why is this type of loan considered to be high-risk? First, the value of mobile or manufactured homes tends to decrease over time rather than increase, as is the case with more traditional housing. Second, as the name implies, the home can be moved away, making it hard to foreclose. Third, the home is not considered a part of the land it sits on; the owner usually rents land in mobile home villages or parks. Most loans on these types of homes are conditional on the owner's qualifying to enter a park.

The loan is on the actual home, so the buyer must select a mobile home first rather than become prequalified or preapproved for a certain amount of money. The home must be inspected and appraised, and the buyer must have a site on which to place the home. Therefore, lenders have to evaluate the borrower's ability to pay both the monthly loan payment and the monthly land rental payment. If a buyer defaults on the loan for the home, the lender can repossess the home but still has to pay the rent on the land while looking for another buyer.

HUD offers a financing option under the Title I program in which the FHA insures approved lenders against loss if an eligible borrower defaults on a loan to finance the purchase of a manufactured home, a lot on which to place the home or a home/lot combination. The home must be used as the principal residence of the borrower, and there is a maximum loan amount and loan term.

Visit **www.hud.gov/offices/hsg/sfh/title/repair.cfm** for more information.

Although this type of home has its disadvantages, it does provide the tax advantages of homeownership and can provide low-cost housing for low-income families, senior citizens or people who want to live in rural areas.

Important Mortgage Details

When you are shopping for a mortgage, there are a few important issues to consider.

Down Payment

A down payment is a critical factor in any mortgage. Review all the information about down payments in Chapter 3, which also discusses buying with a low or no down payment or a letter of credit.

In addition, there are down payment assistance programs (DAPs) to help many prospective home buyers. DAP assistance is not free. Typically, the seller adds the cost of the DAP to the price of the home. For example, as a last resort in selling his or her home, the seller agrees to donate between 2 percent and 10 percent of the value of the house to help the buyers make a down payment or pay for closing costs. Once the home sells, the seller donates the amount to the DAP along with a service fee. Sellers can then write off the donation on their income taxes.

In essence, the buyers are financing their down payment. As a result, they have little equity in their new home until they start making monthly payments and adding improvements. Nevertheless, the buyers have a home and a foundation for building equity and a sound investment.

Among the DAP programs are the following:

- American Dream Downpayment Initiative (ADDI), sponsored by HUD, offers an average of $5,000 assistance to each household. ADDI aims to increase the homeownership rate, especially among lower-income and minority households, and to revitalize and stabilize communities. The program was created to assist low-income, first-time home buyers in purchasing single family homes by providing funds for down payment, closing costs, and rehabilitation carried out in conjunction with the assisted home purchase. Visit **www.hud.gov/offices/cpd/affordablehousing/programs/home/addi/index.cfm** for more information.

- Housing Action Resource Trust (HART) operates nationally and tries to focus on homes in HUD-designated revitalization areas. Visit **www.hartprogram.com** for more information.

- The Nehemiah Program claims to be the country's largest DAP. Since its founding in 1997, the program has awarded almost $8 million in funds. Visit **www.nehemiahcorp.org** for more information.

- AmeriDream operates the AmeriDream Redevelopment Program that builds housing for low- and moderate-income buyers and rehabilitates older homes to sell. Visit **www.ameridream.org** for more information.

Warning
If you have made no down payment or a small down payment, and you need to sell your home during a slump in housing prices, you may have to come up with thousands of dollars above your sale price in order to pay off your loan.

Private Mortgage Insurance (PMI)

If you put less than 20 percent down on a home mortgage, lenders often require you to have private mortgage insurance. PMI protects the lender in the event that you default on the loan. The Homeowners Protection Act of 1998 establishes rules for automatic termination and borrower cancellation of PMI on home mortgages. These protections apply to certain home mortgages signed on or after July 29, 1999 for the purchase, initial construction or refinance of a single family home. They do not apply to government-insured FHA or VA loans or to loans with lender-paid PMI.

For home mortgages signed on or after July 29, 1999, your PMI must–with certain exceptions–be terminated automatically when you reach 22 percent equity in your home based on the original property value provided your mortgage payments are current. Your PMI also can be canceled at your request–again, with certain exceptions–when you reach 20 percent equity in your home based on the original property value provided your mortgage payments are current.

One exception is if your loan is high-risk. Another is if you have not been current on your payments during the year prior to the time for termination or cancellation. A third is if you have other liens on your property. For these loans, your PMI may continue. Ask your lender or mortgage servicer for more information about these requirements.

If you signed your mortgage before July 29, 1999, you can ask to have the PMI canceled once you exceed 20 percent equity in your home, but federal law does not require your lender or mortgage servicer to cancel the insurance.

On a $100,000 loan with 10 percent down–$10,000–PMI might cost you $40 a month. If you can cancel the PMI, you can save $480 a year and many thousands of dollars over the loan. Check your annual escrow account statement or call your lender to find out exactly how much PMI is costing you each year. Also ask how and when it can be terminated or canceled.

Visit **www.ftc.gov** or call toll-free, 877.FTC.HELP (877.382.4357), TTY: 866.653.4261 for more information.

Tip
Some lenders may require credit life insurance, in which the amount of the policy matches the loan balance at any given time so that the loan will be paid off in full in the event of the borrower's death.

Interest Rates and Points

Interest is money paid for the use of money. A lender charges interest rates on the principal of the loan as a reward for allowing the use of its money. Mortgage interest rates may vary depending on the market, the risk factors and the type of loan.

As a home buyer, it is obvious that you want to borrow money at the lowest possible interest rate. One way to do that is to pay points. A mortgage point equals 1 percent of the mortgage loan amount; it is collected from the borrower in a lump sum at the beginning of the loan period. In return for points, most lenders will reduce your interest rate, usually by a quarter of a percentage point for each point you buy upfront when you take out the loan. You have to calculate the advantages for your individual case, but in general, settling on a lower monthly payment at a lower interest rate is more advantageous than taking the money you pay in points and adding it to the down payment, especially on a long-term loan. Of course, by lowering the total interest you pay on the loan, you also are decreasing the amount of mortgage interest you can deduct from future taxes.

Points can be deducted from your taxes. For federal income tax purposes, points are classified as interest expense to the borrower and can be deducted on the borrower's income tax return. If you are buying a new home, you have the option of deducting the points completely in the year of purchase. On the other hand, if you purchase the home late in the year and do not have enough expenses to qualify for itemizing in the first year, you can deduct the points evenly over the duration of the loan.

When you have selected the mortgage you want, ask for a written statement that locks in the interest rate. This will include the agreed upon interest rate, the duration of the lock-in period and the number of points to be paid. Although a fee may be charged for locking in the interest rate, it protects you from high interest rate fluctuation, which can be particularly costly while your loan is being processed.

Applying for the Loan

Once you have selected a lender for your mortgage using the guidelines set out in Chapter 4, it is time to submit your mortgage application. The lender will need at least the following information to process your application:

- Social Security numbers for you and your spouse or anyone else applying for the loan with you;
- copies of checking and savings accounts statements for the past 6 months;
- evidence of other assets such as bonds or stocks;
- a recent paycheck stub detailing your earnings;
- a list of all credit card debts and the approximate monthly amounts owed on each;
- a list of account numbers and balances due on outstanding loans, such as car loans;
- copies of your last 2 years' income tax returns; and
- name and contact information for someone who can verify your employment.

You will complete the loan application with your mortgage lender. You also will pay several fees, including the loan processing fee, the property appraisal fee and credit reporting fee. If the mortgage you are applying for includes points, you will pay these. If you are assuming a seller's mortgage, you will pay a loan assumption fee.

The mortgage lender should inform you of the following:

- the interest rate for the loan and whether or not it can be locked in;
- the amount of the loan origination fee–usually 1 percent of the loan–and when it should be paid;
- a requirement for PMI;
- the amount of the closing costs; and
- any other factors that may influence your approval.

> **Note**
>
> The law requires that you receive a good faith estimate of the closing costs within 3 business days of submitting your loan application. If you do not, call your lender and ask that it be sent to you.

The lender will review your documentation and initiate certain services: an appraisal will be conducted to determine and confirm the market value of the home; a title search will comb the public records for unpaid taxes, judgments, mortgage payments or outstanding liens; and a survey may be conducted to verify the location of the property.

When you are approved, the lender will send a letter of commitment that states the terms and conditions of the mortgage. Read the letter carefully and look for errors or misstatements. If you find a mistake, phone your lender and have the problem corrected. When you are satisfied with the letter of commitment, sign and date it, make copies for your file and return the original to the lender.

It usually takes time for a mortgage application to be approved, but if you do not hear from your lender within 2 weeks, call and ask about the status of your application. For a list of Web sites that provide additional information about mortgages and down payments, go to the Resources section in Appendix A.

Preventing Problems

Mortgage lenders are bound by laws and regulations, but that does not absolve you from the responsibility of protecting yourself from loan fraud and legal problems. HUD recommends that you perform all of the following steps as you apply for a loan:

- Be sure to read and understand everything before you sign.
- Refuse to sign any blank documents.
- Do not buy property for someone else.
- Do not overstate your income.
- Do not overstate your assets.
- Do not overstate how long you have been employed.
- Report your debts accurately.
- Do not change your income tax return for any reason.
- Tell the truth about gifts.

- Do not list fake co-borrowers on your loan application.
- Be truthful abut your credit problems, past and present.
- Be honest about your intention to occupy the house.
- Do not provide false supporting documents.

> **Note**
>
> The Real Estate Settlement Procedures Act, also known as RESPA, requires lenders to disclose information to potential customers throughout the mortgage process in order to protect borrowers from abuses by lending institutions. RESPA mandates that lenders fully inform borrowers about all closing costs, lender servicing and escrow account practices, and business relationships between closing service providers and other parties to the transaction.

Final Steps

At closing, you will be required to sign the mortgage note that secures the loan. By signing the note, you give the lender a lien on your property, which allows the lender to bring a lawsuit if you default in making payments. Alternatively, you may be asked to sign a deed of trust that gives the lender the right to have the property sold in the event of a default.

Discrimination

Lenders are not allowed to discriminate in any way against potential borrowers. The Equal Credit Opportunity Act prohibits lenders from refusing to provide services to you on the basis of race, color, nationality, religion, sex, familial status, marital status, age or disability. Furthermore, lenders cannot discriminate if all or part of your income derives from a public assistance program or whether or not you have in good faith exercised a right under the Consumer Credit Protection Act. You cannot be refused a loan, charged more for a loan or offered less favorable terms based on these characteristics.

If you think you have been discriminated against, contact HUD's Office of Fair Housing and Equal Opportunity at 800.669.9777 (800.927.9275 for hearing impaired) or visit **www.hud/offices/fheo/index.cfm** for more information. To document the discrimination, make a record of every meeting and phone call and what occurred. Keep all written papers, business cards or applications that may be relevant to the discrimination.

Mortgage Shopping Worksheet

	Lender 1	Lender 2
Name of lender		
Name of contact		
Date of contact		
Mortgage amount		
Type of mortgage: fixed rate, adjustable, conventional, FHA, other		
Minimum down payment		
Loan term		
Contract interest rate		
Annual percentage rate		
Points		
PMI premium		
Length PMI must be kept		
Estimated monthly escrow for taxes and insurance		
Estimated monthly payment—principal, interest, taxes, insurance, PMI		
Application fee or loan processing fee		
Origination fee or underwriting fee		
Lender fee or funding fee		
Appraisal fee		
Attorney fees		
Documentation and recording fees		
Broker fees—may be quoted as points, origination fees or interest rate add-on		
Credit report fee		
Other fees		
Other costs at closing		

Title search/title insurance: For lender For you		
Estimated prepaid amounts for interest, taxes, casualty insurance, escrow payments		
State and local taxes, stamp taxes, transfer taxes		
Flood determination		
Prepaid PMI		
Surveys and home inspections		
Total fees/closing costs		
Can any fees be waived?		
Prepayment penalties		
Length of penalty period		
Extra principal payments allowed?		
Statement of locked in interest rate?		
Fee to lock in the interest rate?		
When does lock-in occur—application, approval, other?		
Length of interest rate lock-in		
If rate drops before closing, can we lock in at lower rate?		
ARM initial rate		
ARM maximum rate next year		
ARM rate and payment caps each year and over life of loan		
ARM frequency of rate change and of any changes in monthly payment		
ARM index lender will use		
ARM margin lender will add to index		
Credit life insurance required as condition of loan?		

Credit life insurance cost		
How much lower would monthly payment be without credit life insurance?		
If lender does not require credit life insurance and you want it, what rate can you get from other insurance providers?		

Summary

When you begin searching for a mortgage, it is beneficial for you to speak to several different lenders. This will help you evaluate the type of mortgage you need and determine which lender can provide you with the best deal. Create a checklist with specific questions that you can compare to determine the right morgage and lender for you.

What You Have Learned

- The various types of mortgages you can choose from when selecting a lender.
- How to evaluate a mortgage lender.
- What other options exist besides the traditional mortgage.
- The different finance options when looking at buying a condo, manufactured or mobile home.
- Once you select a lender, how to apply for a loan.

Free Forms and Checklists

Visit **Socrates.com** and register to receive a variety of useful FREE forms, letters and checklists. See page iv for details on how to register (you will need the seven-digit registration code provided on the enclosed CD).

Section Four

. . . . .

Making It Yours

14

· · · · · ·

Insuring Your Home

In This Chapter

- Discover the different types of insurance you can get for your home.
- Learn how you can save money on your home insurance policy.
- Understand what a home warranty covers and determine if you need to invest in one.

Toward the end of the home buying process, it is important that you obtain insurance. In fact, as you discovered when you applied for a mortgage, your lender will require proof of a valid insurance policy before the closing. Insurance will protect not only your investment but also the lender's investment, which is higher than yours at the beginning of the mortgage loan.

While finding insurance coverage should not be a daunting task, it also should not be a casual undertaking. Do not simply buy the minimal coverage for the least amount of money just to satisfy the lender's requirement. Be prepared to evaluate insurance coverage and carriers carefully in order to buy yourself the best protection.

Types of Coverage

There are three basic types of coverage:

- casualty
- personal property
- liability

Casualty Insurance

Casualty insurance covers losses caused by hazards. The most common hazard is fire, but the policy may cover losses caused by other hazards such as wind or hail. It is crucial that you find out exactly what is and what is not covered. For example, if your new home is in a flood-prone area, you must buy a separate flood insurance policy. Also, ask about wildfire as well as hurricane, tornado and other types of storm damages.

Some insurance companies are expanding their list of exclusions for property damage. The increased number of claims for damage resulting from mold, for instance, has led some carriers to exclude mold coverage. That is why it is important that you make certain your home insurance policy includes what you want and does not exclude what you may need.

Flood Insurance

In 1968, the U.S. Congress created the National Flood Insurance Program (NFIP) in response to the rising cost of taxpayer-funded disaster relief for flood victims and the increasing amount of damage caused by floods. The Mitigation Division, a component of FEMA, manages the NFIP and oversees the floodplain management and mapping components of the program.

Nearly 20,000 communities across the United States and its territories participate in the NFIP by adopting and enforcing the floodplain management ordinances to reduce future flood damage. In exchange, the NFIP makes federally backed flood insurance available to homeowners, renters and business owners in these communities.

Flood insurance is required by law to obtain secured financing to buy a home in special flood hazard areas (SFHAs). Lending institutions that are federally regulated or federally insured must determine if a structure is located in an SFHA and must provide written notice requiring flood insurance.

Flood insurance is available to any property owner located in a community participating in the NFIP. All areas in an SFHA are susceptible to flooding to varying degrees. In fact, 25 percent of all flood claims occur in the low to moderate risk areas. Flooding can be caused by heavy rains, melting snow, inadequate drainage systems and failed protective devices, such as levees and dams, as well as by tropical storms and hurricanes.

There is a big difference between having to buy flood insurance to comply with the law and choosing to buy flood coverage because it is in your best interest. Even if you are not buying in an SFHA, you may want to consider purchasing flood insurance as the best way to recover from flood damages. Visit **www.fema.gov/nfip** for more information.

Personal Property Insurance

Personal property insurance coverage protects what is inside the home. This includes furniture, clothing, books or any belongings found inside the home.

Because the contents of each home vary widely, the amount of coverage also will vary. No matter what is covered within your home, be certain that you understand the limits of the coverage. Does the policy you are considering cover replacement costs of an item at today's price, or is the replacement value based on the item's original cost or depreciated cost?

> **Tip**
>
> Some personal property requires additional coverage because it may cost more to replace than the typical insurance policy allows. If you have jewelry, furs, antiques, artwork, musical instruments, computers or other top-of-the-line equipment, you may need to arrange for additional coverage.

Liability Insurance

Liability insurance protects you against lawsuits resulting from injuries your guests or visitors may suffer in your home or on your property. Specifically, liability coverage provides insurance coverage for medical expenses and legal costs when you are legally responsible for physical injury or property damage to guests in your home or on your property. Your cost for this kind of coverage may depend on the dollar amount limits.

Liability coverage is extremely important. Lawsuits can be costly, and medical expenses can be high. Protect your assets, including your home, from being used to settle a legal dispute.

Should You Carry Liability Coverage?

You should by all means carry liability coverage. Everyone should have liability protection no matter what type of home they have.

> **Note**
>
> Mobile home coverage offers protection against losses to a mobile home, other structures and contents. This type of policy also includes liability and medical payments coverage.

The Basic Homeowners Insurance Policy

Every homeowners insurance policy is tailored to meet the needs of a particular home and its owner. However, every policy should contain some standard clauses.

Coverage for the Structure

There are four possible ways to insure the actual structure of your home:

- replacement cost—the cost of replacing the property without deduction for depreciation, but limited to a maximum dollar amount;
- guaranteed replacement cost—the full cost of replacing the property without considering depreciation and without a dollar cap, this provides the most protection;
- extended replacement cost—coverage up to a specified amount or cap, for example, if structure coverage was $200,000 with a cap of $250,000, the insurance would pay up to $250,000 in rebuilding costs for a home destroyed by fire; and

- actual cash value—coverage for the depreciated amount of the replacement value.

Structural coverage usually covers the home and its attached structures as well as unattached structures–up to 10 percent of the structural coverage amount for the home itself–from damage caused by:

- fire and lightning;
- wind, hail, tornadoes and hurricanes in most states;
- theft, vandalism;
- explosions;
- damage from vehicles;
- accidental damage from smoke;
- weight of snow, ice and sleet;
- freezing of plumbing;
- accidental overflow of water from plumbing;
- sudden and accidental tearing, cracking, bulging or steam pipe or hot water heating system;
- objects falling from the sky; and
- riot and civil unrest.

Structural coverage does not include covering damage caused by:

- earthquakes and flood, depending on where you live hurricanes may not be covered either, but you may be able to purchase additional coverage for each of these; and
- theft by someone who is named as an insured party on your homeowners insurance.

Uninsurable Risks

These are certain conditions for which most insurance carriers will not write coverage, such as:

- war;
- nuclear accident;
- damage from pets;
- rodent, termite or pest damage; and
- deliberate damage caused by you or another insured person in your household.

How Much Coverage Do You Need?

You need enough coverage to be able to rebuild your home completely. If you have a mortgage, your lender will tell you how much coverage it requires. However, the lender only may require the amount needed to repay your mortgage, which probably will underestimate the actual amount it will cost to rebuild. Therefore, you should calculate an estimate of the expense to rebuild. A fast way to estimate how much it would cost to rebuild is to multiply the total square footage of your home by the local building costs per square foot.

You can find out the local building costs by talking to a local real estate agent, insurance agent or builders' association. Visit **www.countryside.com** for a homeowners insurance calculator to determine how much coverage you need.

You also should investigate other factors that will influence the cost to rebuild:

- the type of exterior wall—frame, veneer, brick or stone
- the style of the house—colonial, ranch, Victorian, modern
- the type of roof
- the number or rooms and bathrooms
- special features—attached garages, custom windows, fireplaces, exterior trim or treatments

Before settling on any amount, check the building codes in your community. If your home is damaged severely, it may have to be rebuilt to conform to new building code standards, which may require a different design or different building materials. This can create an extra expense, so you may want to look into an insurance company that will accept a change in policy to pay a specified amount toward these costs.

Coverage for Personal Property

As a rule, personal property coverage protects your personal property from the same risks as the home's structural coverage.

This section of the policy, however, often carries limits on the amount the insurance company will pay in the event of a loss. Personal property coverage may fall between 50 percent to 75 percent of the amount of your home's structural coverage.

How Much Coverage Do You Need?

As a rule, personal property coverage is for actual cash value at the time of the loss, which is the cost of the item less depreciation. What you want is actual replacement value. Purchasing guaranteed replacement coverage can increase your coverage and is a good investment since the current depreciated value of a piece of personal property may be considerably less than it would cost to replace it.

As mentioned earlier, be certain that you have adequate coverage for expensive or unusual items, such as jewelry, antiques or office equipment. You may have to buy extra coverage for these items. Do not forget to include outdoor furniture, sound or stereo equipment, computers and electronic equipment, sports equipment, firearms, silverware, china and special or vintage clothing—your heirloom wedding dress, for example.

> **Tip**
>
> Keep an inventory of your personal property for loss claims. Take either still or video photos of each item to which you can attach any available receipts. Keep your inventory in a safe place away from the house—perhaps in a safe-deposit box. Do not forget to add new purchases or acquisitions to the list and the photo album as time goes by.

Coverage for Loss of Use

Homeowners insurance often includes coverage for temporary living expenses. If your home is damaged to the point that you cannot live in it, this coverage will pay for temporary housing, meals and even fees for car storage and pet kennels.

This type of coverage also has limits. As a rule, it will cover up to 20 percent of the amount of your home's structural coverage for a set period of time.

Coverage for Personal Liability

Liability coverage provides insurance coverage for medical expenses and legal costs when you are legally responsible for physical injury or property damage to guests in your home or on your property. Some insurance carriers also include medical payment coverage in this section of a homeowners insurance policy. Generally limited to $1,000, this coverage pays for certain minor medical costs, such as examinations or X-rays, incurred by a guest with a minor injury.

How Much Coverage Do You Need?

A standard homeowners insurance policy includes $100,000 of liability insurance. However, most insurance professionals recommend a minimum of $300,000 for each occurrence. You can buy a policy addendum for this amount.

If you have personal assets of $300,000 to $500,000 or more, you also may want to add personal umbrella coverage up to $1 million, which is extra protection that takes effect once your regular coverage is exhausted. For example, an injured visitor sues you for $500,000. Your homeowners policy pays out to its limit of $300,000, and then your umbrella coverage kicks in to pay the remaining $200,000. Your cost for the $1 million umbrella coverage will be approximately $200 per year, a small price to pay to protect all of your assets.

Other Homeowners Policy Considerations

Protect yourself from being underinsured in the future by including an inflation protection clause in your homeowners policy. The inflation protection clause adjusts your insurance coverage each year to account for increases in a home's value and the accompanying increases in rebuilding costs due to inflation.

You also should develop the habit of reviewing your insurance policy at least once a year. Make it a New Year's resolution or select an arbitrary time to look at your policy. If you have made any home improvements or major purchases, you may want to increase your coverage.

Condo Coverage

The basic principles of the standard homeowners insurance policy, including the advisability of buying coverage for replacement cost rather than actual cost, apply to condos, co-ops and townhouses. However, there are some differences.

For condos and similar types of homes, the standard structural coverage is divided into two areas: building coverage and dwelling coverage. The building usually is covered under a master policy obtained by the condo association; you buy the dwelling coverage to protect the contents and structures within the unit, including wall coverings, flooring, light fixtures, carpeting and personal belongings.

How Much Coverage Do You Need?

A rule of thumb you can follow is to assume $40,000 worth of personal property for the first 1,000 square feet of the condo; for each additional 500 square feet, add about $5,000 coverage. As with any home insurance policy, be certain to add additional coverage for special items, such as jewelry, antiques or other special pieces of property.

Most policies have a loss of use clause that provides temporary living expenses if your condo is being repaired after a loss. A condo owners policy, however, often differs from a standard homeowners policy in that it covers:

- necessary increase in living costs to maintain your normal standard of living while your condo is uninhabitable; or
- fair rental value for the condo minus any expenses you do not have while the unit is uninhabited—this may not be available if the condo is not your primary home.

Saving Money on Insurance

The premiums you pay on your homeowners policy can vary by hundreds of dollars depending on the carrier you choose and type of insurance you buy. Following are some tips on how to save money when purchasing homeowners insurance:

- **Shop around**—Talk to your friends, check the Yellow Pages or contact your state insurance department (**www.consumeraction.gov/insurance.shtml**) or National Association of Insurance Commissioners (NAIC—**www.naic.org**). Under the "Consumer Information Source" section of the NAIC Web site, you can find information about insurance carriers, including rates and complaints. Also, check consumer guides, insurance agents and online insurance quote services to determine who has the lowest rates. But do not base the entire decision on rates; look for quality service and speedy claim processing as well. Check the carriers' financial stability by going to A.M. Best (**www.ambest.com**) or S&P's (**www.standardandpoors.com**).

- **Raise your deductible**—Deductibles are the amount of money you have to pay toward a loss before your insurance company starts to pay a claim. The higher your deductible the more money you save on your premiums. Most companies recommend a deductible of $500, but if you can raise that to $1,000, you can save as much as 25 percent on the premium. Remember, your policy may have a separate deductible for certain kinds of damage. For instance, if you live near the East Coast, you may have a separate windstorm deductible; if you live in an area subject to hurricanes, you may have a separate deductible for hurricanes; and if you live in an earthquake zone, your earthquake policy may have a separate deductible.

- **Do not insure the land under your home**—The land under your home is not susceptible to damage from theft, wind, fire and other hazards covered in your policy. Therefore, do not include it as an insurable part of your home. This will only increase the value of your home and thus the premiums.

- **Buy your home and auto policies from the same carrier**—Some companies offer a discount if you buy homeowner, auto and liability coverage from them. But be certain that the final price, even with discount, is still lower than buying different policies from different companies.

- **Look for other discounts**—Seniors or retired people, for example, may be entitled to a discount of up to 10 percent because they are at home more than working people and can, therefore, head off disasters or maintain the home in better condition. In addition, some employers and professional associations offer group insurance programs that may offer better rates than elsewhere.

- **Stop smoking**—Since smoking contributes to more than 20,000 home fires a year, some insurance companies offer discounts if all the residents in a home are nonsmokers.

- **Stay with the same insurer**—Some companies offer a discount to long-term policyholders by reducing the premium by 5 percent if you stay for 3 to 5 years and by 10 percent if you remain a policyholder for 6 or more years. Be sure, however, to compare this discounted price with those of other companies.

- **Improve your home security**—You may be able to get discounts of at least 5 percent for a smoke detector, deadbolt locks or a burglar alarm, especially one that rings at the police or fire stations. Consider a sprinkler system as well. Many of these items are expensive, however, and some do not qualify for a discount. You should ask your insurer for recommendations and weigh the cost of purchase and installation against the cost of the premiums.

- **Look for and point out to insurance carriers other features of the home that may affect insurance premiums**—Newer construction, reinforced roofs, storm shutters, upgraded wiring, new plumbing, close proximity to fire hydrants and fire stations all may earn you discounts on your premiums.

- **Review your coverage at least once a year**—Just as you do not want to be underinsured because of inflation, you also do not want to continue to pay premiums on coverage you no longer need. A new purchase requires an upgrade, but discarding an insured item can lower your coverage needs and your premium.

- **Look for private insurance if you have a government plan**—If you live in a disaster-prone area and have been buying your insurance through a government plan, check with your insurance agent to see if there may be some companies who might be interested in your business. You may be able to buy insurance at a lower price in the private sector.

- **Maintain a good credit rating**—Insurers are increasingly using credit information to price homeowners policies. In most states, your insurer must tell you about any adverse action, such as a higher rate; verify the accuracy of the information on which the insurer based the change.

Property Insurance Score

Insurance companies now use insurance scores and information from claims databases to underwrite insurance applications.

An insurance score is a statistical analysis of a buyer's likelihood of filing an insurance claim within a given period of time in the future. Your insurance score is tied to your credit rating; according to insurance companies, there is a correlation between a buyer's financial history and his or her likelihood of filing insurance loss claims in the future. Therefore, insurance companies are depending more and more on credit information to write insurance at a cost that reflects their risks. Maintaining a good credit rating can save money on insurance premiums.

Insurance companies have been using the standard credit bureau databases to obtain credit information and the Comprehensive Loss Underwriting Exchange (CLUE) database to learn a person's claims history. However, now consumers can access their claims history on the CLUE database as well. By periodically checking your credit rating and going to the CLUE database, you can track your ratings and rectify or question anything that is incorrect or out-of-date.

Selecting an Insurance Company

As you search for the most economical insurance premium rates, you will be learning about various insurance carriers. Visit these sites again and talk to friends, colleagues and real estate professionals for sources.

In addition, the Internet is an excellent way to look for insurance companies. As mentioned earlier, visiting the sites for your state insurance office, the NAIC and the financial rating companies is a good way to begin the search. For a list that includes other online resources to help you make decisions about your home insurance, turn to the Resources section in Appendix A.

Home Warranties

A home warranty covers repair or replacement costs that are not covered by homeowners insurance. Warranties cover specific items, such as heating, air conditioning, plumbing and home appliances. Typically, home warranties cover such appliances as washers, dryers, refrigerators, range and oven, and for an additional fee, microwave, garbage disposals, doorbells, ceiling fans and water softeners.

Warranties are essentially service contracts that repair and replace major home systems that malfunction because of normal wear and tear. Warranties should never be considered replacements for homeowners insurance; rather, they overlap the coverage that the homeowners insurance provides. For example, if your refrigerator stops working, there could be damage to your floor from leakage. The homeowners insurance will repair the floor, while the warranty will replace the refrigerator.

Home warranties usually cost between $300 and $400 a year plus a fee for a service call. If your home is new and the systems and appliances are in good condition, you may not want to invest in warranties. However, in an older home, a warranty can prevent unexpected expenses from denting your budget.

As with any purchase, you should find out as much as you can about the company standing behind the warranty. Find a company with financial stability and a good reputation. Ask your real estate agent for suggestions and check with your state's department of consumer protection before selecting a warranty company. Also, be certain you are clear about what the warranty covers before you sign. Ask questions about what is and is not covered and find out how to file a claim. Visit the Resources section in Appendix A for Web sites that provied information about home warranties.

Summary

Finding home insurance is an amportant part of the home buying process. Before you close, your lender will requiare some proof that you have valid home insurance. To find the best protection, evaluate your needs based on the type of home you are buying. This will help you narrow your choics on the type of insurance coverage you will need to get. After you have done this you can shop around for the best rates.

What You Have Learned?

- The type of insurance you need to get for your home.
- What the basic homewoners insurance policy covers.
- Different tips to help you save money on your homeowners insurance policy.
- How home warranties cover the costs that home insurance did not cover.

15
· · · · · ·
Closing the Deal

In This Chapter

- Determine what you need to do for the final walk-through of your new home.
- Determine what paperwork and documentation you need to have with you during the closing process.
- Get an estimate of the closing costs and fees.
- Find out what you need to do when you get the title to your home and title insurance.

The day you finally close on your new home is always exciting. At last, the long, tedious process of finding a home and obtaining a loan is over, and by the end of the day, you will be a homeowner.

Before that day ends, you will be asked to sign a seemingly endless number of documents and hand over seemingly endless fees. It may seem confusing, but you can prepare for the closing by knowing what to expect.

The Final Walk-Through

You have already seen the home several times and it has passed several inspections. Nevertheless, before the final closing, you should make another inspection of the home. The final, or presettlement, walk-through is done to discover only those changes that may have occurred since the contract was accepted and the professional inspection was completed. It may be your first opportunity to see the home without furniture and other decorating.

Be sure to take all your paperwork with you, including the sales contract and any addenda, any inspection reports, a list of what is to be included in the home and a record of any repairs or replacements agreed to in the contract. Examine the house carefully, attic to basement and any common areas you may share. As you walk around, be sure to:

- look at the walls and ceilings and check for cracks, water damage or other signs of structural problems;
- inspect floors where rugs or furniture had been placed to see if there are any defects in the floors or carpeting that had been covered previously;

- verify that everything that is supposed to be included with the home is there, such as drapery rods, chandelier or appliances, and be certain that these items are the originals and not cheap replacements—check everything against your contract and lists;

- test the various systems to be certain that everything is in working order;

- look for any items or trash the seller has left behind and bring them to the attention of the agent—you should not have to clean out the house before your movers arrive; and

- check to see if the seller has completed all the work he or she agreed to do; if any of the problems have not been corrected, point this out and handle it before closing.

In fact, this is the time to handle any problems. If you identify a problem or potential problem, tell your real estate agent so that he or she can take care of it before the home closes.

Final Walk-Through Checklist	
Items to Inspect	Completed/Notes
Garage	
Yard and lot	
Storage shed(s)	
Basement	
Crawl spaces	
Attic	
Common areas	
Living room	
Dining room	
Kitchen	
Family or great room	
Bedroom 1	
Bedroom 2	
Bedroom 3	
Bedroom 4—home office, den	
Other room(s)	
Furnace	
Air conditioning	
Refrigerator	
Stove/oven	
Dishwasher	
Washer and dryer	
Other appliances	
Trash to be removed	
Items to remain in home—real property	
Repairs/replacements agreed to in contract	

See also the fixtures inventory checklist in the Moving section of Appendix B.

The Closing Process

Closing often occurs at a title company, an escrow company or an attorney's office. The buyer and seller usually attend along with real estate agents and review and sign closing documents. If you have not already provided a paid homeowners insurance policy or a binder and receipt showing that the premium has been paid, this is the time to do so. The closing agent will present forms listing all of the money you owe the seller, such as the remainder of the down payment, and any money the seller owes you, such as a previously agreed upon rent payment for staying in the home for a longer period of time. The seller also provides proof of any warranties agreed on or repairs made.

The forms that you will deal with at the closing include:

- the closing cost estimate, which your agent should give you with the contract, and a good faith estimate, which your lender will give you after you apply for the loan; these should provide an estimate of the funds you will need at the closing;

- truth-in-lending statement, which requires that good faith estimates be provided within 3 days of a loan application;

- the settlement statement, which will inform you of the total amount of cash you will need at the closing and how these funds will be allotted; as a rule, this may not be available until a few days before the actual closing, but that still gives you an opportunity to eliminate any discrepancies;

- disclosure documents;

- the real estate contract;

- the loan papers, including the mortgage note;

- homeowners insurance, which must be obtained before the closing;

- title insurance; and

- the title or deed.

Disclosure Documents

At the closing, you will receive a packet of disclosure statements, many of which are required by law. These documents may include:

- the appraisal notice, which informs you of your right to receive a copy of the appraisal report;

- the private mortgage insurance disclosure, which generally permits the lender to offer a loan with a down payment that is lower than usual;

- the transfer of mortgage servicing disclosure statement, which will state that your lender has the right to transfer your loan payments to another lender;

- the truth-in-lending disclosure statement, which will list the annual percentage rate of your loan, the finance charge, the amount financed and the total of payments; and

- the good faith estimate of settlement costs, which lists the final closing expenses and settlement charge in your loan and property purchase, including:
    - the appraisal fee
    - the credit report fee
    - tax-related service fees
    - underwriting fee
    - yield spread premium to the mortgage broker
    - courier fee, flood certification fee
    - processing fee, wiring fee
    - prorated interest
    - mortgage insurance premium
    - hazard insurance premium
    - city tax escrow fee
    - settlement or closing fees
    - document preparation fee
    - title insurance fee
    - lender's title insurance fee
    - recording fee
    - city or tax stamps

Upon completing the transaction, your lender should give you duplicate copies of these forms. Store these copies in a safe place to use when preparing your tax returns or when writing to your lender or insurance agent.

Note

While federal law requires that a lender provide a good faith estimate to a buyer, the law does not require a service provider to make good on the estimate. Many mortgage lenders, however, are recommending mandatory redisclosure if the final fees represent an increase of 10 percent or more over the good faith estimates.

What to Bring to the Closing

The buyer must bring the following to the closing:

- the down payment—usually a certified check;
- a deposit for prepaid taxes and insurance to the escrow account;
- various fees for the lender and attorney;
- proof of insurance on the home; and
- certified funds.

The seller must bring the following to the closing:

- the deed, title and keys to the home;

- inspection reports not previously submitted;
- any documents that will be transferred, such as for property taxes or insurance policies;
- a bill of sale for any furniture or personal property included in the sale; and
- the real estate agent's commission.

When all of the paperwork has been handled, you will review and sign the mortgage as well as the mortgage promissory note. At this point, you will receive the deed to the property.

> **Tip**
>
> Be sure to check the deed to see that you and your co-owner's names are spelled correctly and that your title designation is correct, that is, you and your co-owner are listed as joint tenants with right of survivorship or as tenants in common.

Recording the Deed

The deed and mortgage are recorded with the local authority, such as the county recorder or registry of deeds office. The closing agent should complete this within a reasonable amount of time.

This is a very important step, and you should make a point of following up to be certain that it is completed. Recorded documents, including deeds, affect the title to a property. Unrecorded deeds may be valid as far as the buyer and seller are concerned, but they do not give constructive notice to the rest of the world. Regardless of your opinion about the trustworthiness of the parties involved, you do not truly hold the title to a home until the deed is recorded. Recording your deed will prevent problems later in the event of other claimants developing an interest in the property or the property becoming part of divorce proceedings or inheritance documents.

Closing Costs and Fees

At closing, the closing agent receives payment from you for the closing costs and gives you a settlement statement. As a rule, closing costs are 2 percent to 4 percent of the loan, excluding points. Closing fees vary but usually cover:

- attorney or escrow fees;
- property taxes for the remainder of taxes due during the tax period to date;
- interest paid from the closing date to 30 days before the first monthly payment;
- a loan origination fee of approximately 1 percent of the loan, covering the lender's administrative costs;
- deed recording fee;
- a survey fee;
- the first premium covering the mortgage insurance;

- title insurance fee;
- loan discount points;
- the first payment of the escrow account for future real estate taxes and insurance;
- homeowners insurance policy, other insurance policy receipts—such as fire or flood; and
- miscellaneous fees, such as document preparation fee.

> **Tip**
>
> Some closing costs may be waived by the closing agent before the actual closing. Federal law guarantees you the right to choose your own settlement service provider, so shop for closing agents as carefully as you did for a mortgage lender or a real estate agent. Talk to closing agents to determine who will provide the requested services at the lowest cost and have them send you a list of the fees they will charge. Some fees, however, such as the fee for recording the deed, cannot be waived.

Contesting Closing Fees

As the fees begin to pile up, you may wonder if all of these fees are necessary and reasonable. In any case, how would you be able to determine whether or not you are being overcharged?

The National Mortgage Complaint Center can help you avoid what is known in the industry as junk fees. To avoid paying too much, the center recommends examining the good faith estimate as soon as you receive it. If you do not feel you are capable of evaluating whether or not the fees are inflated, for a small fee, the center will analyze your good faith estimate and point out excessive or duplicated fees as well as terms and conditions you may be unaware of, such as prepayment penalties and hidden charges that your lender may be paying to the mortgage broker who originates the loan. The latter, behind-the-back fees are known as yield spread premiums.

Other fees that the Mortgage Complaint Center recommends you contest include:

- application fee—you already are paying a loan origination fee that covers the lender's administrative costs;
- document preparation fee—the loan origination fee should cover this;
- processing fee—the loan origination fee should cover this;
- underwriting fee—the loan origination fee should cover this; and
- funding fee—you should not be charged a fee to give you the money you applied for.

If you decide to contest the closing fees, you must do so before the closing and in writing. Write the lender and ask that the fees in question be explained or waived. Request a response in writing, including any offer to lower the fees. You must take all of this correspondence to the closing and be prepared to walk away from the deal if you are not satisfied with the final resolution of the fees. If you walk away, you may lose the money you already have paid for a credit report and an appraisal; to protect yourself, the center suggests that you insist on paying the credit report and appraisal fee at the closing rather than up front.

Visit **http://nationalmortgagecomplaintcenter.com** for more information about the National Mortgage Complaint Center.

Attorney Need at the Closing?

With the exception of nine states—Alabama, Connecticut, Delaware, Georgia, Massachusetts, New York, South Carolina, Vermont and West Virginia—most states do not require an attorney to be present at the closing of a home. However, state regulations do require the participation of a qualified real estate professional, such as an escrow agent or a title company.

Even if you are not required to hire an attorney, it is a good idea to have an attorney review the sales contract and help you in the negotiations. At the very least, you should include a contingency clause in your contract that requires the offer and sales contracts to be subject to review and approval by your attorney. You also may want to have your attorney represent you at the closing.

For more information about real estate attorneys, review the information in Chapter 4.

Title to the Home

The title to a home is your proof of ownership and should be treated with great care. It should be recorded as soon as possible. The first person to claim the property legally is the rightful owner. Thus, even if you hold the title in your hand, it is not final until you have recorded it with the proper authority.

Ownership Interest in a Property

There are several ways to hold title to your home. If you are single and no one else will own or have an interest in the home with you, you will hold title to the home in fee simple without limitation to any other person. This is the most common form of property ownership and reflects the type of estate you have in the property.

If you are a typical married couple buying your first home, you will more than likely select joint tenancy with right of survivorship. This is a situation in which two or more persons own and have equal interest in the same property; if one person predeceases the other, the survivor is the sole title owner. You also may hold a property as tenants in common, in which two or more persons own and have equal interests in the same property.

There are advantages and disadvantages to joint tenancy with right of survivorship. A major advantage is the avoidance of probate court costs and delays after one joint tenant dies; when one joint tenant dies, the surviving joint tenant automatically receives the ownership share of the deceased joint tenant without the complications of probate. On the other hand, this can be a problem in second marriages when each spouse wants to leave his or her share of joint tenancy to the children from a first marriage.

Avoiding probate and delays may not always be enough of a reason to opt for joint tenancy or tenancy in common. Because all joint tenants have the right to occupy and manage the property, for example, a problem may arise if the tenants cannot agree on management decisions, such as refinancing the mortgage. If one tenant is incapacitated, a conservator may be appointed by the court to represent the incapacitated tenant's interests.

The law of partition in most states permits one joint tenant or tenant in common to force a sale of the property even if the other owner resists. In addition, most states allow a joint tenant to secretly transfer his or her share of the property by gift or sale without approval of the other joint tenant.

Despite the fact that joint tenancy ownership is not subject to the wills of the tenants, joint tenants may want to provide their own share of the property in their wills anyway. For example, if all joint tenants are killed in an accident, it may be impossible to determine who survived the longest. Therefore, their individual shares in the property will pass to their heirs according to their wills just as if they were tenants in common.

Joint tenancy with right of survivorship may not be the best way to hold title in a house, depending on your individual situation. Talk to your real estate attorney or a tax adviser about other alternatives, such as revocable living trusts.

Title Insurance

Title insurance is issued by a title company and protects the buyer against loss from a defective title. The title company searches and examines public records at the county recorder's office or registry of deeds and looks for unpaid taxes, judgments or mortgage payments, outstanding liens, or belated probate claims. The examiner also looks for third-party claims, such as monies owed to a former spouse, a business partner or a homeowners association, or for problems if a previous owner sells a home without a co-owner's permission.

Title insurance protects home buyers and lenders if a property has problems from the past. If the title company misses a problem that is discovered later, the insurance carrier makes a reimbursement if there is a loss.

If there are unpaid monies owed or third-party claims, the title will be designated as not clear or marked-up or with encumbrances. These are problems that must be corrected before a lender will approve a mortgage loan. Do not accept a title that is not clear; you undoubtedly will encounter future problems. Either demand that the title be made clear before you purchase the home or cancel the purchase if the problems appear significant. Also, have your attorney take a look at the title and its status.

You should always purchase title insurance in the event that problems appear after the purchase, but shop around for a good price. You may qualify for a discount rate, but you have to inquire about it. Ask about a binder rate if you plan to keep the home for just a few years. Although this is not available in every state, binder rates discount title insurance for short-term ownership of up to 2 or 3 years.

Remember that title insurance is an indemnity policy—that is, it only pays when there is an actual title loss.

Depending on your mortgage, title insurance can cost from a few hundred to a few thousand dollars. The person who actually pays may depend on the home's location. For example, in some states, particularly on the West Coast, sellers pay for title insurance. On the East Coast, buyers often pay this cost.

Escrow Account

As you have been reading about the closing process, you have seen such terms as escrow account, escrow fee, escrow agent and escrow company. Exactly what is an escrow account?

Established by your lender, an escrow account is a place to set aside a portion of your monthly mortgage payment to cover annual charges for homeowners insurance, mortgage insurance—if applicable—and property taxes. Escrow accounts ensure that money always will be available for these payments.

At the closing, your lender will require an escrow account containing up to 14 months of prepaid taxes and insurance premiums. The escrow account may be waived by the lender once you have 20 percent equity in your home, but you may want to continue the account so that money for these recurring expenses is always set aside. Some states require interest to be paid on escrow accounts, but others do not have that requirement. Check with your lender.

If you do use an escrow account to pay property taxes or homeowners insurance, make sure that you are not penalized for late payments since it is the lender's responsibility to make these payments.

The Final Step

As you complete the closing process, you will be tempted to take your new keys and move into your new home. But before you stuff all the closing documents into a moving box, take some time to set up a working filing system. Create a tax file, an insurance file, a home document file and a file for receipts and canceled checks. Sort and classify all the information you have gathered about the property in a way that is useful to you.

Safe-deposit storage is recommended for items that have high monetary value or are difficult to replace. Most experts recommend that certificates of ownership, such as title, deeds and purchase contracts, be stored in a safe-deposit box. You also may want to keep a household inventory, such as bills of sale, appraisals and receipts in the safe-deposit box. A list of financial advisers, insurance policies, the location of important papers and Social Security numbers also can go into the safe-deposit box, but you may want to keep a photocopy of such lists at home for convenience.

Records that are kept at home should be stored in a fireproof box. These records include your tax, insurance and home documents files as well as photocopies of helpful lists.

> **Note**
>
> A copy of each person's will and plan for transfer of property and personal items should be kept in the safe-deposit box, but the original will should be stored in the fireproof box at home where it can be accessed easily. Living wills or power of attorney for health care also should be kept at home and not in the safe-deposit box.

Summary

Before you sit down and sign all the forms it is wise to do one last walk through around the home and make sure everything you and the seller agreed upon has been done. Once you have completed the walk-through you are ready to close on the home. Have your real estate agent and attorney review the forms and advise you on what you ned to bring at closing. Being prepared and knowing what to expect at closing will help ease your mind during thie final step before homeownership.

What You Have Learned

- What to inspect and check when you make the final walk-through before you close on the property.
- What to expect during the closing process, including closing costs and fees.
- How to hold the title of your home, what title insurance is and how it protects you.

16

. . . . . .

Moving In

In This Chapter

- How to find a reliable moving company and save money on the moving process.
- Best way to plan your move and packing tips.
- What to expect on moving day.
- Getting settled in to your new neighborhood.

Moving is not an easy task, but when you are moving into your own home for the first time, moving day can be exciting. The work seems less arduous when you are celebrating the end of the long process of buying a home and the beginning of a new chapter in your life.

Nevertheless, moving day can become frantic if you have not planned ahead. Advance planning is the key to preventing problems and expenses, not to mention unnecessary stress. There are ways to make the job less stressful.

Finding a Mover

It is well worth the effort to take some time and investigate moving companies. Although the U.S. Congress included some consumer protection clauses in its Highway Reauthorization Bill in 2005, it is still essential that you investigate your options carefully. Following is a list of steps you can take as you begin to search for a reputable mover:

- **Ask friends, relatives, co-workers and your real estate agent to recommend movers with whom they have had good experiences**— Gather at least six names and then check to see which ones are members of the American Moving and Storage Association (AMSA). The AMSA does not recommend a mover, but its members do agree to abide by the organization's arbitration program–mandated under the auspices of the U.S. Department of Transportation–for disputes involving loss or damages during a move. Visit their Web site at **www.moving.org** for more information.

- **Be sure that the mover has insurance and is licensed by the proper authority**—For example, for moves from one state to another, a U.S. Department of Transportation number is issued by the Federal Motor Carrier Safety Administration (FMCSA). You can double-check a mover's license by visiting **www.protectyourmove.gov**. If you are moving within a state, check with your state, county or local consumer affairs agency or your state's attorney general.

- **Narrow down the list by checking references**—Contact each company and ask if they can offer references or have had contracts with corporate relocation departments. Contact the references to discuss their experiences with the moving companies. You also can check with the Better Business Bureau for complaints about individual companies.

- **Call the best three moving companies and ask for a walk-through and a written estimate based on an actual inspection of your household goods**—Be sure to find out if the bid is binding or nonbinding. A binding bid may be a higher quote, but the mover is not going to increase the price on moving day. On the other hand, movers are required by law to move your goods for no more than 10 percent above the price of a nonbinding bid.

- **Find out how the mover calculates charges**—Some movers charge by weight and distance; others charge by number of man-hours to complete the move. Movers also may charge by the number of workers to do the job. If you find a mover who charges by the hour and by the worker, you may want to determine the most economical way to use the mover. Is it cheaper to pay for one more person if it will cut down on the hours it takes to complete the move? Also, be sure to ask how much it will cost for the mover to do the packing and to provide the boxes. These may be extra charges that inflate the bill tremendously.

- **Be alert to red flags indicating that the mover may not be reputable**—There are four signs you should watch for:
  ○ low estimates that undercut competitors, the mover may impose extra charges once your possession are in the truck;
  ○ immediate estimates over the phone or Internet, an on-site inspection of your household is the safest way to get an accurate estimate;
  ○ cubic foot rather than weight charges; and
  ○ cash ahead of time, be wary of movers who demand cash payment or a large cash deposit before the move.

- **Think carefully before deciding to use a broker of moving services from the Internet**—Brokers usually do not own or operate trucks or equipment themselves. Instead, they collect a deposit from you and then contract with another company to carry out the actual move. Thus, you have no control over who actually moves your household. In addition, you often will not have the same consumer protection as you would with a licensed mover; the broker already has your deposit, so he or she may lose interest in helping you settle a claim for damaged or lost goods.

- **Look at your insurance needs carefully**—Most movers include insurance coverage as part of their standard bid, but the coverage may be limited to 60 cents per pound. That is usually insufficient. If a mover drops and breaks your 100-pound glass-top dining room table, for example, you will receive $60, certainly not enough to replace the furniture. You must buy additional insurance coverage, either from the mover or from your insurance company. Full replacement coverage is the goal, and you may have to do some comparison shopping to get the best rate.

> **Tip**
>
> You may need to prove ownership if you file an insurance claim for a missing or damaged possession. A file with receipts and serial numbers is a good way to present proof. You also can photograph or videotape everything being loaded on the truck.

Saving Money on the Move

After tapping into your funds for closing costs and other expenses related to buying a home, you may want to look for ways to save money during the move. There are ways to save money if you plan ahead. Consider the following options:

- Read the estimate bids to see if there are extra charges for packing materials or travel time. You may be able to negotiate these fees. Movers work in a competitive industry and definitely want your business.

- Help the movers develop an accurate picture of what you want to move. When the estimators come to your home to prepare the quote, show them everything you want to move. Do not forget the basement, attic, garage, outbuildings, closets and under beds. Anything you want to move that is not included in the original bid will add to the total cost at the end. This is also a good way to take stock of your belongings and decide what you can discard before moving day.

- Gather free cartons from grocery or beverage stores to use for books and other sturdy objects. Boxes with divider inserts are excellent for moving glasses and bottles.

- Find out if buying your own packing material–boxes, wardrobes, packing tape or Bubble Wrap®–is cheaper at self-moving companies than it is from your mover.

- Calculate whether or not it is more economical to pack and move your own small valuables while leaving the large appliances, furniture and big boxes for the movers.

- Throw away or donate anything you do not need or have not used within 1 year or so. Movers often charge by weight, so why move something that you will end up throwing away later?

- Pack your possessions yourself. The exceptions might be valuables or fragile items that a professional mover or packer must pack in order to have the valuables insured. Be sure to ask if your mover will insure boxes you have packed yourself. In many cases, they will refuse to provide coverage for those boxes.

- Consider you load, we haul moving companies. You pack your belongings and load them onto a trailer that the moving company leaves at your house for a few days. A professional driver then picks up the load and drives it to your new home where you unload it yourself. This is a good option for people who want to move themselves but are uncomfortable driving a large van or truck.

- Select a moving date during off-peak times. If you are able to do so, avoiding moves during the peak times of May through September or at the beginning and end of each month may mean a savings because of lower rates. You also may get a more experienced moving crew during off-peak times.

Is Your Appliance Worth Moving?

Life Span of Appliances:

- refrigerator, electric dryer—11 to 13 years
- washing machine—10 to 12 years
- microwave—9 to 11 years

Should You Move Yourself?

If you are thinking about moving yourself, you should take a good look at the costs and effort. Compare your evaluation with the costs and effort of professional moving. Filling in the chart below will give you some idea of the costs of a do-it-yourself move.

Moving Cost Estimate	
Truck rental	$
Rental deposit	$
Car hitch	$
Insurance on truck	$
Fuel charge	$
Additional mileage charge	$
Appliance service cost	$
Furniture pads	$
Dollies or handcarts	$
Packing materials—boxes, tape, Bubble Wrap	$
Loading and unloading help	$
Warehouse storage charge	$
Additional truck rental to deliver from storage	$
Extra costs—tolls, hotels, food, child-care, liniment, painkillers	$
Total	$

> **Tip**
>
> The IRS may allow tax deductions for moving expenses if the move is job-related and is 50 miles or more away from the old employment location. If you qualify, you may be able to deduct the moving company's bill, packing costs and storing costs within 30 days of relocating. One-way travel expenses also may be deductible. Deducting moving expenses is complex, so you should obtain IRS Publication 521, "Moving Expenses," by calling 800.829.1040 or visiting **www.irs.gov.**

Planning the Move

Moving into a new home can be exciting, but it also can be stressful. Begin your planning by breaking the move down into before, during and after segments.

Before the Move

Find a mover. If you are moving during the peak moving seasons–summer and at the beginning and end of each month–you should allow at least 2 months' advance notice. During the off-peak times, you may be able to schedule a mover 4 to 6 weeks before moving day.

If you are moving yourself, book a rental truck at least 1 month in advance and be sure to ask about discounts or coupons on midweek or midmonth rentals. Also, start collecting empty boxes from grocers or other stores.

Refer to the preceding section on finding a mover, and remember to:

- obtain three written estimates;
- never pay a deposit;
- negotiate for free boxes or discounts during off-peak moving times;
- check out insurance coverage—the mover's standard coverage, your own extra coverage and any in-transit coverage your homeowners or renters policy may have, also ask if the mover will insure items that you personally pack;
- ask movers about their policies for handling complaints or claims; and
- insist on as specific a cost estimate as possible and ask for a binding estimate.

> **Tip**
>
> 10 percent to 15 percent of the bill is the general tip to be split among the movers and the supervisor if you are satisfied with their work.

Change of Address

When you have set the moving date, send out change of address notifications. File a change of address form with the U.S. Post Office at **www.moversguide.usps.com** or in person at your local branch. Notify credit card companies and magazine and newspaper subscriptions of your new address about 1 month before the move. Also arrange for utilities at the new home in case there is a wait for installation, but arrange to continue service at your current home through the moving day.

As you pay bills, look for a change of address section on the statement and fill it out when you pay.

Address Change Notice

Date: _____

To: _____

Dear _____:

Please be advised that effective _____, 20_____, my/our address has been changed

from: _____

_____

_____

to: _____

_____

_____

My/our new telephone number is: _____

Please make note of the above information and direct all correspondence to me/us at my/our new address.

Sincerely,

_____

Important Documents

Before it gets too hectic and while you are doing some preliminary sorting, take the time to construct a file of important documents. Include all paperwork pertaining to the move, including bids, final estimates and any signed contracts.

Next, gather any documents that you keep at home rather than in a safe-deposit box. This may include all the paperwork for your new home, calendars, health records, school papers, bank statements, canceled checks, paycheck stubs, tax returns, receipts for household items—in short, any important legal, financial or personal documents you keep at home. Place them in an accordion file or some sort of folder or container for quick access. You may want to move this file yourself so that it does not get misplaced or lost in a mass of cartons.

Think Ahead

When you know your moving date, reevaluate the way you shop. Do not stock up on perishable foods during the week or so before you move. Put a moratorium on catalog or online ordering and refrain from buying unnecessary products. Everything you buy now will have to be packed and moved.

Retrieve anything you have loaned to neighbors or friends and return anything you have borrowed. Pick up layaway items, dry cleaning, film being developed or items being repaired. Use up coupons and free movie or pool passes.

Donate items to charity or give them to friends. This might include any unused passes or coupons. Be sure to get a receipt for tax purposes.

In fact, try to assess the impact on your move of anything you do in the last few weeks before a move. Your goal is to keep the move as simple as possible, so try not to complicate it by purchasing new furniture or extending an invitation for houseguests to visit.

As you make final arrangements for the move, make a note of contact information for the mover. Be ready to tell the mover where you can be reached while in transit to your new home. If it is a local move, all you may need to give the mover is your cell phone number. If it is a long-distance move involving several days, be prepared to tell the mover where you will be during those few days.

During the Move

Proper packing by a professional packer is a critical component of any move. Professionals use special packing materials and techniques that protect your belongings. In addition, moving companies are more willing to insure goods that have been professionally packed than those that you pack. Schedule packing 1 to 2 days before the moving van arrives to be loaded.

Make a point of being present when your belongings are packed. You and the packer should make an inventory of your goods and resolve any questions about the condition of items–scratches, dents, water damage–before you sign the inventory. List valuable items separately. Be certain that all items are numbered and that the numbers correspond to those on the inventory sheet. Also, check that all copies of the inventory sheet are legible.

Schedule any required servicing of appliances before the move. For example, dishwashers and washing machine may require a special packing block to be inserted to immobilize the agitators.

Double-check that all boxes are clearly labeled. The packer will tag each box with an inventory sticker, but you should write your name and the name of the room the box belongs in on the top and both sides of the box. There is nothing more frustrating than having to rotate a box or dig it out of a stack to find out its contents. You should be able to read the labels from both sides of the box. Also, identify the boxes that contain fragile items with a distinctive mark. That way, you can check them first for damage after they are unloaded in the new home.

Remember, the mover is responsible for loss or damage to any box he or she takes possession of, even if he or she did not pack the carton. However, if you pack the carton, the mover is not responsible for damage to the contents of the carton unless external damage to the carton causes damage to its contents. In addition, the mover can refuse to move a carton you have packed if he or she thinks it is improperly packed or is too heavy. Once the van is loaded, ask to see the inventory sheet and the bill of lading. Keep a copy.

Packing Tips

If you pack any or all of your household goods, the following tips may be helpful:

- Pack nonessential or seldom used articles weeks before the move. Books or out-of-season clothing, for example, can be packed early and labeled.
- Be sure to pack heavy items like books in smaller cartons so that the boxes can be lifted without strain.
- Reinforce the bottoms of boxes, especially boxes from the grocery, with heavy-duty tape.
- Wrap household items in blankets, bedding or towels for protection and for more efficient packing.
- Pack all the items from one room together and label the boxes with the name of the room.
- Fill each box to capacity and fill in empty spaces with newspaper or Bubble Wrap so that items do not bang together when moved.
- Tape appliance doors or lids closed and tie or secure furniture drawers. Most movers will move a dresser or bureau with drawers full if the piece is not too heavy.
- Use masking tape to attach cords to their appliances or equipment.
- Pack special items in appropriate containers. For example, dish barrels, which can be bought for $5 to $7 each, are double-walled to protect fragile items. Wardrobe containers allow you to hang garments. Long, flat boxes are necessary for artwork and mirrors. Tape an X with masking tape across picture frame glass to prevent cracking or shattering.

- Label boxes on all sides and the top and include your name, the room where the contents belong and any special or unusual items in the boxes.

After the Move

Be at your new home before the movers arrive. Post someone at the door to direct movers where to take each box or piece of furniture. When unloading, focus on the kitchen and bathroom first. These are the rooms you will be using immediately.

Warning
Be sure the mover knows how to contact you upon delivery. Since your belongings may be transported in the same truck with those of other families moving to the same area at the same time, delivery of your goods may be made on any of several consecutive days previously agreed upon. If the mover cannot reach you at the destination, he or she may place your shipment in temporary storage to prevent delaying delivery of other households on the truck. You will then be charged extra for storage and handling.

Most movers prefer to disassemble and reassemble furniture themselves. Be certain that they do not leave until the beds and any other furniture are unpacked and reconstructed.

Upon delivery, check everything for damage. Use your inventory sheet while you inspect your belongings and cartons for damage. If there is damage, note the facts in detail on the original copy of the inventory sheet. Do not sign the inventory sheet or the bill of lading until you have inspected for damage and noted any problems on it.

You have 9 months to file for loss or damage, but it is best to report damage as soon as possible. You will have to save the cartons and packing material until the mover has inspected the damage, so the sooner you report it the sooner you can finish unpacking. The mover must acknowledge receipt of your damage claim within 30 days and must settle—either by denying the claim or making an offer within 120 days of your claim.

Moving Day

It is difficult to avoid all stress and tension on moving day. The following steps, however, can minimize problems:

- Place everything you plan to take with you in your car before the movers arrive so that the movers do not inadvertently load these items on the van. This includes the moving day box—see below.
- Have your phone number, new address and directions to your new home ready for the movers.
- Block off a place on the street or in the back for the moving truck before the movers arrive if you live in an urban area or do not have a private driveway.

- Assign someone to photograph or videotape your belongings as they are loaded onto the truck. This is to be used when you check the inventory sheet for losses and damage.

- Buy some paper or plastic cups and soft drinks for the movers.

- Be sure you have payment, including the tip, for the movers.

- Be prepared to protect your floors or carpeting at the new and old houses. Home improvement stores sell rolls of kraft paper to place on pathways to protect floors from water, snow or dirt.

- Ask the movers to load kitchen and bathroom items, beds and carpets last so that they come off first. You want to lay the carpets before the furniture is put in place, and you will need to set up your bathroom, a minimally functional kitchen and sleeping arrangements as soon as possible.

- Arrange for baby sitters to pick up your children as early in the day as possible. Infants and young children are difficult to work around on moving day, so removing them from the premises is a good idea.

- Arrange for someone to sweep out, check over and lock up the house after the van pulls away. If the van is traveling directly to your new home to be unloaded, you will have to leave to meet it, but you can ask a family member or friend to close up the old house after you leave.

Whether you are moving across town or across the country, you want to be in your new home before the movers arrive. You or someone you assign should stand at the entrance and direct the movers to the final destination of each box or piece of furniture. You also may need to ask someone to supervise the laying of carpet and the reassembling and placement of furniture. That may be the last task the movers tackle.

When the movers are ready to leave, do not forget to check the inventory sheet carefully and note any damage or loss in writing before signing it and the bill of lading. Be sure to retain a copy of both for your file.

Meanwhile, another person can be setting up the bathroom and kitchen and making up the beds. By the time the movers finish unloading and leave, you should be able to eat, take a bath and go to bed. The rest of the unpacking can wait—by this time you will have decided that moving day has gone on long enough anyway. See Appendix A for the moving checklist.

Moving Day Box

Moving day will go more smoothly if you have prepared a moving day box, also known as the last box. This box should include everything you will need before the rest of your household goods are unpacked. These are basics items you will use up to the last minute before leaving and will need immediately upon arriving.

The moving day box must be unloaded first. In most cases, it should travel with you in your car, but if it goes on the van, it should be loaded last and unloaded first and should be included on the inventory list. Be sure to label it Moving Day

Box with a bold, broad-tipped pen. In both the old and new houses, this box should be placed where you will have unobstructed access to it.

Place the following items in the box:

- toilet paper
- trash bags
- cleaning supplies, bucket, cleanser, rags, sponges, rubber gloves
- hand soap, bath soap, dish soap, hand towels, dish towels
- toothpaste, toothbrushes for everyone, wash cloths
- shower curtain, bath mat, shampoo
- bath towels, sheets, pillowcases, blankets
- paper towels, facial tissue, paper cups, paper plates, napkins, plastic utensils
- aluminum foil, plastic wrap
- coffee maker or teapot
- coffee, tea, creamer, sugar, powered drinks, instant hot cereal, canned soups, peanut butter, crackers, raisins
- pot or pan
- can opener, bottle opener
- screwdriver, hammer, scissors
- box of nails, screws, hooks
- extension cords
- flashlight
- radio
- first-aid kit, including aspirin, ibuprofen or acetaminophen
- clothes hangers
- notepad and pencil
- books, toys
- phone book from your previous home

Also include anything that you or any family member uses on a daily basis. Be certain, for instance, to take along medications you or any family member takes on a regular basis and a change of clothes for everyone in your family. If you have a baby, pack plenty of diapers and feeding supplies.

Leaving the Old Neighborhood

Although moving into your first new home can be a thrilling experience, leaving the old neighborhood and old friends can be difficult. This may be especially true for children who may have more issues leaving playmates and familiar surroundings.

Again, planning ahead can help. Begin talking about the move and your new neighborhood as soon as you have closed on a home. You can set the tone by being upbeat and enthusiastic about the new neighborhood. This does not have to diminish the concerns your family may have about leaving the old home; rather, you should strive to portray the new home and neighborhood as a positive move forward and an exciting adventure.

Even though you may feel rushed and pressured to get ready for the move, take the time to get adjusted or help your family get adjusted, especially the children. The following suggestions may ease the transition:

- Encourage family members to talk about fears or concerns they may have. If everyone is open, you often can transform a negative concern into a positive anticipation.

- Visit favorite places in the old neighborhood before the move.

- Let the children have a party with friends before leaving. You also can throw a farewell party for your friends.

- Make plans to invite friends from the old neighborhood to the new neighborhood once you are settled in to your new home.

- Exchange addresses, phone numbers and e-mail addresses.

- Go online to look up the new neighborhood and read about it, or contact the chamber of commerce in your new neighborhood for information. Read about the area's history, look up recreational facilities and review points of interest or tourist attractions. After all, you will be a tourist when you first arrive.

- Go for a tour or take the family on a tour of the new neighborhood or show them photos.

- Include the children in the unpacking phase and allow them to decorate their new rooms.

- If you have children, try to move at beginning of a new school year or even during the school year. It is difficult to make new friends during summer vacation.

You may encounter different kinds of problems with very young children, whose universe is enclosed within the family and the family home. Expect some regressive behavior—being clingy, whining, sleep disturbances, bed-wetting. It may be best to shelve toilet training and other routine changes temporarily until you are fully settled into the new home. Be reassuring and calm. Most children calm down when they see that their parents are still in control and at the center of everything.

Tip
Unpack and arrange your toddlers' bedrooms first—after the bathroom and kitchen, of course. Very young children relax when they see their rooms are basically the same and all their toys and belongings are safe and accounted for.

Settling into the New Neighborhood

As soon as the movers leave, you can begin to settle in and adjust to the new surroundings. Once you have taken care of the basics, such as unpacking enough to establish a functioning household, you may want to take a break to visit the neighborhood. Show your family the neighborhood attractions that drew you there in the first place.

First Stop

Your first stop in the new neighborhood probably will be the grocery store. Not only will you stock up on perishable foods, but you also will have an opportunity to gather all types of information about the neighborhood. Grocery shoppers often are friendly and willing to offer advice.

Schools

If you have not already done so, enroll your children in school. Ask the principal for a tour for you and your children. Try to talk to your children's teachers. Clarify how your children will get to school—walk or by bus. Be sure to point out the bus stops to your children or walk the route to school with them. Most children find it easier to adjust to a new school if they know what to expect, and getting lost, either on the way to school or at school, can be frightening.

School is also an ideal way for you to become involved in the neighborhood. While you are enrolling your children, ask about volunteer activities and parent groups. These are good places to meet new friends with similar interests.

Other Points of Interest

On a day when the entire family can go along, prepare an itinerary of local places of interest to visit. Start at city hall or the chamber of commerce to pick up brochures and flyers. Tour nearby playgrounds or parks. Visit the library and sign up for new library cards for everyone in the family. Be sure to pick up any brochures or calendars of events. Stop at museums and ask about classes or special programs for both children and adults. Check the phone book for a YMCA or swimming clubs.

On all of these outings, be alert for opportunities for you as well as for your children. Community involvement is the best way to have a stake in your neighborhood. Plus, you will meet new people, develop new friendships and foster new interests.

Neighbors

Some neighborhoods are particularly welcoming, but do not wait for neighbors to call. If the weather is warm, you can walk through the neighborhood, introducing yourself to neighbors who are working in their yards. If you have moved into a condo, speak to neighbors at the mailboxes or in the hallways. Take your children along so that they can meet the neighbors, particularly those with children of the same age.

Most people are quite willing to share information about the neighborhood and display their knowledge. Take advantage of any source of information. In return, share information about yourself and what you are planning to do with your new home. In no time, you will have the names of some people who may become friends or even surrogate family.

Home Attractions

Some people have helped their children find new friends by providing opportunities for neighborhood children to play at their home. For example, a sandbox or swing set can be enticing to small children. Older youngsters may be attracted to a basketball backboard or a frozen ice rink in the backyard. Remember, however, that these kinds of home attractions mean that you must provide some adult supervision. You also may want to reevaluate your liability insurance.

> **Note**
>
> Whatever you do to help your family adjust to their new surroundings, be ready to give it time. No one should be expected to move from a familiar home to an unfamiliar home and adjust immediately. As time goes by, you and your children will make friends and become involved in the school and the community. One day you will realize that you are no longer adjusting—you are a part of the neighborhood.

Summary

Moving into your own home for the first time is very exciting. However, moving and packing up all your things may become stressful if you haven't prepared yourself and planned ahead. To make this job less stressful, follow a moving checklist that organizes your tasks weeks in advance up until the day you move. This way come moving day you'll be ready to supervise the entire move, without worry or distraction.

Once you move into your new home and get settled into your neighborhood take time to walk around and visit the local points of interest to familiarize yourself with the community. Also, take time to meet your neighbors, as they will be a great source of information and can tell you about the neighborhood and local events that are happening in the area.

What You Have Learned

- How to find a reputable moving company and estimate your moving costs.
- Ways you can save money during the move.
- How to prepare before the move, and what to expect during and after the move.
- What you can do to prepare yourself for leaving your old neighborhood and how to settle into the new neighborhood.

> **Free Forms and Checklists**
>
> Visit **Socrates.com** and register to receive a variety of useful FREE forms, letters and checklists. See page iv for details on how to register (you will need the seven-digit registration code provided on the enclosed CD).

Appendix A
· · · · · ·
Resources

Over the past decade, the world of information has changed considerably, particularly for first-time home buyers. Today, the Internet has created a wealth of real estate property search options that puts you in control of information as never before.

Web resources are spread throughout this book, but here is a summary of some of the most useful home buying sites you can find on the Web.

Government Sites

U.S. Department of Housing and Urban Development
www.hud.gov

How to Buy a HUD Home
www.hud.gov/offices/hsg/sfh/reo/reobuyfaq.cfm

Home Ownership for All (HUD)
www.hud.gov/webcasts/archives/homeforall.cfm

FirstGov for Consumers
www.consumer.gov/yourhome.htm

U.S. Government's Official Web Portal
www.firstgov.gov

Federal Deposit Insurance Corporation
www.fdic.gov

Federal Trade Commission
www.ftc.gov

Federal Citizen Information Center
www.pueblo.gsa.gov

Office of Federal Housing Enterprise Oversight
www.ofheo.gov

GovLoans
www.govloans.gov

Useful Resources for Information about Shopping for Homes

Realtor.com—Official Site for the National Association of Realtors®
www.realtor.com

House For Sale Online
www.house-for-sale-online.com

Helpful Resources for Information about FSBO Transactions

Virtual FSBO
www.virtualfsbo.com

For Sale by Owner
www.forsalebyowner.com

FSBO Advertising Service
www.fsboadvertisingservice.com

Owners.com
www.owners.com

MSN Real Estate
http://realestate.msn.com

Newspaper Ads Online

News Voyager
www.newspaperlinks.com

Homescape
www.homescape.com

Useful Resources for Information about Personal Finance and Loans

American Consumer Credit Counseling
www.consumercredit.com

Bill Payment Score
www.prbc.com

Center for Debt Management
www.center4debtmanagement.com

Commerce Clearing House
www.toolkit.cch.com

E-Loan
www.eloan.com

Equifax
www.equifax.com

Experian
www.experian.com

Federal Trade Commission
www.ftc.gov/credit

FICO Scores
www.myfico.com

Free Annual Credit Report
www.annualcreditreport.com

Get Smart
www.getsmart.com

Home Loan Search
www.homeloansearch.securesites.com

HSH Associates, Financial Publishers
www.hsh.com

LoanWeb
www.loanweb.com

Useful Resources for Information about Mortgages

Mortgage Grader
www.mortgagegrader.com

Mortgage Minder
www.mortgageminder.com

National Mortgage Complaint Center
www.nationalmortgagecomplaintcenter.com

Mortgage Bankers Association
www.mbaa.org

Mortgage Insurance Companies of America
www.privatemi.com

Useful Resources for Information about Energy

Home Energy Magazine
www.homeenergy.org

BuildingGreen Suite
www.buildinggreen.com

Green Home Building
www.greenhomebuilding.com

Environmental Design and Construction
www.edcmag.com

Natural Home and Garden
www.naturalhomemagazine.com

Useful Resources for Information about Home Inspections

American Society of Home Inspectors
www.ashi.com

National Association of Home Inspectors
www.nahi.org

National Institute of Building Inspectors
www.nibi.org

National Academy of Building Inspection Engineers
www.nabie.org

National Society of Professional Engineers
www.nspe.org

American Home Inspector Directory
www.americanhomeinspectordirectory.com

World Inspection Network
www.wini.com/find.html

Home Inspection Supersite
www.inspectamerica.com

Useful Resources for Information about Manufactured Housing

MHVillage.com
www.mhvillage.com

My Great Home
www.mygreathome.com

ModulorCenter.com
www.modularcenter.com

Buying a Home
www.allamericahomes.com

Manufactured Housing Glorbal Network
www.mobilehome.com

Useful Resources for Information about Home Owner's Insurance

Insurance Information Institute
www.insurance.info

4Insurance
www.forinsurance.com

Insurance Finder®
www.insurancefinder.com

NetQuote®
www.netquote.com

State Insurance Departments
www.consumeraction.gov/insurance.shtml

National Association of Insurance Commissioners
www.naic.org

Useful Resources for Information about Warranties

2-10 Home Buyers Warranty®
www.2-10.com

HMS® Home Warranty
www.warrantyofchoice.com

Home Warranty of America
www.hwahomewarranty.com

Useful Resources for Information about Schools

School Matters
www.schoolmatters.com

GreatSchools.net
www.greatschools.net

The School Report
www.theschoolreport.com

School Match
www.schoolmatch.com

Additional Web Sites of Interest

American Bar Association
www.abanet.org/publiced/practical/buyinghome.html

Consumer Federation of America
www.consumerfed.org

Craig's List
www.craigslist.org

Department of Veterans Affairs
www.va.gov

Federal National Mortgage Association (Fannie Mae)
www.homebuyingguide.com

Freddie Mac
www.freddiemac.com/homebuyers

Insurance Information Institute
www.insurance.info

National Consumers League
www.nclnet.org

Standard & Poor's
www.standardandpoors.com

UDSA Rural Housing Service
www.usda.gov

Appendix B

· · · · · ·

Moving

A local move may cost a few hundred dollars, while a long-distance move may cost several thousand dollars. When figuring the cost of a move and hiring a mover, it is recommended that you obtain a minimum of three quotes from reputable moving companies. It is also a good idea to inquire about replacement insurance for lost and stolen items.

> **Tip**
>
> Planning a move with children is more challenging. Make your travel arrangements well in advance and aim to make the trip as stress free as possible. If flying, try to book a direct flight. If driving, estimate how far you will get each day and book accommodations in advance. Plan sightseeing stops along the way to break up travel time. Try to pack younger children's belongings last and unpack them first to minimize the disruption of a move for them.

Moving Checklist

Careful preplanning is essential to a successful move. Start by making a plan for packing—which rooms get packed first, next and last.

Use the following checklist to help you and your loved ones have the smoothest move possible:

_____ Set up appointments for important services such as telephone and cable television hookups and Internet access to be installed prior to arriving in your new home.

_____ Assign every family member a sorting, packing and moving day job–or two–to increase efficiency and ensure that everyone feels as though they are part of the process.

_____ If you have young children, plan ahead of time how you will keep them safe and occupied on moving day.

_____ Keep pets safe and out of the way on moving day when doors are open and moving trucks are in the driveway. If you are moving a long distance, think about how best to transport them to their new home.

_____ Keep all essential records in a secure folder that is not packed away but goes with you, especially anything needed for children's enrollment in their new schools, including birth certificates and medical, dental and school records.

_____ Identify irreplaceable family keepsakes that can easily be carried—baby books, photographs, art projects, etc. Take them with you in the car or on the plane.

_____ Pack a bag, box or suitcase with the necessities you will need to unpack immediately when you arrive in your new home—toilet paper, soap, shampoo, bath towels, paper towels, shower curtain, etc. Carry it with you in the car or on the plane. It will be easier than having to run out and buy these things upon arrival.

_____ Make sure every family member has an overnight bag of clothing, special favorites–toy, blanket, CD–things to read or do en route to the new home, favorite snacks, toothbrushes and toothpaste. These are considered essentials for getting to the new home, getting through the first night and tackling unpacking in the morning.

_____ Develop a contingency plan for sleeping in your new home the first night, especially if you arrive before your beds do. Plan on taking sleeping bags or air mattresses with you or make a hotel reservation that can be canceled if not needed.

_____ Locate nearby restaurants and supermarkets in your new community. Assign one member of the family to stock up on groceries or order takeout to keep everyone fed.

_____ Number each box and identify the contents of each. Group items packed in each box by room. This will help you identify which box contains an item you need immediately and you will know quickly if a box is missing. If a box does get lost, you will have a detailed list of all items included in it to provide to the insurance company.

_____ Do not pack chemicals or hazardous cleaning supplies in boxes to be transported on a moving truck. Heat, cold and damage to containers may cause leaking. Give away extra cleaning supplies or leave them for the new owners to use or safely dispose of.

Moving Timeline

1 Month before Moving

_____ Fill out change of address order form for post office.

_____ Fill out an IRS change of address form.

_____ Notify credit card and other financial service companies of your new address.

_____ Notify magazine subscription companies of your change of address.

_____ Make arrangements with a moving company or reserve a rental truck.

_____ Make travel arrangements with airlines, buses, car rental agencies and hotels, if necessary.

_____ Transfer memberships in churches, clubs and civic organizations.

_____ Obtain medical and dental records, X-rays and prescription histories. Ask your doctor and dentist for referrals and to transfer prescriptions.

_____ Set up new bank accounts.

_____ Check into the laws and requirements of your new location regarding home-based businesses, professional tests, business licenses and any special laws that might be applicable to you.

_____ Take inventory of your belongings before packing, in the event you need to file an insurance claim later. If possible, take pictures or videotape your belongings. Record serial numbers of electronic equipment.

_____ Make arrangements for transporting pets.

_____ Start using up food items, so that there is less left to pack and possibly spoil.

1 to 2 Weeks before Moving

_____ Switch utility services to new address. Inform electric, disposal, water, newspaper, telephone and cable companies of your move.

_____ Arrange for help on moving day.

_____ Confirm travel reservations.

_____ Reserve elevator if moving from an apartment.

_____ Have appliances serviced for moving.

_____ Clean rugs and clothing and have them wrapped for moving.

_____ Plan ahead for special needs of infants.

_____ Close bank accounts and have your funds transferred to your new bank. Before closing, be sure there are no outstanding checks or automatic payments that have not been processed.

_____ Collect valuables from safe-deposit boxes. Make copies of any important documents before mailing or hand carry them to your new address.

_____ Check with your insurance agent to ensure that you will be covered through your homeowners' or renters' policy during the move.

_____ Defrost the freezer and refrigerator. Place deodorizer inside each to control odors.

_____ Give a close friend or relative your travel route and schedule so you may be reached if needed.

On Moving Day

_____ Double-check closets, drawers, shelves, attic and garage to be sure they are empty.

_____ Carry important documents, currency and jewelry yourself or use registered mail.

_____ Carry traveler's checks for quick, available funds.

_____ When the moving truck arrives, you will be required to pay for the move before the workers start unloading the truck. Make sure you have a cashier's check for the exact amount made out to the moving company. Most movers do not like to handle that much cash and will not accept personal checks.

Arriving at New Home

_____ Renew your driver's license, auto registrations and tags within 30 days. Also, register bikes and pets with the municipality.

_____ Shop around for new insurance policies, especially auto coverage.

_____ Revise your will and other legal papers to avoid longer probate and higher legal fees.

_____ Locate the hospitals, police stations, veterinarian and fire stations near your home.

Miscellaneous Packing Tips

• Keep the following supplies handy for packing: boxes, marking pen, bubble wrap, newspaper and tissue, tape, scissors and tape measure.

• Use strong boxes and containers that can be tightly secured. Purchase special boxes for dishes, wardrobe and other special items.

• Pack audio and video equipment in the original boxes. Label cables and tighten transit screws. If you remove screws, tape them to the objects they are removed from.

• Avoid loading more than 50 pounds into one box.

• Label each box and indicate the following: (a) which room it should go in, (b) whether it is fragile and (c) if it should be loaded last so it will be unloaded first.

• Cushion contents with packing material. Save room by using towels and blankets to wrap fragile items.

• Pack books tightly on end in small boxes. If they are musty smelling, sprinkle talcum powder between the pages and wrap them before packing. Leave them stored for a couple of months to eliminate the smell.

• Have rugs and draperies cleaned before moving and leave them in wrappings for the move.

• Pack medicines in a leak-proof container.

• Carry all valuables with you.

- Check with your local U.S. Department of Agriculture branch for regulations regarding moving plants from one state to another. Many states have restrictions on bringing certain plants into the state to prevent importing insects or other pests that can destroy valuable cash crops.

Tips for Moving Pets

The following are tips for moving your pets to their new home:

- Cats and dogs can be taken in your car. If your pets travel with you, remember to take along food, water and a leash for letting your pet out of the car. Keep a number of plastic bags to clean up after your pet.

- Put a blanket or sheet over the seats to keep your car clean.

- Animals can get carsick and will require frequent stops along the way. Also, check ahead to see if the hotel where you are staying allows pets. Depending on the animal's age, temperament and size, it might be better to have it shipped by air. Be sure to check if your destination has any local requirements or restrictions on animals. Some vets may prescribe a light sedative to keep pets calm during the move.

- If you are shipping your pet by air, make sure to arrange for someone to meet your pet at the destination airport and take care of it until you arrive. A kennel can do this for you and keep your pet until you have completed your move.

If you are flying to your new destination, your cat or dog can ride in the baggage compartment. You may need the following items:

- Health certificate—obtain this from your veterinarian.

- Pet container—the airline might have a special container available, or you can use your own as long as it complies with airline regulations.

- Tranquilizers—your vet can provide tranquilizers to give to your pet immediately before going to the airport.

- Your scent—your pet can be comforted by having a piece of cloth with your scent on it.

Tips for Successfully Moving Houseplants

Two weeks before you move, prune your plants to facilitate packing. Consult a florist or a plant book for instructions.

One week before you move, place your plants in a black plastic bag along with a bug/pest strip, conventional flea collar or bug powder. Close the bag and place it in a cool area overnight to kill any pests on the plant or in the soil. You also may add dish soap to the soil and water. The liquid dish soap will not harm the plant but will kill any bugs burrowed in the soil.

One day before you move, place the plants in cardboard containers. Hold them in place with dampened newspaper or packing paper. Use paper to cushion the leaves and place a final layer of wet paper on top to keep them moist. If you must leave your plants behind, then take cuttings. Put them in a plastic bag with wet paper towels around them.

On the day of your move set the boxes aside and mark "DO NOT LOAD" so they will not be taken on the moving van. Close the boxes and punch air holes in the top before loading them into your car.

Park your car in a shaded area in the summer and a sunny spot in the winter. Upon arrival, unpack the plants as soon as possible. Remove plants through the bottom of the box to avoid breaking the stems. Do not expose the plants to much sunlight at first. Let them gradually become accustomed to more light.

Hiring a Moving Company

Consumer complaints against moving companies have been rising. The following are some tips that can help your move go smoothly:

- Get a binding estimate from the moving company. Make sure the amount is written in the contract.
- Inquire about their on-time record and check for complaints with the local Better Business Bureau or consumer complaints department.
- Movers are limited by law regarding what they can reimburse you for lost or damaged goods. To cover potential damage, check your existing homeowners' or renters' policy. Most movers offer separate insurance to cover lost or damaged items. Inquire about the costs, the length of coverage and deductibles.
- Ask about expected gratuities.
- Make sure the contract includes a guarantee of how many hours the job will take; allow an overrun of no more than 10 percent.
- Be sure that all charges are listed on the contract.
- Inform the moving company of how many stairs are at your new home.
- Watch loading and unloading and examine all items carefully before signing a receipt.
- Document an inventory of your belongings before you pack.

Home Checklist

What part of town, city or area do you want to live in?_____
_____

Do you need to be close to public transportation?

____ Yes   ____ No

What price range would you consider?

No less than _____ No more than_____

Do you want an older home?_____ Or a newer home? _____

What type of house are you looking for?

____ Single family detached

        ____ One-story   ____ Two-story

        ____ Bi-level   ____ Tri-level

____ Townhouse   ____ Condo   ____ Co-op

____ Manufactured ____ Farmhouse

What style of house appeals to you?

____ Contemporary   ____ Traditional

____ Colonial   ____ Southwestern

How much renovation would you be willing to do?

A lot_____ A little_____ None_____

Do you or any of your family members have any physical needs that must be met, such as wheelchair access?

____ Yes   ____ No

Are there other needs besides access?

_____
_____
_____

Do you have any animals that will require special facilities?

____ Yes   ____ No

Your Home's Community

Do you want to live in an area with a homeowners association?

___ Yes   ___ No

What else do you want in a community?	Must have	Would like
Schools	_____	_____
Parks	_____	_____
Library	_____	_____
Community pool	_____	_____
Ice rink	_____	_____
Basketball courts	_____	_____
Tennis courts	_____	_____
Local shops/shopping centers	_____	_____
Medical clinic or hospital	_____	_____
Gated community or doorman	_____	_____

Is there anything else that you want?

_____

_____

_____

_____

_____

_____

The following checklist can be used to rate the features of individual homes. You may want to make a copy for each house you visit. When you have narrowed down your choices, you can compare the checklists to help you decide which house you find the most suitable. If a feature is not available in a home, mark the entry N/A to help you remember that the house lacked that particular feature. You also may want to save the checklist for the house you finally select to compare against the disclosure form that the seller must provide at the time of the offer. See Chapters 11 and 12 for more information about the disclosure form.

Home Ratings Checklist

Date:_____

Age of home:_____

Price:_____

Address:_____

_____

Directions:_____

_____

_____

Name of owner(s):_____

_____

Name of real estate agent:_____

Telephone:_____

Fax:_____

e-Mail:_____

Square footage:_____Lot size:_____

Type of home: _____ Style of home: _____

Number of bedrooms:_____

Number of bathrooms:_____

Interior	Good condition	Average condition	Poor condition—unacceptable
Appearance			
Air conditioning			
Heating			
Security system			
Cable hookup			
Energy efficiency			
Storage space			
Interior walls			
Floor plan			
Basement			
Attic			
Carpeting			
Hardwood floors			
Ceramic tile baths			
Walk-in closets			
Kitchen			
Eat-in kitchen			
Pantry			
Dishwasher			
Refrigerator			
Mudroom			
Separate dining room			
Living room			
Family room			
Den/home office			
Great room			
Playroom			

Interior	Good condition	Average condition	Poor Conition—unacceptable
Laundry room			
Fireplace			
Natural light			
Thermopanes			
Cross ventilation			

Exterior	Good condition	Average condition	Poor condition—unacceptable
Appearance			
Yard			
Fence			
Patio/deck			
Front porch			
Pool			
Outbuildings			
Driveway			
Garage			
Garage attic			
Carport			
Street parking			
Flat lot—drainage			
Room to add on			
Exterior walls			
Foundation			
Windows			
Roof			
Gutters/downspouts			
A good view			

Neighborhood	Good	Average	Poor — unacceptable
Appearance			
Noise			
Traffic			
Safety			
Diversity			
Children in area			
Pet regulations			
Zoning regulations			
Parking space			
Parking regulations			
Fire protection			
Police protection			
Snow removal			
Garbage removal			
Homeowners association			
Shopping			
Grocery			
Medical services			
Parks/recreation			
Library			
Community pool			
Ice rink			
Basketball courts			
Tennis courts			
Restaurants			
Church/synagogue			
Airport			
Highways			

Neighborhood	Good	Average	Poor—unacceptable
Industrial areas			
Public transportation			
View			
Gated community			

Schools	Good	Average	Poor — unacceptable
Appearance/age			
Reputation			
Teacher credentials			
Test scores			
Class size			
Distance from house			
Busing/walking			
Percent graduating			

The fixtures inventory checklist can be used to check off the fixtures and other property that are included in the price of the house. You maybe able to buy those that are not included as part of the property, but there must be a clear understanding between you and the seller about these features. That is why you should ask the owner to sign this list or another appropriate document before you agree to buy the house.

Fixtures Inventory Checklist

Exterior

___ Security system	___ Outside lights
___ Garden equipment or furniture	___ Toolshed
___ Garden ornaments	___ Distinctive trees or plants
___ Garbage cans	___ Satellite dish or TV antenna
___ Porch furniture or swing	___ Patio furniture
___ Gas barbecue grill	___ Automatic garage door opener

Interior

___ Carpeting

Rooms:_____

_____

_____

___ Curtains, drapes, blinds

Rooms:_____

_____

_____

___ Light fixtures

Rooms:_____

_____

_____

___ Wall fixtures—shelves, mirrors, cabinets

Rooms:_____

_____

_____

___ Furniture

Description/location:_____

_____

_____

Kitchen

___ Stove ___ Microwave

___ Refrigerator ___ Dishwasher

___ Cabinets, pantry shelves ___ Washer/dryer units

___ Built-in appliances

Description:_____

_____

_____

Bathroom

__ Medicine cabinet ___ Mirrors

__ Built-in cupboards/shelves ___ Towel racks

__ Shower/tub fittings

Other

Description:_____

_____

_____

I certify that the items checked and noted on this list are included in the price of the property.

Signature:_____

Home seller:_____

The objectives of the structural checklist are to allow you to make a preliminary evaluation of the structure of a house in order to see if you:

- want to pursue buying the house; and
- need to arrange a professional inspection.

Structural Checklist

Is the foundation in good condition?

__ Yes __ No

Are the bridging and joints solid?

__ Yes __ No

Are the roof, gutters and drainpipes in good condition?

__ Yes __ No

Are the floors and walls in good condition?

__ Yes   __ No

Is drainage from the lot adequate?

__ Yes   __ No

Is drainage in the basement good?

__ Yes   __ No

Are there signs of water dampness or seepage on walls or floors?

__ Yes   __ No

Are there signs of water leaking from bathroom and toilet fixtures?

__ Yes   __ No

Is the flooring in good condition?

__ Yes   __ No

Are the windows easy to open and close?

__ Yes   __ No

Is the attic insulated and ventilated?

__ Yes   __ No

Are the chimneys open and clean?

__ Yes   __ No

Do all of the appliances—stove, refrigerator, dishwasher, disposal, washer/dryer—work?

__ Yes   __ No

Is the electrical wiring safe and adequate?

__ Yes   __ No

Are the fences, patio and driveway in good condition?

__ Yes   __ No

Free Forms and Checklists

Visit Socrates.com and register to receive a variety of useful FREE forms, letters and checklists. See page iv for details on how to register (you will need the seven-digit registration code provided on the enclosed CD).

Appendix C
Glossary

A

abatement A reduction or decrease in the value of a property that affects its market value or the amount of rent that may be charged to a tenant. Abatement usually occurs as the result of a discovery of something negative about the property (e.g., the roof must be replaced, the furnace will not make it through the winter, there is serious termite damage to the house) that decreases its worth and the price or rent it can command, or, in the case of a sale in progress, it affects the price already agreed on by the buyer and seller. The term can also refer to a decrease in the local government's valuation of a property, which in turn leads to lower taxes.

abut To share a common (property) boundary or even share a portion of that boundary.

accelerated depreciation Depreciation is a reduction in the value of a property resulting from the passage of time or changes in economic circumstances. Homeowners in recent years have come to think that property can only become more valuable (e.g., appreciate) but property does depreciate. For example, even though it may be well maintained, a property that is located in an area that becomes a hopeless slum or is beside the planned route for an expressway can depreciate. Depreciation may be used as a tax reduction. If a property loses its value quickly, this depreciation may be speeded-up and claimed in the first few years of ownership; the depreciation deduction then decreases later in the property's life. Any income tax expert can provide details. Another term for depreciation is writing down**.**

acceleration clause Most mortgages or loans include such a clause, which allows the lender to demand payment in full of the outstanding balance (e.g., to accelerate the loan) if the borrower fails to live up to the provisions of the agreement.

acceptance A positive (and voluntary) response to an offer or counteroffer for a property that sets out price and terms. This positive response creates a binding agreement between the buyer and seller. Acceptance may be conditional (e.g., based on certain events taking place). For example, in buying a new residence, the buyer may make his or her offer conditional on the sale of his or her current home within a certain number of months.

accepted offer *see* AO.

access The right to enter a property. This may be restricted to certain times and to certain categories of people (e.g., those who read gas or electric meters or deliver the mail).

access right The right of an owner to enter or leave a property; this right may be expressed or implied.

accessible/accessibility The ease (or not) by which one may reach a property.

accessory building A structure on a property (e.g., a garage, a garden shed) that serves a specific purpose for the home or main building.

accrued depreciation Depreciation in the value of a property that has not yet been claimed against taxes.

accrued interest Interest that has been earned but not yet claimed by the person to whom it is owed.

acquisition The act of taking title to a property.

acquisition cost The cost to the buyer of obtaining title to any property, outside of the actual purchase price. These costs can include escrow fees, title insurance, lender's fees and interest, legal fees, and land transfer fees.

act of God Damage to property caused by natural forces such as rain, lightning, floods, mudslides, snow, forest fires, or earthquakes.

actual authority The power a real estate agent, broker, or other representative may or may not have to bind a buyer or seller to an agreement.

actual cash value A term used in the insurance industry to describe the valuation of a building . It is determined by subtracting the decrease in value that is caused by such factors as age and wear-and-tear from the actual current cost of replacing the building.

addendum Something added to a document (e.g., lease, contract, purchase agreement) that then forms part of it. May be used to add some provision to the original document or to clarify some aspect of that original document.

additional principal payment Making an additional payment on a mortgage. With a monthly mortgage payment of $2,000, the interest portion may be $1,750 and the principal portion may be $250. If the lender offers this sort of provision (and most do), the borrower may opt occasionally to pay an additional amount to reduce the principal (e.g., the amount owed) by more than the fixed amount of $250. Sometimes borrowers who have acquired a sum of money through means such as the sale of another asset, a tax refund, or an inheritance choose to make a substantial one-time payment of this kind. The advantage is that the total interest over the life of the loan is reduced.

adjacent/adjoining land A term that may have a different meaning in different locales. In general, it refers to land that is located very near a particular piece of property, sometimes abutting it (e.g., sharing the same boundary).

adjustable-rate mortgage (ARM) Also called a variable-rate mortgage. This kind of loan has an interest rate that is determined by some outside index—such as the federal prime rate or the interest paid on government bonds. This kind of mortgage is most popular when this rate is lower, especially when it is much lower, than the interest on a fixed-rate mortgage would be. People who choose this kind of mortgage are hoping that the adjustable rate will remain below the fixed rate for a long time—or at least until their income improves. The savings in interest on an ARM, at least in the short term, can be substantial.

adjusted cost base A calculation that is used to determine capital gains (or losses), by taking the purchase price of a property and adding the costs of any improvements made to it. A homeowner who paid $300,000 for a house, then added a swimming pool for $25,000 and a new garage for $30,000, has an adjusted cost base of $355,000.

adjusted sales price A way of deciding what the price of a property should be according to the following method: taking the price of a comparable property that has recently been sold, adding the value of any recent improvements to the subject property not matched by the comparable property, and subtracting the value of any improvements or features in the comparable property not matched by the subject property.

adjustment date A date soon after the completion of a purchase of property when the mortgage comes into force and the buyer must make a payment of interest only. This is a device used to ensure that the mortgage payment subsequently will be due on the first of the month. For example, if a mortgage comes into effect June 15th, the adjustment date is July 1st (e.g., the interest owed for the last 15 days of June must be paid on June 15th). The first regular mortgage payment will be due on August 1st (interest is paid in arrears; the borrower pays the interest owed for July on August 1st). Often, interest that is due on the adjustment date is paid at closing**.**

adjustment interval/period With an adjustable-rate mortgage, this is the interval between potential changes in the interest rate. It may be as short as a week or as long as a year. With some ARMs, the rate can change at the end of each calendar year.

adjustments Anything that, at closing, changes the value of the property (e.g., taxes overpaid or underpaid by the seller, fuel for several months stored on the premises and provided to the buyer, rent collected from tenants for the following month). A statement of adjustments is presented by the closing officer to the buyer or seller.

aesthetic value The value that is added to the price of a property by its overall physical appearance and presentation. A beautifully landscaped house may be worth more to a potential buyer than the same house in the same neighborhood that is less pleasing in appearance.

affidavit of title The seller's statement that the title (e.g., proof of ownership) is valid, can be sold, and is subject to no defects except those set out in the agreement of sale.

affirmative fair housing marketing plan A plan that is sponsored by the U.S. Department of Housing and Urban Development (HUD) to foster the integration of different races in new housing projects. Such a plan must be presented by a developer before a project is eligible for certain U.S. government grants.

after-tax proceeds The net proceeds from the sale of a property; that is, the sale price less the legal fees and expenses, the realtor's commission, any taxes paid, etc.

agency agreement *see* nonexclusive listing.

agent Anyone (albeit usually a real estate agent) who is authorized by a buyer or seller of property to act on that person's behalf in any dealings with third parties. The third party may rely on the agreement and assurances of the agent as being binding on the person represented.

agreement of sale Also called purchase agreement, agreement of purchase and sale, land agreement, etc. A legal contract in which the buyer agrees to buy and the seller agrees to sell a specific property. The agreement of sale contains all the terms and conditions of the transaction and is signed by both parties. These documents are essentially the same but differ slightly from state to state.

agricultural property Land that is zoned for farming or other agricultural activities.

alienation The transfer of property from one owner to another.

alienation clause A provision in a mortgage that allows the lender to demand payment in full of the outstanding debt upon the sale of the property (e.g., not an assumable mortgage). Also called a due-on-sale clause.

allocation/abstraction method A method for estimating the value of the land component of any property by subtracting the value of the buildings or development from the market value of the property as a whole.

amenities Improvements to a property (other than necessities) that increase its desirability and enhance its value such as a swimming pool, central air conditioning, a patio or deck, or nearby attractions such as highways, good schools or public transportation.

American Society of Appraisers (ASA) A professional society composed of persons involved in the appraisal of both real estate and personal property.

American Society of Home Inspectors (ASHI) Specialists in the inspection of and determination of the physical condition of homes.

American Society of Real Estate Counselors (ASREC) Individuals who specialize in helping people to buy and sell homes.

amortization/amortization period The payment of a mortgage loan in equal (usually monthly) installments that include both principal and interest rather than interest only. If every payment is made on time, the loan will be repaid completely at the end of the agreed period (e.g., the amortization period).

amortization schedule A statement of the payments to be made on an amortized mortgage loan. This statement generally shows the date and amount of each payment, the portions of each payment that will be applied to interest and to principal, and the balance (of principal) still outstanding on the loan after the payment has been made.

annual debt service The amount that is required to service a loan in any given year; that is, the interest that must be paid to keep the loan current.

annual mortgagor statement A document that is sent each year, usually at the end of the year, by the lender to the borrower regarding a mortgage loan. It details amounts paid for principal, interest, and (if the mortgage company pays the borrower's property taxes) taxes paid; it also notes the amount still owed on the mortgage.

annual percentage rate (APR) The total cost of a loan (e.g., of borrowing the money to buy a property) in any given year expressed as a percentage of a loan amount (e.g., 6.5 percent). It includes compounded interest. The lender (e.g., the institution or person that holds the mortgage) is required by the Federal Truth-in-Lending Act to disclose the APR to the borrower.

AO An acronym (e.g., abbreviation) used by real estate agents to indicate that the buyer's offer to purchase has been accepted by the seller, or by the agent on behalf of the seller.

application A form filled out by an applicant for a mortgage that allows the lender to consider whether the applicant is a good candidate. It contains financial information on the potential borrower that allows the lender to assess the candidate's suitability (e.g., whether she or he seems financially stable or has an income adequate to pay off the mortgage).

application fees The fees that a lender charges an applicant to apply for a mortgage. These fees usually include the costs of a property appraisal and a credit report (from one of the three main U.S. credit agencies), and they often are not returned to the applicant even if the mortgage loan is not approved.

apportionment *see* adjustments.

appraisal An estimate of the value of a property on a certain date, usually provided by a qualified appraiser, after both an inspection of the property and a comparison of that property with other comparable properties that have recently been sold.

appraisal principles Factors that a qualified appraiser will consider in making an appraisal. These include the value (as determined by recent sale) of comparable properties, the appraised property's location, the level of competition in the current sales market, the current supply of comparable properties, and current market interest in such properties (e.g., supply and demand).

appraisal process In a particular market, appraisers try to use a standardized approach (e.g., to use the same appraisal principles) to ensure consistency and accuracy.

appraisal report A document, issued by an appraiser to the seller (or buyer), that documents the factors the appraiser has used to arrive at the appraisal amount. It also sets out the positive and negative aspects of a property, so that the client can understand the appraiser's "thinking." Finally, it sets out the appraiser's valuation.

appraiser A professional who is trained to assess the value of commercial or residential property.

appreciation The increase in value of a property over time. This increase can be the result of many factors, such as inflation, increased demand for property resulting from low interest rates, the condition of the market, or the gentrification of a particular area.

approaches to value Ways in which an appraiser determines the value of a property. The appraiser may consider the condition of the property, upgrades made to the property, the location of the property, the potential of the property to produce income, etc. See cost approach and income approach. Probably the most common approach used is the comparison approach, in which the value of a property is determined by investigating the price of comparable properties that have recently been sold.

approved attorney Any lawyer who is acceptable to title companies. This is usually any lawyer who can complete transactions having to do with title insurance (e.g., is capable of rendering opinions about the validity of title).

appurtenance A right, or entitlement, that is included within the ownership of a property and passes to the new owner when the title passes. An easement is one example: the new owner may be entitled to use a driveway to a garage on the previous owner's property even though that driveway is partially built on a neighbor's property.

APR *see* annual percentage rate

arbitration A way of settling property disputes without going to court. The parties to the dispute appoint a third party as judge and agree to be bound by her or his decision.

arrears Money that, under an amortization schedule, was not paid when it was due. The mortgagee is usually given the chance to make up the arrears. If he or she fails to do so, the mortgage holder can call in the loan (e.g., demand that it be paid in full).

as is/as-is agreement The situation in which a property is accepted by the buyer (or tenant) in the condition existing at the time of the sale or lease; the seller (or lessor) is released from any liability after closing. Most agreements of sale contain such a provision.

ASA *see* American Society of Appraisers.

ASHI *see* American Society of Home Inspectors.

asking price The amount at which a property is offered, by a seller, for sale. This price may change as a result of negotiations between the buyer and seller. In a tight market, a good property in a desirable location may bring more than the initial asking price as a result of bidding by numerous potential buyers.

ARM *see* adjusted rate mortgage.

ASREC *see* American Society of Real Estate Counselors.

assessed value The value placed on a property by a tax assessor for the purpose of determining property taxes.

assessment Estimating the value of land or other property for tax purposes. It can also refer to the means by which a municipality raises taxes, or to the fees that a condominium association charges owners for basic (and common) services such as upkeep and maintenance or utility fees such as gas or oil for heating. See special assessment.

assessment base The total of assessed values of all properties in a particular municipality.

assessment roll The public record of the assessed values of properties. It includes an assessment roll number for each property, which is the number by which the property can be identified in municipal records.

assessor Also called the tax assessor. The person who is employed by a municipality to estimate the value of properties to provide a basis for the municipality to levy real estate taxes.

assign To transfer interest in a property. An elderly person might decide to transfer ownership in a piece of land to children who might be more likely to develop it.

assignee The person to whom an interest in property is transferred.

assignment The transfer of interest from one person (or entity) to another. The term also refers to the transfer of a mortgage from one lender to another, and to the document that effects such a transfer.

assignor The person responsible for an assignment.

associate broker An otherwise qualified real estate agent or broker who is working for or with another broker.

assumable mortgage A mortgage that can be taken over (e.g., assumed) by the buyer from the seller when a property is sold. If interest rates are high, a low-rate assumable mortgage can be a great selling point for a property. However, this is not necessarily a common provision in mortgages. Buyers and sellers should always determine whether the mortgage contract contains such a clause.

assumption fee The amount the lender charges the person who is taking over an assumable mortgage. There is almost always such a fee, and buyers should always inquire as to its amount.

assumption of mortgage The formal agreement whereby one takes on the responsibilities of an assumable mortgage.

attached housing Two or more houses, occupied by different people, that have a common wall (e.g., townhouses).

attachment The binding, or seizing, by a court of a property as security for, or to settle, a debt.

attestation/attestation clause A statement by a witness to the finalization (e.g., closing) of a deed or mortgage that the document was properly execute, and that the persons signing the document were aware of what they were doing (e.g., they understood the contents and responsibilities of the document). Such witnessing is required by various states.

attorney's opinion of title A statement of a lawyer's conclusions about the legal condition of title to (e.g., ownership of) a property that is issued after the lawyer's investigation of that title.

authority The right of an agent, conferred by the person the agent represents, to deal with third parties. In property transactions, for example, the buyer customarily gives a real estate agent the right to deal with the seller on the buyer's behalf.

authorization to sell The contract between a seller and a real estate agent that allows the agent to sell a property. It also sets out the rights and obligations of the seller and agent. Some such agreements involve a time limit, after which both sides are allowed to terminate the agreement.

B
....

back-end ratio An analysis, by a lender, of a potential borrower's ability to carry a mortgage or other loan, conducted by comparing the applicant's current expenses in relation to his or her gross monthly income. If the applicant wants to spend too great a percentage of his or her income on the mortgage (40 percent or more), the lender will conclude that borrower will probably fail to do so, and will almost certainly refuse to offer a mortgage loan.

back-title letter/certificate In states in which lawyers are required to examine title for title insurance purposes, this document is given to the attorney by the title insurance company to certify the condition of a title as of a certain date.

back-up contract A secondary offer (from a potential buyer) for a property on which an offer from another buyer has already been made. This contract will come into effect if the first offer is not accepted or, is withdrawn.

balance The amount of principal that is still outstanding on a mortgage or other loan at any given time.

balloon mortgage A mortgage loan that is repaid in fixed, periodic (probably monthly) payments until a given date. On that date, either the balance of the loan becomes due in one large payment or the amount of the payments rises significantly.

balloon payment The final payment that pays off a balloon mortgage.

below-market interest rate (BMIR) A subsidized interest rate on a mortgage or loan. This kind of subsidy is often provided by the government to allow for the acquisition of property by people who earn less than average salaries.

bequeath To leave land, a dwelling, or other personal property to someone in a will. See devise.

bequest That which is bequeathed. See bequeath.

betterment Any improvement of real estate that leads to an increase in its value. Landscaping, renovation, and improvements in outbuildings (e.g., a garage) are all forms of betterment.

bill of sale A document that certifies that, in return for a certain price, ownership of property has passed from the seller to the purchaser.

binder In real estate, this term has two meanings. It is a report issued by a title company that sets forth the condition of a title as of a certain date, as well as the conditions under which a policy of title insurance will be issued. It is also a preliminary agreement to purchase a property, accompanied by a deposit that is lost if the purchaser does not complete the purchase.

bi-weekly mortgage A mortgage in which one half of the monthly payment is made every two weeks. With this kind of mortgage, 26 payments will be made in a year; the extra monthly payment that is made each year reduces the duration of the mortgage and the total amount of interest the borrower will ultimately pay. Many people find such plans to be a fairly painless way to reduce the principal on a mortgage more quickly.

bond The term has several different meanings in real estate. It can be an interest-bearing instrument. It also can be a sum of money that is paid to a court as an assurance of the performance of some obligation, or as security for payment of a claim (this may be used, at the discretion of the court, to allow for the removal of a claim for lien from a property). Finally, it can be an insurance agreement insuring against loss by acts or default of a third party, such as a performance bond that a contractor will finish the construction of a house.

borrower (mortgagor) A person who receives money from a lender to buy property, in exchange for a written promise to repay that money with interest. The borrower also accepts the lender's lien on that property until the debt is paid in full.

breach of contract In law, the failure to live up to the terms of any contract.

bridge loan/financing A form of interim loan that is most commonly used when a buyer has bought a new house or condominium unit but has yet to sell his or her current residence. Thus, he or she may lack the funds necessary to make the down payment on the new residence or to pay two mortgages simultaneously. The bridge loan usually covers the down payment on the new premises and the monthly mortgage payment for a stated number of months. The bridge loan customarily ends when the buyer has sold the old premises and has the funds to pay off the lender.

broker Refers to two kinds of agents: a mortgage broker, who brings potential borrowers together with potential lenders; and a real estate broker, who brings buyers together with sellers. Real estate broker is a professional designation; it requires training and licensing.

brokerage The act by brokers of bringing together principals (e.g., buyer and seller, landlord and tenant) in return for a fee, often a percentage of a transaction's value (5 percent to 10 percent).

budget mortgage An all-in mortgage under which the borrower is required to make payments that cover not only principal and interest but also insurance and real estate tax payments.

builder warranty A guarantee, which is enforceable, of the quality of construction that is given by either a builder or a developer.

building code Regulations that are established and enforced by a municipality to guarantee standards and quality of construction.

building contract A contract that sets forth the terms (and price) of planned construction.

building line/setback The minimum distance from a property line or boundary that a building may be constructed; this is established by agreement or by municipal ordinances.

building permit A permit that is issued by a local government to allow a builder to construct a building or to make improvements to existing structures.

building restrictions Rules in the building code (e.g., zoning restrictions) that control the size, placement, design and materials of new construction.

buy-back agreement A contract between a buyer and a seller in which the seller agrees to buy the property back from the buyer if a certain event occurs within a set period. The price of such a buy-back is usually set out in the contract.

buy down The payment of extra money on a loan, such as the payment of additional principal when making a monthly mortgage payment, to reduce the interest rate and/or the life of the loan.

buyer's broker/agent A real estate agent who represents the potential buyer. Agents commonly represent the seller, but potential buyers increasingly are engaging real estate agents to watch out for their interests also.

buyer's market A market in which there is more property for sale than there are buyers available to purchase it. This situation usually causes the value of available property to decrease. It most commonly occurs in over-built markets or when a poor economy results in few buyers being present in the marketplace.

buy-sell offer An offer by one owner to buy out the interests of another owner or partner.

by-laws Rules and regulations enacted by a governing body. The term commonly refers to the rules of a condominium management board, which usually are agreed to by a poll of the condominium-unit owners.

C
....

cancellation clause A clause in a contract, such as a mortgage, that sets forth the conditions under which each party may cancel or terminate the agreement.

cap A limit. A cap is important in adjustable-rate mortgages, where it represents the limit on how high payments may go or how much the interest rate may change within a given period or over the life of the mortgage.

capital asset Any property to which the tax rules of capital gains and capital assets applies.

capital expenditure/improvement Money that is spent to improve a property and thus enhance its value, excluding repairs. Such expenditures may include building a new garage and adding a room to a house.

capital gain An increase in the value of capital property (e.g., property other than a principal residence) on which tax is payable, usually upon sale of the property.

capital loss A decrease in the value of capital property (e.g., property other than a principal residence), which the owner may use against capital gains or against regular income when paying his or her taxes, depending on the tax rules.

carrying charges/costs A general term for those expenses (other than the basic, original purchase price) that are required to maintain a property over a given period, including such items as property taxes, upkeep, insurance, and interest charges on a mortgage.

cash equivalent The amount a seller would have realized on the sale of a property had she or he not accepted the proceeds of the buyer's financing but had received cash instead.

cash reserve The amount of money a buyer of a property still has on hand after she or he has made a down payment and paid out the fees of closing. Some lenders ascertain that such a reserve exists (commonly, the equivalent of two mortgage payments) before granting a mortgage.

cash sale The sale of a property for cash; no mortgage or other financing is involved.

caveat emptor (Latin: let the buyer beware). A legal maxim suggesting that the buyer of any property takes a risk regarding the condition of the property and, that it is the responsibility of the buyer to determine the condition before the purchase is completed. Many states now have laws that place more responsibility for disclosure on the seller and the real estate broker. Potential buyers should always check on their rights with their real estate broker.

CC&Rs *see* covenants, conditions and restrictions.

ceiling The limit to which an interest rate may rise, over the life of the loan, on an adjustable-rate mortgage.

certificate of eligibility A document issued by the U.S. Department of Veteran's Affairs (VA) that allows qualified veterans to apply for either subsidized or guaranteed housing loans.

certificate of insurance Issued by an insurance company, this document sets out the particulars of the coverage that is being provided for a specific property.

certificate of occupancy A document issued by a local municipality certifying that a particular dwelling is in proper condition for human occupation (e.g., that it complies with local building and safety by-laws).

certificate of reasonable value (CRV) A document issued by the U.S. Department of Veteran's Affairs (VA) that sets out the market value, based on an appraisal, of a certain property. It purpose is to establish the maximum principal that will be available on a VA mortgage on that property.

certificate of sale A certificate issued at a court sale that entitles the buyer to a deed to a particular property.

certificate of satisfaction A document provided by a lender and subsequently registered on a title certifying that a mortgage has been paid out and that the property has been released to the buyer (e.g., it has no claims against it).

certificate of title A written opinion by a lawyer as to the validity of a person's claim to ownership of a particular property; such opinions may also be issued through a title.

certificate of veteran status A document issued by the U.S. Department of Veteran's Affairs (VA) confirming that the person named in the document has served in the U.S. military forces for at least 90 days of active duty (including training) and is therefore eligible for VA benefits, including a VA mortgage.

certified copy A declaration, usually by the holder of the original document or by a lawyer, that the copy is a true (e.g., exact) copy of the original.

certified general appraiser Someone who is licensed, after training, to appraise the value of property (qualification requirements can vary, depending on the particular jurisdiction).

certified home inspector (CHI) Someone who is licensed, after training, to inspect and report on the physical condition of property (qualification requirements may vary, depending on the particular jurisdiction).

certified residential appraiser (CRA) Someone who has met the licensing requirements to appraise the value of only and specifically residential property. See certified general appraiser.

certified residential broker (CRB) Someone who has met the requirements of the Realtors National Marketing Institute to be an agent or broker for residential properties. The Realtors National Marketing Institute is affiliated with the National Association of Realtors.

chattel A word that is not used much in common speech but is often used in real estate documents to describe personal property that is part of the property but is not fixed to the land or to a building. This is different from a fixture, which is part of the land or building. A homeowner's dining room table and chairs are a form of chattel; the chandelier above the table, which is secured to the ceiling, is a fixture. Fixtures are commonly included in the sale of a property, whereas chattels usually are not unless they are itemized in the agreement of sale.

CHI *see* certified home inspector.

claim Any legal right that one asserts against another person or institution: in real estate, often a formal request for some right that the claimant feels he or she is due, such as a right of way; in insurance, the request by a person insured by an insurance company, to that company, to be paid on some aspect of his or her insurance policy.

closed mortgage Any loan that cannot be prepaid or renegotiated before the end of its term without the borrower's having to pay a penalty.

closed-end mortgage A mortgage with a set amount of principal; this amount cannot be increased and the loan cannot be extended.

closing The final procedure in any real estate transaction in which the parties to the transaction (or their representatives) meet to execute documents, exchange funds, and complete the sale (and, if a mortgage is involved, the loan). A closing typically takes place at the offices of a title company.

closing costs Expenses, usually those of the buyer, that are over and above the cost (e.g., the sale price) of the property itself, such as legal fees, mortgage application fees, taxes, appraisal fees, title registration fees, etc.

closing date The date set out in the agreement of sale on which the final real estate transaction (e.g., the closing) is to take place. On that date, the appropriate documents will be completed, the purchase price paid, and the transfer of title (e.g., ownership) recorded. Also known as completion date.

closing statement A document that lists the financial settlement between the buyer and seller of real estate, including the costs that each must pay at closing. This statement usually is circulated to the buyer and seller before the closing date. Also known as a HUD-I settlement statement.

code Laws or regulations that are drawn up (often by the government) to cover a particular aspect of life in a municipality or state (e.g., a building code, a traffic code).

code of ethics A set of rules governing the activity of members of the organization or profession that establishes them. Lawyers and real estate agents and brokers have their own codes of ethics.

collateral/collateral security A term used most commonly to mean some guarantee for a loan other than the personal guarantee of the borrower. Also refers to the property (real or personal) that is pledged against a loan or a mortgage. If the debt is not paid, the lender has the right to sell the collateral to recoup the outstanding principal and interest.

collateral assignment The assignment of property as collateral security. The intention is not to transfer ownership but to guarantee a loan or mortgage.

co-maker A person who signs a loan document along with the principal borrower. The co-maker promises to be responsible for the loan should the borrower fail to pay it. If a lender believes there is a chance the borrower might default because she or he is a young person, someone in a first job, or someone buying a first house or condominium unit, the lender may require a co-maker on the loan. Also referred to as co-signer or guarantor.

commission The amount paid to a real estate agent or broker as compensation for services rendered in the purchase, sale, or rental of property. The amount is usually a percentage of the sales price or the total rental.

commission split The dividing-up of a commission when two or more real estate agents have been involved in the sale (or purchase) of property.

commitment/commitment letter A written promise, by a lender or insurance company, to make a loan or insure a loan for a specified amount and on specified terms.

commitment fee The fee that may be charged by a potential lender in return for the lender's promise to provide a mortgage to a potential borrower when that person finds property he or she wishes to buy.

common-area assessments A periodic charge (usually monthly) that is levied against owners in a condominium complex. These fees are used by the condominium owners' association to pay for the maintenance of common areas in the building. Some assessments also include fees for utilities such as central heating or air conditioning. Also known as common-element fees or assessments.

common areas/common elements Those portions of a condominium or co-operative that are intended for the use of all tenants, such as the lobby, a work-out room, a swimming pool, or a sun terrace. With rental properties, such as an apartment building, the term is often used to mean the same thing.

community association Any organization created by property owners in a particular area to represent them collectively in dealing with the government, planning bodies, developers, etc.

community home-buyer's program A scheme to find ways to finance home purchases for people with low incomes.

comparison approach *see* approaches to value.

completion date *see* closing date.

concessions Any sacrifice (in price or terms) that is made by one person to persuade another to enter into a real estate contract. An example might be the seller of a house or condominium unit offering to include some of his or her furniture in the already announced sale price as an inducement to a potential buyer.

condition(s) Requirements in a real estate agreement to purchase that must be fulfilled before the agreement becomes firm and binding. If the conditions are not fulfilled, the agreement will usually be regarded as cancelled and any deposit will be returned to the buyer.

conditional acceptance *see* qualified acceptance.

conditional offer/conditional sales contract An offer to purchase or sell a property that comes into effect only if certain conditions are fulfilled.

condominium A structure comprised of two or more units in which the units are individually owned but the remainder of the property (e.g., the land, buildings, and amenities) is owned in common. The maintenance of these common areas is supervised by the condominium corporation, in which each unit owner owns a share and has voting rights.

condominium board of directors An organization comprised of some of the unit owners in a condominium building or development, who are elected to their posts at specified intervals by all the unit owners. The purpose of the condominium board is to govern relations between all the owners, to administer the rules and regulations (e.g., the by-laws) of the condominium, and generally to manage the condominium's operations. The last function particularly comes into force when there is no on-site, full-time manager.

co-signer *see* co-maker

constant-payment loan A mortgage that requires equal and periodic payments over a certain period (e.g., 15 years, 30 years), at the end of which the amount owed under the loan (both principal and interest) will be completely paid.

consumer reporting agency or bureau The source to which lenders turn for the credit history of any applicant for a loan. Also called a credit bureau.

contiguous Sharing a common boundary.

contingency A condition that must be fulfilled before a contract can become firm and binding. For example, the sale of a house may depend on whether the potential buyer can obtain financing.

contingency fees Fees that are paid only if a particular event takes place in the future For example, a real estate agent's fees are usually payable only if that agent succeeds in selling or leasing a property.

contract An agreement between two or more persons (or entities) that creates (or modifies) a legal relationship. In real estate, a contract is usually an offer for property and an acceptance of that offer (e.g., an agreement of sale).

contract of sale The written agreement between the seller and buyer for the sale of a property. It includes all the terms and financial details of the transaction. Also known as contract or agreement of purchase and sale, offer to purchase, and contract of purchase.

conventional loan There are two meanings: 1) a loan or mortgage with a fixed interest rate, fixed payments, and a fixed term (e.g., life); and 2) a mortgage or deed or trust not insured by the government.

conversion/convertibility clause The provision in an adjustable-rate mortgage that allows the borrower to change the mortgage to a fixed-rate mortgage upon the occurrence of certain stated events.

convey To transfer title to a property to someone else.

conveyance The act of transferring title to (or other interest in) a property to someone else. Also, the document that effects that transfer; such documents include most instruments by which an interest in real estate is created, mortgaged or assigned.

co-op Abbreviated term for co-operative, a form of ownership in which the occupiers of individual units in a building have shares in the co-operative corporation that owns the entire property. Co-ops are still popular in large American cities, such as New York and Chicago, but condominiums are the more usual form of apartment ownership in most American cities and suburbs.

cooperating broker A broker who is not the main (listing) broker in any real estate transaction but has assisted in the transaction and is therefore entitled to share in the commission. Often, the cooperating broker is the one who has found the buyer.

co-operative *see* co-op.

cost approach An appraisal method in which a property's value is estimated by adding the cost of the property and the cost of improvements and subtracting depreciation.

co-tenancy A situation in which more than one person owns a piece of property. Title is held by the owners in one of two ways: 1) as joint tenants, where each tenant owns the land equally and, in the event of the death of one of the tenants, his or her surviving co-tenant(s) will continue to own title equally by right of survivorship; or 2) as tenants in common, where each owner owns a specific portion of the property and may sell, mortgage or bequeath that interest to a third party without the consent of the other owners.

counteroffer A response to an offer. If a prospective buyer makes an offer to purchase a property (e.g., offers a price for that property), the seller may do one of three things: 1) accept the offer; 2) reject the offer outright; or 3) suggest an alternative. For example, the listed or advertised price of a condominium is $350,000 and the prospective buyer offers $325,000. The seller makes a counteroffer of $340,000. By suggesting this alternative, the seller is legally regarded as having rejected the buyer's original offer. The buyer in turn may also counteroffer (e.g., suggest a price of $330,000).

covenants, conditions and restrictions Abbreviated term for covenants, conditions and restrictions, which are the obligations of any real estate contract.

CRA *see* certified residential appraiser.

CRB *see* certified residential broker.

creative financing Any means of financing the purchase of a property that is unusual, (e.g., different from the normal ways of financing such a purchase).

credit bureau *see* consumer reporting agency.

credit history/credit report A statement of debts and obligations, both current and past, and of the record of payment of such debts. The lender obtains a credit history for an applicant to assess the risk in making a loan to that applicant. The lender is interested in determining whether a potential applicant is likely (and willing) to make the payments on a mortgage, and believes that her or his past behavior as a borrower will be a good indication of future behavior.

credit limit The maximum amount that an individual can borrow to buy property. This amount is set by the lender after an examination of the individual's credit history/credit report.

credit rating/credit risk An evaluation of a person's ability to manage current and future debt.

CRV *see* certificate of reasonable value.

cumulative interest The total amount of interest that will be charged on a loan or mortgage to a certain date. In offering a mortgage, lenders usually set out both the principal (e.g., the amount borrowed) and the cumulative interest for the life of the loan.

D

debt-equity ratio A comparison of what is owed on a property with its equity (e.g., the current market value of the property less the amount owed on the mortgage or loan).

debt financing The purchase of a property using any kind of credit rather than paying cash.

debt ratio A simple means of assessing whether a potential buyer of property can pay a mortgage: the total monthly payments of all the buyer's debts, including the proposed mortgage, are compared with the buyer's gross monthly income. If very little income is left over for such things as food, transportation or entertainment, the potential lender may conclude that the potential buyer is a bad risk.

debt service Another term for a mortgage payment over a given period.

debtor's position The value over and above the amount owed (e.g., the principal and accumulated interest on the mortgage) on a property at any given time. With each monthly mortgage payment, the debtor's position improves. Also known as equity.

decree of foreclosure A court decree made when a borrower is seriously in default on a mortgage and the lender decides that the borrower will not (or cannot) pay. The decree declares the amount outstanding on the delinquent mortgage and orders the sale of the property to pay off the mortgage. The lender is then repaid to the extent possible (sales that result from foreclosure do not necessarily achieve full market value of the property).

deed The legal instrument by which title to (e.g., ownership of) property is conveyed from one owner to another when a sale occurs.

deed books The record of deeds registered in the appropriate registry office in a particular jurisdiction. Also known as libers.

deed of reconveyance A legal instrument that conveys title from a trustee back to a buyer once that buyer has completely paid off the mortgage.

deed of trust Used in many states in place of a mortgage. Property is transferred by the buyer or borrower to a trustee. The beneficiary is the lender, and the property is re-conveyed to the buyer when the loan obligation is paid.

deed restrictions A clause (or clauses) in a deed that limits the use of the property in some way.

default The failure to make mortgage payments in full or on time, or to live up to any other obligations of the mortgage agreement.

default judgment A decision of the court that a default has taken place.

deferred interest Interest that is not paid as it is incurred but instead is added to the loan's principal.

deferred-interest mortgage A way of reducing the amount of the payments on a loan by postponing payment of the interest (or a portion of the interest) until some future date or until the eventual sale of the property. This kind of mortgage appeals to buyers who believe that their income will be higher in the future or that the property will appreciate greatly before it is resold.

deficiency judgment A court order used in foreclosure stipulating that the lender may sell the property to recover what is owed. If the proceeds are less than what the lender is owed, the court may order the borrower to make up the difference.

delinquency Being late in making a mortgage payment but not yet in default.

delivery Turning over any legal document, particularly a deed, to another party, and in doing so making it legally nonrevocable.

demand loan A kind of loan that stipulates no fixed date for repayment but is due in full (e.g., principal with accumulated interest) if the lender asks for payment.

Department of Housing and Urban Development (HUD) The federal agency that concentrates on housing programs and on the renewal of urban and suburban communities.

department of real estate That department of the state government that is responsible for the licensing and regulation of persons engaged in the real estate business. The individual who heads the department is normally called the real estate commissioner. Other names for this department, depending on the state, are the division of real estate and the real estate commission. There is such a department in each of the 50 states.

Department of Veterans' Affairs (VA) The federal government agency that administers benefits for American military veterans, including property loans and mortgage programs.

deposit Money that is paid up front by a buyer to guarantee that she or he will actually complete a transaction to buy a particular property—in effect, it is a guarantee to the seller that the seller may remove the property from the market (e.g., that the sale is "firm"). If the buyer later fails to complete the transaction, she or he generally loses the deposit. Also called earnest money.

deposit of title deeds Some lenders require that ownership documents be left with the lender as an additional security for a loan or mortgage.

depreciation The decrease in value of a property over time, which can also lead to a reduction in the owner's taxes (e.g., a capital loss).

description *see* legal description.

designated real estate broker An individual who has a real estate broker's license and who is appointed by a corporation or institution to oversee all of its real estate activities.

designated real estate instructor Anyone who has met the requirements of the Real Estate Educators' Association and may therefore teach courses in real estate practice.

detached single-family home A freestanding house; that is, a house that does not share walls with another house, and is designed to house just one family. Most houses in the United States are of this type.

development A planned construction project, such as a shopping mall or a new housing project, on what was formerly unused land or land used for other purposes, such as farming.

direction regarding funds A statement by the seller informing the buyer how the seller wishes to be paid at closing.

direction regarding title A statement made by the buyer to the seller informing the seller how the buyer wishes to take title; it also includes the buyer's particulars. Also called title direction.

discharge A document that is registered to remove a mortgage lien from the title to a property.

disclosed principal The announcement of the name of a potential buyer by a real estate agent or broker to a seller.

disclosure In some U.S. jurisdictions, the seller of a property must provide a written statement to the buyer listing those defects in the property of which the seller is aware. For example, the seller may know that the roof of the property needs to be replaced, but may be unaware that there is severe termite damage to the property. Also called vendor's disclosure.

disclosure statement A legal requirement in some jurisdictions that the lender issue a document to a potential borrower outlining the terms and conditions of the loan or mortgage.

disinterested appraisal An estimate of the value of real property by someone, such as a professional appraiser, who has no personal interest in the property.

dispossess To remove a person from a property as a result of legal action.

documentary stamp/documentary tax stamp A levy charged by the local government for the registration of a deed or mortgage; the stamp shows the amount of transfer tax paid.

documentary transfer tax State tax on the sale of real estate, often calculated as a percentage of the sale price.

dominant estate A property that enjoys an easement over another property, which is known as the servient estate.

down payment The amount of money that is provided by the buyer toward the total price of the property (not including fees, taxes or other costs). In general, the down payment plus the principal of the mortgage equals the purchase price. The down payment is customarily cash paid by the buyer from his or her own funds—as opposed to that part of the purchase price that is financed by a lender. A down payment amount that is common in the United States is 20 percent of the total purchase price. However, if the borrower agrees to insure this part of the mortgage, some lenders will accept a 10-percent down payment.

DREI *see* designated real estate instructor.

dual agency In general, dual agency is a breach of real estate brokerage rules. If a single real estate agent is representing both the buyer and the seller in a particular transaction, the agent must disclose this fact to both sides. Otherwise, the agent is involved in a conflict of interest that is not allowed by most real estate brokerages.

due date The date in a loan agreement on which the loan is payable in full.

due-on-sale clause *see* alienation clause.

E

earnest money *see* deposit.

easement The right of the owner of one property to use part of the land of another for a specific purpose. The property that enjoys the right in this arrangement is said to be in the dominant position; the other is said to be in the servient position.

easement appurtenant An easement for the benefit of another parcel of land, such as the right to cross parcel A to get to parcel B (this kind of easement usually passes with the transfer of property to a new owner).

easement in gross An easement for the benefit of a person or company rather than another parcel of land. These easements commonly are for the equipment of public utilities.

easement by necessity A landowner's right to make use of the property of another person (or a portion of it) when such use is necessary to allow the landowner to enjoy his or her own land (e.g., an easement that allows a property owner to gain access to landlocked property).

easement by prescription The continuing use of all or part of a property by the owner of a neighboring or nearby property for a specific period.

economic depreciation A reduction in the value of a property that is caused by reasons aside from the condition of the property itself. For example, a shopping mall that is built across from a row of houses may result in traffic and noise that make the street a less desirable residential area, and the houses may decline in value.

effective age The age of a structure as estimated by its condition rather than by its actual chronological age. This estimate may take into account both renovation and maintenance.

egress The right to come and go across the land, public or private, of another, most often to a road.

employment letter A letter from an employer stating the length of time a person has been employed and how much she or he earns. Lenders often ask for such letters when considering whether to grant a mortgage to a potential borrower.

encumbrance Any right, lien or charge attached to and binding on a property. An encumbrance can affect the owner's ability or right to sell that property until such time as it is removed.

energy-efficient Containing features that reduce the use of electricity or heating fuel, such as effective insulation, double-glazed windows, skylights, or a state-of-the-art furnace. The fact that a property is energy efficient can be a selling point in its favor.

energy tax credits A tax write-off that is available to property owners who take steps to reduce energy consumption.

Equal Credit Opportunity Act A U.S. law guaranteeing that people of all races, ages, genders and religions must have an equal chance to borrow money.

equity The market value of a property, less the debts of that property. Likely debts include the principal and accumulated interest on the mortgage, unpaid taxes, and a home equity loan.

equity buildup The increase over time of an owner's interest in a property (e.g., the difference between the market value of the property and the amount owed on the mortgage and any other outstanding liens). With most mortgages, the mortgage holder may accelerate the process of building equity by making an extra payment on the principal each month. In addition, property in desirable areas of major American cities has risen in value significantly in recent years, further increasing owners' equity.

equity loan A loan to a home or condominium owner that is secured by the lender against the equity the owner has built up in the property. Equity loans have become increasingly popular in recent years as a way of consolidating credit card debt (the interest rate on equity loans is usually far less than that charged by credit card companies) and tapping into what is often a large amount of money to use for home repairs and renovation or to fund some major expense such as an expensive vacation or a child's college education.

equity purchaser A person who buys the equity of another in a property, often by assuming (e.g., taking over) a mortgage that the borrower can no longer afford to pay.

equity of redemption The right of a borrower to pay in full a mortgage on a property that has gone into foreclosure, thus saving that borrower's rights in the property. This often happens because the borrower has a new source of financing, such as a relative or a bank that is willing to loan the money because the borrower has a new job with a stable employer.

escape clause A provision in a contract that allows one or more of the parties involved to end the contract if certain events occur. For example, a potential buyer of a house may stipulate in the sale agreement that the agreement comes into effect only if the buyer is able to sell her or his current residence by the anticipated closing date.

escrow In real estate, the delivery of a deed by the seller to a third party (e.g., the escrow agent), to be delivered to the buyer at a certain time, usually the closing date. In some states, all instruments having to do with the sale (including the funds) are delivered to the escrow agent for dispersal on the closing date.

escrow account A form of trust. This is the account in which the funds required to effect a closing are held.

escrow agent A third party who is independent of the buyer and seller (usually an agent), and who receives items to be held in escrow, holds them until transfer is allowed, and then delivers them.

escrow collections/deposit Money that is deposited with the escrow agent and held for future payments as required by the contract (e.g., taxes and insurance on the property). Also known as reserves.

escrow disbursements The act of paying out escrow funds as required by the real estate contract. Also known as escrow payments.

escrow reimbursement Returning to the borrower any excess funds that are present in an escrow account after all debts have been paid.

estate The term has two meanings: 1) the assets of a deceased person; and 2) in real estate, a person's interest in real property.

estoppel certificate A document outlining the terms and conditions to which the receiver agrees to be bound. A mortgage company sets out the terms and conditions of the mortgage, such as the outstanding principal and the interest rate. A condominium corporation might set out assessments for a particular unit, a special assessment against unit owners, or the amount in the condominium's reserve fund.

evidence of title A document that establishes ownership to property, most commonly a deed.

examination of title A review of the current title to a property for the purpose of establishing the rightful owner of, or any encumbrance to, that property.

exception In an insurance policy, any exclusion (e.g., that which the insurer is unwilling to insure). In California, for example, an insurer might be unwilling to insure damage to property by earthquakes. In Florida, an insurer might be unwilling to insure against hurricanes.

exclusive listing/exclusive agency listing/exclusive right to sell A written contract in which a property owner grants a single real estate agent or brokerage the right to sell that property. The owner promises to pay a fee or commission if the property is sold within a specific period, regardless of whether the agent or brokerage is the direct cause of the sale. In turn, the agent or broker may make specific promises, such as to advertise the property, to conduct open-house viewings, and to list the property on the brokerage's website.

exculpatory clause A provision of a mortgage that gives the borrower the right to surrender the property to the lender as payment for the loan without any other personal liability.

executed contract A real estate contract that has been signed by the parties to the contract, and is therefore complete, legal, and in force.

F
....

face rate of interest The rate of interest to be charged on a loan, as set out in the loan document itself.

face value The value of a mortgage as stated in the mortgage document.

Fair Credit Reporting Act A federal law that protects consumers by establishing procedures whereby they can correct errors on credit reports; it gives consumers specific rights in dealing with credit-reporting agencies.

fair market value The price that is likely to be agreed on by a buyer and seller for a specific property at a specific time. This price is typically arrived at by considering the sales prices of comparable properties in the area, taking into consideration any special features of or upgrades to the property in question.

Fannie Mae (FNMA) A slang term for the U.S. Federal National Mortgage Association. This association purchases, sells, and guarantees both conventional and government (e.g., VA) mortgages. Fannie Mae is a corporation established by the U.S. Congress; it is the largest supplier in the country of mortgages to home buyers and owners.

farm mortgage Any mortgage that is secured (e.g., guaranteed) by agricultural land.

Farmer's Home Administration (FMHA) An agency of the U.S. Department of Agriculture that provides financing for farmers and others who live in rural areas.

Federal Fair Housing Law Article VIII of the U.S. Civil Rights Act, this law forbids discrimination in either the sale or rental of residential property because of race, color, sex, religion or nationality.

Federal Home Loan Mortgage Corporation (FHLMC) see Freddie Mac.

Federal Housing Administration (FHA) A federal agency (a division of the U.S. Department of Housing and Urban Development, or HUD) that purchases first mortgages, both conventional and federally insured, from members of the Federal Reserve System and the Federal Home Loan Bank system. It also sets standards for the underwriting of private mortgages and insures residential mortgages made by private lenders.

federal land banks Banks, usually in rural areas, that provide mortgages to farmers and owners of agricultural land.

Federal National Mortgage Association (FNMA) *see* Fannie Mae.

Federal Savings and Loan Insurance Corporation (FSLC) A federally chartered institution that insures mortgages issued by savings and loan associations.

federal tax lien An encumbrance registered on title to a property as security against a tax debt owed by the owner to the federal government.

Federal Truth in Lending Act A U.S. federal law that requires lenders to disclose all the terms of a loan arrangement (e.g., a mortgage) to the borrower in a specific, understandable way.

fee appraiser Another term for a professional appraiser, that is, someone who appraises property in return for a fee.

fee simple The best title to a property that is available—ownership that is not subject to dispute.

fees There are two meanings for this term: 1) the fees that are charged for services provided by a real estate professional such as an appraiser or property inspector; and 2) the service charges that are required of a borrower by a lender in return for making a loan (these fees are either charged at the outset or held back from the mortgage).

FHA *see* Federal Housing Administration.

FHLMC *see* Federal Home Loan Mortgage Corporation

fiduciary A person who is acting in a relationship of trust (with another person) in a financial transaction. A fiduciary is required by law to place the other person's interests ahead of the fiduciary's own in any dealings that involve that other person. Real estate agents, investment brokers, and lawyers all can be fiduciaries in their professional practice.

fiduciary relationship The arrangements between a fiduciary and the person the fiduciary represents. Because of his or her special skills, the fiduciary has more power and knowledge than the person represented and therefore is held by law to a very high standard of conduct.

fifteen-year mortgage A loan that is paid off in 15 years rather than the usual 25 or 30 years. The interest savings with a 15-year mortgage are substantial, though the monthly payments are higher than with a 30-year mortgage. Fifteen-year mortgages are increasingly popular with buyers of houses and condominium units.

final value estimate The final statement of an appraiser, outlining the appraiser's valuation of a particular property. Often, this statement includes the appraiser's comments on the evaluation method(s) used.

finance charge The entire cost of a loan or mortgage, including the principal and interest charged over the life of the loan, appraisal and application fees, title insurance fees, and recording fees.

financing The way in which a potential purchaser intends to make up the difference between the cash that she or he has on hand and the purchase price of a property (e.g., by obtaining a loan from a mortgage lender or borrowing the money from a bank).

financing costs The interest and other charges involved in borrowing money to buy or build property.

finder's fee The commission that is paid to a mortgage broker by a lending institution when the broker places a mortgage with that institution. This practice does not affect the broker's objectivity when acting on behalf of his or her client (e.g., the potential borrower) because virtually all lending institutions pay mortgage brokers such a fee.

firm commitment A promise from a lender to lend a potential borrower a specific amount of money (on specific terms) to be secured against a specific property—in other words, a promise by the lender to give the potential borrower a mortgage.

firm offer An offer from a potential buyer of a property to the owner of that property indicating that the buyer will not negotiate any changes to that offer. For example, if a buyer offers $300,000 for a residence and indicates that the offer is firm, he or she will not consider the seller's counteroffer.

firm price An indication that the seller will not enter into negotiations with any potential buyer to change the price at which a property is offered. The indication that a price is "firm" is often included in any announcement or advertisement of the sale of the property.

fixed installment The periodic payment, usually monthly, for the principal and interest on a mortgage or other kind of loan. This is an amount that, in practice, is always the same.

fixed-rate mortgage (FRM) *see* adjustable-rate mortgage. A loan on which the interest rate does not change over the term (e.g., the life) of the mortgage.

fixture Personal property that is attached to real property; this is treated legally as real property while it is so attached. Fixtures, unless they are specifically exempted from an accepted offer to purchase, are regarded as part of the property when that property is bought or sold. Furniture is generally not a fixture (see chattel), with the exception of furniture that is built-in (e.g., a bookcase). A lamp is not a fixture, whereas track lighting that is attached to the ceiling is a fixture.

floating rate The rate of interest that is charged on an adjustable-rate mortgage. This rate usually is set according to a specified index or is tied to the national prime rate. For example, a loan that is set at prime plus 2 percent will carry an interest rate of 7 percent if the prime rate is 5 percent.

flood insurance Insurance that covers loss by water damage. Such insurance is required by lenders in areas known to be potential flood areas. The insurance is written by private insurance companies but is subsidized by the federal government.

floodplain The area of land that is adjacent to a body of water. This land is under water sometimes and dry at other times. Houses built on such land are usually constructed on some type of stilts that keep them above water during times of flooding.

floor The lowest interest rate that will be charged on an adjustable-rate mortgage. This rate is stated in the mortgage agreement.

floor plan A layout drawing of a building (or portion of a building) showing the size and the purpose of each room. Usually provided (by the seller's agent) to any potential buyer of the property. Floor plans may be quite specific, including doors, windows, stairways, and other features.

FMHA *see* Farmer's Home Administration

FNMA *see* Federal National Mortgage Association.

for sale by owner (FSBO) The situation when a seller tries to find a buyer on his or her own, without using a real estate agent or broker.

foreclosure A proceeding that is usually instigated by a lender, in a court or not, to cancel all rights and title of an owner in a particular property when that owner has defaulted on payment of a mortgage. The purpose of the lender's action is to claim the title, so that the property can be sold to satisfy the debt still outstanding on the mortgage.

foreclosure sale *see* foreclosure. The sale of a property in foreclosure. The lender sells the property to satisfy the debt on the mortgage.

forfeiture The loss of one's right in a property because of failure to meet one's legal obligations in that property. A secondary meaning is the taking by the government of an individual's property if that individual has committed a crime.

FRM *see* fixed-rate mortgage.

Freddie Mac The Federal Home Loan Mortgage Corporation (also FHLMC), a private corporation that is federally chartered to purchases and sells mortgage loans.

FSBO *see* for sale by owner.

FSLC *see* Federal Savings and Loan Insurance Corporation.

G

graduated-payment mortgage (GPM) A mortgage in which the payments increase over time, according to a predetermined schedule set out in the mortgage agreement. Often, the increases level off at some point and remain fixed thereafter.

graduation period The (announced) interval between payment increases on a graduated-payment mortgage.

graduation rate The rate, expressed as a percentage, at which payments increase in a graduated-payment mortgage.

grandfather clause An exemption. A clause in a law or an agreement that permits the continuation of some use or practice that was permissible when established but is now no longer permissible. Such clauses ensure that property owners will not be penalized by retroactive laws. For instance, if a property owner, at great expense, has created a brick wall around her or his house for privacy purposes, and a new law dictates that such fences must be made of metal, a grandfather clause in the new law may allow the owner to keep her or his brick fence.

grant The act of transferring title (e.g., ownership), typically from a seller to a buyer.

grantee One who receives title, typically a buyer.

grantor One who gives title (or property rights), typically a seller.

grantor/grantee index A public document that contains an alphabetical listing of all parties to all transfers of land, cross-indexed by grantor, grantee and property transferred.

guarantee/guarantee mortgage An agreement by a third (e.g., outside) party to join in a land transaction (usually a mortgage) and to be responsible for the outstanding balance if the principal debtor or borrower fails to pay (e.g., defaults). Often, parents provide such a guarantee for a child's first purchase of a house or condominium unit.

guaranty fee Fannie Mae's fee for insuring a mortgage.

H

HAC *see* Housing Assistance Council.

HAM *see* hedged-account mortgage.

handyman's special A property that requires substantial work to bring it up to normal standards. Such a property is often sold at a lower price than it would be if it were in excellent repair.

hazard insurance A policy on property (or on property improvements) that covers damage by natural causes, such as fire or flooding.

hedged-account mortgage (HAM) The payment of funds into an account that is set up to reduce mortgage payments at a later date.

heterogeneous An appraisal term describing an area comprised of buildings of varying styles or uses. Not as desirable as homogenous property.

hidden amenities Qualities that may not be immediately (or visually) apparent but that add to the value of a particular property, such as the fact that a building has been constructed of high-quality materials.

high-ratio mortgage A mortgage in which the amount of money borrowed is 75 percent (or more) of the purchase price. The lender on such a mortgage usually requires the sort of insurance that is provided by various U.S. government agencies as a guarantee of the lender's risk in making the mortgage.

historic district A classification (from a zoning, heritage or other agency) of a particular area of a community, usually within a city, denoting that the buildings within that area have historical value or significance. Such districts include Greenwich Village in New York City, Old Town in Chicago, the French Quarter in New Orleans, and Beacon Hill in Boston. The historic district designation usually enhances the value of individual properties in the district because buyers know that the area will be preserved, maintaining its current charm. Such designations may also involve very strict rules regarding the ways in which buildings may be renovated or changed; in a commercial area, this may be resisted by property owners.

historical scenario A prediction of how interest rates on an adjustable-rate mortgage will fluctuate in the future based on their performance in the past.

home inspection report The official statement provided by a professional home inspector detailing the results of her or his examination of a specific property. This report may show problems (or potential problems) not obvious to a potential buyer, such as problems with the structure of a building. Many buyers, especially those who are considering the purchase of an older building, make their offer conditional on obtaining a satisfactory home inspection report.

home inspector Someone who offers his or her services as an examiner of the physical condition of property. Qualifications for this profession differ between jurisdictions.

homeowners' association A group of property owners in a particular area who band together in an informal co-operative so that they may have a stronger voice in combating specific ills in their neighborhood. One purpose of such an association could be to achieve a more powerful political voice than each property owner would have separately.

homeowner's insurance Liability coverage that provides for both loss and damage to property. Most mortgage lenders require this kind of insurance of borrowers, and many lenders require evidence, provided each year, that the policy has been renewed.

homeowner's once-in-a-lifetime tax exclusion A superseded law. Before 1997, homeowners were subject to capital gains tax on the profit (e.g., the difference between the original purchase price and the current sales price, less any allowable expenses for renovation or improvement) they made on the sale of their homes, unless they were older than 55 years of age, in which case a capital gains exemption of the first $125,000 in profit was allowed. As the term implies, this exemption could be claimed only once in a lifetime. Since 1997, any homeowner may claim an exemption of $250,000 ($500,000 if married and the spouse has met the same requirements) if the homeowner has lived in the home for two of the previous five years. In addition, the homeowner may claim this exemption more than once in a lifetime (e.g., on the sale of any subsequent home in which the owner has resided for at least two years).

homogenous In appraisal, this is an area that contains properties of similar style or properties that are used for a similar or complementary purpose. Such an area is considered more valuable than a heterogeneous area.

house-poor A slang term for someone who has very little disposable income left after she or he has paid for the principal, interest, and insurance on a mortgage and the cost of upkeep on a property.

housing affordability index An analysis by the National Association of Realtors, issued on a monthly basis, of the ability of the average-income family in the United States to afford a mortgage on the average-priced home, after making a 20 percent down payment.

Housing and Urban Development (HUD) see Department of Housing and Urban Development.

Housing Assistance Council (HAC) A federal agency, funded by the U.S. Department of Housing and Urban Development, that supports the development of low-income housing in rural areas.

housing code The rules of a particular municipality that set out the minimum standards for dwellings in that area.

housing expense ratio A figure that is obtaining by comparing a family's monthly gross income with the costs of their home (e.g., the principal and interest on a mortgage plus the cost of upkeep).

housing finance agency A state agency whose function is to provide loans to residents of the state who cannot obtain property loans through commercial lenders.

HUD *see* Department of Housing and Urban Development.

HUD median income A figure that is used by the U.S. Department of Housing and Urban Department (HUD) in determining eligibility for various HUD programs; it is the average income for a family in a specific area of the United States.

HUD-I settlement statement *see* closing statement.

I
...

impound That portion of a borrower's mortgage loan payment that pays for expenses other than principal or interest (e.g., real estate taxes, insurance premiums).

impound account The trust in which a lender keeps the portion of the borrower's monthly loan payment that must be disbursed, on due dates, to third parties for such expenses as real estate taxes and insurance premiums. Also known as escrow account.

imputed interest The interest that a court determines has been charged on a loan.

independent appraisal An estimate of the value of a property in which the appraiser has no interest in the property (e.g., is not a representative of the potential lender).

index A factor that is used to calculate the interest on an adjustable-rate mortgage. For example, a lender may use the Federal Reserve Bank's prime rate as an index from which to calculate the interest rate on the mortgage. The index usually only provides a base, to which is added a further percentage (e.g., prime plus 2 percent).

indexed loan Any loan in which the interest rate may change in accordance with an index that is announced periodically by an independent third party. One example is an adjustable-rate mortgage.

initial interest rate The interest rate that is being charged on a mortgage on the day that it is first signed.

initial rate period The period for which the initial interest rate is guaranteed on an adjustable-rate mortgage; that is, the length of time before it can change as a result of a change in its index.

installment Any regular, periodic payment, such as the monthly payment on a mortgage.

installment loan Any loan that is paid back in periodic installments, usually either weekly or monthly.

installment sale A property sale in which the seller retains title (e.g., ownership) but the buyer takes possession of the property and thereafter makes installment payments to the seller consisting of principal plus interest. In effect, the seller is providing the mortgage. The seller is not liable for any taxes on the sale until the principal is paid.

institutional lender An accredited financial organization or company (e.g., a bank, a trust company, savings and loan, credit union) that offers loans or mortgages.

institutional mortgage A loan offered by an institutional lender that is secured against real estate.

insurable value The value of property for insurance purposes. Any one of the following determinants of value may be used: the sale price, the current market value, or the replacement value.

insurance A contract in which one party (the insurer) agrees to indemnify another (the insured) against possible losses under specific conditions. Such conditions may include compensation of the insured for loss of job and income, in which case the insurer would pay the insured's debts, including mortgage payments, and compensation of the insured for any damage to the insured's property caused by natural phenomena (e.g., fire, storms).

insurance binder A temporary measure or device that provides written evidence that insurance is in effect even though a permanent, formal policy has not been issued.

insured mortgage A mortgage that is insured against loss to the lender in the event that the borrower defaults. It usually covers both the mortgage balance and the costs of foreclosure. This type of insurance is provided by such government agencies as the FHA or VA, as well as by independent insurance companies.

interest There are two meanings for this term: 1) a person's legal right to property; and 2) the cost of borrowing money for any purpose, such as to buy property, charged as a percentage of the outstanding balanced that is owed.

interest adjustment date A concept that is confusing to many borrowers. Mortgage interest is paid in arrears; that is, most mortgages involve a monthly payment that includes the interest owed for the preceding, rather than the following, month (e.g., a mortgage payment due July first contains the interest that is owed for June and not July). The closing date of a mortgage may not be on the first or last day of the month, however. If the closing date is May 15th and the first payment date is July 1st, only the interest for June will be paid on July 1st and not the interest for May 15th through 31st. The interest adjustment date, in this instance June 1st, is when the interest for May 15th through 31st is due. This amount usually is not paid on a particular day, however, but rather at closing.

interest-only mortgage A type of mortgage that is increasingly popular in which the borrower pays only the interest and none of the principal during a certain period (e.g., three years, five years). After that, the borrower makes conventional payments containing both principal and interest for the remainder of the loan's term. Such mortgages are appealing to those who want initial payments on a mortgage to be as low as possible or those who expect the value of the property to rise very quickly, providing them with a profit without substantial principal investment.

interest payment That portion of each periodic payment on a loan or mortgage (expressed in dollars, not as a percentage) that is allocated toward accrued interest as opposed to principal.

interest rate The amount that a borrower pays to service a loan (e.g., to use the borrowed money), usually expressed as a percentage.

interest rate adjustment period The length of time, usually stated on the mortgage, between possible interest rate changes on an adjustable-rate mortgage.

interest rate cap The clause in an adjustable-rate mortgage that states the limitations on the amount of interest that can be charged. It may limit changes in one of two ways: 1) over a single adjustment period; or 2) over the life of the mortgage.

interest rate ceiling The clause in an adjustable-rate mortgage that states the highest rate of interest that can be charged on that mortgage.

interest rate floor The clause in an adjustable-rate mortgage that states the lowest rate of interest that can be charged on that mortgage.

interim financing *see* bridge loan/financing.

Interstate Land Sales Act A federal law that is administered by the U.S. Department of Housing and Urban Development (HUD). It regulates the practices associated with sales of land between people residing in different American states.

involuntary conversion Loss of land through natural forces or government action.

involuntary lien A claim that is registered against a property without the consent (and sometimes the knowledge) of the owner, such as a claim by the government for unpaid property taxes. Conversely, a mortgage is a voluntary lien in which the borrower agrees that the lender may register a lien against the property until the loan covered by the mortgage is paid in full.

irrevocability date The time and date specified in a purchase offer for property. The buyer may not retract the offer until that date, and the seller has until that date to accept or reject the offer.

J

joint and several liability When two or more people take on a loan, each may be responsible for a certain portion of the obligation or they all may be responsible for the entire obligation. A joint and several liability clause removes any such ambiguity. In that case, all parties together are responsible for the obligation (joint) and each person individually is responsible for the entire obligation (several). In the event of a default, the lender may sue all or just one of the borrowers to recover the debt.

joint appraisal An appraisal that is conducted by more than one appraiser but states their common conclusions.

joint ownership agreement A contract between two or more people who have an interest in the same property. It sets out their rights and obligations, and may also set out the way in which the parties agree to manage the property.

judgment A decision rendered by a court. If a monetary settlement is involved, it may become a lien on the property of the losing party.

judgment lien A lien that applies to all the property that is owned by the loser in a court action and is located in the county in which the judgment is recorded.

judicial foreclosure/sale An action taken by a lender to sell property in order to recover mortgage debt, after the lender has obtained a judgment of a court that so allows.

jumbo loan/mortgage A loan for an amount that exceeds the usual funding limits of Freddie Mac or Fannie Mae. Offered by some lending institutions to allow for mortgages on very expensive properties.

junk fees A slang term for the extra and sometimes unnecessary services that a lender may charge for on a mortgage.

L

land surveyor A professional who is trained to establish, measure and verify the boundaries of properties and the buildings constructed on those properties.

land-use succession The gradual change in the use of land that occurs in a neighborhood or area over a period of years (e.g., from industrial to residential).

landscaping The act of modifying a landscape, as well as the components used in such modification, such as changes in grade, trees and shrubs, lawns, flowers and other plantings. The object of landscaping is to create a more pleasing appearance for the property, and one of its incidental goals is to enhance the value of that property. Landscaping may accomplish that goal, particularly if it is extensive, professional, and pleasing to a potential buyer.

late charge A penalty fee that is charged by a lender when a borrower is late with a mortgage payment.

latent defect A hidden or concealed defect in a property that, even assuming reasonable care, could not be found in an inspection. A seller must declare to the buyer any latent defect of which she or he is aware.

lease with option to purchase A kind of lease in which the tenant (e.g., lessee) has the right (but not the obligation) to purchase the property during the term of the lease. Payments made under the lease (sometimes wholly and sometimes in part, depending on the lease agreement) may be credited against the purchase price; that is, they may be used as a down payment. This is an ideal arrangement for any potential buyer who lacks the financial means to make a down payment.

lease-purchase mortgage loan A loan offered by Fannie Mae that allows qualified persons to lease a property from a nonprofit organization and includes an option to purchase the property. As in a normal mortgage, payments are credited toward principal and interest, but a portion goes into a savings account that the person leasing the property may use for a down payment when the necessary amount has accumulated.

legal description A description of property that is acceptable in a court of law (e.g., meets legal requirements).

legal notice The act of informing one or more persons of an action or an intention to act, in a manner prescribed by law or by court action.

legal title The rights of ownership that are conferred on a person when he or she purchases a piece of property. These rights may be defended against any other, competing interests.

lender A general term referring to any individual or company that provides money to a borrower in return for periodic payments of principal and interest over time. In real estate, the term most often refers to a person (or institution) who offers a borrower a mortgage (e.g., loans the borrower the money to buy property) and places a lien on that property until the outstanding loan (e.g., the principal) and all the outstanding interest on that loan are paid.

lender option commitments An agreement between a lender and a potential borrower that allows the lender to provide certain loans at certain times on terms set out in the contract; it also allows the lender to choose not to provide such loans (the "option").

lender's title insurance A type of insurance policy that covers the interest of a lender on a mortgage; it is registered on the title to the property involved.

letter of commitment *see* commitment.

letter of intent A formal letter stating that a prospective buyer is interested in a property. This is not a firm offer and it creates no legal obligation. A potential buyer could issue such a letter to a seller of a particular property, indicating that the buyer intends to make an offer for that property.

level-payment mortgage Any property loan that involves consistent, regular and fixed payments.

leverage Any use of debt financing to purchase a property.

levy To assess or make a charge (e.g., a tax levy).

LIBOR An acronym for London Interbank Offered Rate. This rate is sometimes used as an index, particularly for interest-only mortgages.

lien An encumbrance, or legal claim, against a property as security for payment of a debt, such as the lien involved in a mortgage.

lien holder The person or institution who issues a lien; that is, who has a claim against property (e.g., a mortgage) that must be satisfied (e.g., the mortgage must be fully paid) before that claim can be released.

life cap The maximum interest rate that can be charged on an adjustable-rate mortgage. This rate will be clearly stated in the mortgage document.

list/listing An agreement between an owner of a property and a real estate agent or broker in which the agent agrees to find a buyer or tenant in return for either a fee (in the case of rental property) or a commission (in the case of property to be sold). Also, the act of announcing that the property is for rent or for sale.

listing agent/broker The real estate professional who acts for the seller in marketing a property. This is not the same as the selling agent, who represents potential buyers. One agent may act in both capacities for a client (e.g., be responsible for selling a person's current residence, then help them to find a new residence).

loan *see* mortgage.

loan application A form completed by a potential borrower that provides the information that a potential lender requires to determine the borrower's suitability for (e.g., ability to repay) a loan or mortgage.

loan application fee The amount that lenders sometimes charge to consider a loan application. The potential borrower should be advised of this fee before he or she submits the application.

loan commitment *see* commitment.

loan package The complete set of documents that a lender requires to grant a loan or mortgage. This may include the loan application; the potential borrower's credit report, employment verification and financial statement; and a survey and appraisal of the property.

loan-to-value ratio The difference between the appraised value of a property and the amount being loaned on a mortgage.

location The factor that is often cited as the primary factor in determining the worth of a property. It refers to the following phenomenon: if two very similar properties are located in two different areas within the same city or town, and one of those areas is more convenient to the area's most popular amenities (e.g., shopping, entertainment) than the other, the property in the more desirable area will almost certainly be more expensive.

lock or lock-in There are two meanings for this term: 1) the commitment from a lender to guarantee a certain interest rate (or other loan feature) for a designated period; and 2) the restriction that a mortgage may not be prepaid by the borrower for a specific period .

lock period The period during which a lender guarantees a particular loan feature, usually the interest rate.

London Interbank Offered Rate *see* LIBOR

lot In general, any portion or parcel of real estate (e.g., a measured section of land). Often refers to a portion of a subdivision.

lot line The legal boundaries of a property, shown on a survey of that property.

low-ball offer A slang term meaning to offer a purchase price that is much lower than the asking price. Such offers, which are often lower than the appraised market value, are frequently made when a property has been on the market for a long time and potential buyers try to take advantage of pressure on the seller to sell.

M

maintenance costs The expense required to keep a property in a good state of repair.

maintenance fee A term used primarily in reference to condominiums and planned developments. It is the amount that is charged each unit owner to maintain the common areas of the building or development. The maintenance fee is usually charged monthly and is often included as part of the owner's assessment.

manufactured housing *see* prefabricated/prefab housing.

margin In adjustable-rate mortgages, this is the difference between the index interest rate and the interest rate that is actually being charged to the borrower. It is usually expressed as a percentage, and as a percentage on top of the index itself (e.g., "prime plus 2 percent").

market price The amount actually paid for a property. At the moment of sale, that amount is imagined to be its current valuation; subsequently, the market price, depending on economic factors, either appreciates or depreciates.

market segmentation Submarkets within a larger market, such as neighborhoods within a city.

market value An estimation of the price at which a property would sell in the current real estate market.

market-value approach An appraisal technique in which the value of a property is estimated by comparing it with similar properties (e.g., comparables) that have recently been sold.

marketability The probability of selling a particular property within a specified period and price range.

marketable title Ownership of a particular property that can be sold without complications because there are no competing claims to that property (e.g., no liens or encumbrances).

marketing plan A description (usually written) of how a real estate agent or broker intends to market a particular property in order to obtain the best possible price. A good agent should offer his or her clients such plans and solicit their comments on them.

maturity date The specific day on which a mortgage is completely due and payable (e.g., the day on which it must be paid in full).

minimum down payment The smallest amount of money that a purchaser is allowed to provide toward the purchase price of a house under a lender's guidelines for a mortgage. Down payments on residential property in the United States, for many years, have typically been 20 percent of the purchase price. However, down payments of 10 percent or even five percent recently have become more common. With down payments of less than 20 percent, lenders usually require additional insurance on the mortgage. The borrower may cancel this insurance when the principal on the loan reaches 20 percent.

minimum lot size The smallest allowable lot size for development, as stipulated by local zoning ordinances.

minimum payment The lowest amount a borrower is allowed to pay toward a mortgage in any given period.

minimum property standards The basic requirements of construction and lot location, which are required by the FHA before it will underwrite a mortgage on a residential property.

MLS *see* multiple listing service

model home A dwelling, usually the first one built by a developer, that allows potential purchasers to see what other homes in the development will look like when they are completed and furnished. Typically, the developer sells the model home last, and often includes the furniture in the purchase price. Model apartments also are being used increasingly as sales tools in condominium developments.

modular housing *see* manufactured housing.

monthly fixed installment A periodic payment on a loan that is always the same amount and is applied toward both principal and accumulated interest (e.g., the monthly payment on a mortgage).

monthly housing expense The total cost of maintaining a home each month, including the principal and interest on a mortgage, real estate taxes and property (and possibly mortgage) insurance. This figure usually does not include maintenance or improvements, only fixed expenses.

mortgage A loan that is usually granted for the purpose of allowing a borrower to purchase property. The loan is secured (e.g., guaranteed) by that property; in other words, the mortgage is registered on the title (e.g., the ownership record) as a claim on that property.

mortgage back A kind of financing in which the seller agrees to accept only a portion of the purchase price initially and then agrees to hold the rest of the mortgage. With this type of loan, the seller receives periodic payments toward principal and interest for the remainder of the purchase price. Such an arrangement is advantageous to a buyer who is having trouble obtaining a conventional mortgage; it also can be advantageous to the seller, who receives an extra source of income as a result of the sale (e.g., the interest payments over many years). A seller who needs all the money from the sale at once (e.g., to purchase another property) would not find this kind of arrangement attractive. Also known as a vendor take-back mortgage.

mortgage broker A middleman who brings borrowers together with potential lenders, thereby providing a service to borrowers who are not as informed about potential lending sources. Often, the broker collects a fee for this service from the chosen lender.

mortgage commitment *see* commitment.

mortgage disability insurance A policy that will cover mortgage payments for the borrower if he or she becomes incapable of doing so, usually as a result of acquiring some disability.

mortgage insurance A policy that will pay the amount owed on a mortgage if the borrower defaults.

mortgage-interest deduction An income tax deduction offered by the U.S. Internal Revenue Service under which homeowners are allowed to deduct a certain amount of their mortgage interest on their tax returns (the exact amount depends on the homeowner's tax rate). This deduction can represent a substantial savings and serves as an incentive to home ownership.

mortgage life insurance A policy that will pay the outstanding balance on a mortgage if the borrower dies before the mortgage is completely paid. With this insurance, the amount that would be paid by the insurer decreases every year, but the premiums it charges may not.

mortgage-loan servicing The lender's actions in collecting mortgage payments and allocating those payments to principal, interest, and, if the mortgage so stipulates, an escrow account for subsequent payment of property taxes and insurance premiums.

mortgagee In a mortgage transaction, this is the lender; that is, the bank, other institution (private or government), or person making the loan for property.

mortgagee in possession A lender that has taken over control of a property because the borrower has defaulted. This is a first step in foreclosure.

mortgagor *see* borrower.

Multiple Listing Service (MLS) A local service that is created and staffed by real estate professionals. It brings together all property listed for sale in a given area (e.g., a town and its surrounding area or a city and its suburbs) so that real estate agents and brokers can review all available properties on behalf of their clients. The MLS also governs commission splitting and other relations between agents. Licensed real estate professionals have access to the service.

N
.....

National Association of Independent Fee Appraisers (NAIFA) An organization of real estate appraisers; it offers professional licensure to qualified persons.

National Association of Real Estate Brokers (NAREB) A national trade association whose members include not just real estate brokers but also appraisers, property managers and other interested real estate professionals.

National Association of Realtors (NAR) An organization of people engaged in the real estate business. NAR is dedicated to the betterment of the industry through education and legislation. It also sets high ethical and professional standards for its members. Founded in 1908, it currently comprises more than three-quarters of a million members.

negative amortization The situation that exists when the principal amount of a mortgage increases because a payment is not sufficient to cover accumulated interest and the shortfall is therefore added to the principal.

negative amortization cap The limit of negative amortization that is allowed on an adjustable-rate mortgage.

negotiable A term that commonly refers to something that is assignable or transferable (e.g., something that is capable of being negotiated). In real estate, the term refers to the fact that the price of a property is often the result of a negotiation between the buyer and seller, and that many of the charges on a home loan are also subject to negotiation.

negotiable-rate mortgage see adjustable-rate mortgage.

net listing An agreement between a real estate agent and a seller in regard to a sale price (e.g., the net price). In such an agreement, the seller is guaranteed to receive the agreed sale price and the agent to receive as commission the amount that exceeds that price when the property is sold. This kind of arrangement is illegal in some American states.

no bid The situation in which the Veterans' Administration chooses not to acquire a property in foreclosure when that property is in default, but instead opts to pay out the amount it has guaranteed (usually 60 percent of the principal).

no-cash-out refinance The replacement of one loan by another when the principal remains the same; in other words, the borrower is not refinancing to gain cash from his or her equity but usually only to obtain a lower interest rate.

no money down A slang term for the strategy of purchasing real estate using as little of the buyer's own money as possible. Can also refer to an uncommon kind of mortgage that requires very little or no down payment.

nominal loan rate The interest rate that is stated in a loan agreement such as a mortgage.

nonassumption clause A clause in a mortgage contract forbidding the borrower from transferring the mortgage to another person without the consent of the lender.

nonconforming loan/mortgage A loan that is not eligible for backing by Fannie Mae or Freddie Mac because it does not adhere to their requirements.

nonexclusive listing A kind of property agreement. The seller lists a property with a real estate agent, who has the exclusive right to sell that property. However, if the owner sells the property without any help from the agent, the owner is not liable to pay a commission to the agent. Sometimes also called an agency agreement.

nonrecourse loan A loan that allows a lender to claim the borrower's property in the event of default (e.g., failure to make the mortgage payments) but not to hold the borrower personally liable for the remaining principal of the loan.

note rate The interest rate stated in a mortgage or loan contract.

notice of action A recorded notice that property may be subject to a lien, or even that the title is not clear because of pending legal action.

notice of default A written announcement sent by a lender to a borrower, stating that the borrower has not met the obligations of the mortgage loan and that the lender may take legal action to enforce the agreement.

O

objection A buyer's concern about a property being purchased and his or her requirement that the seller correct the problem before closing (e.g., something that is wrong with the heating system and must be fixed before the sale is concluded). Also known as requisition.

obligee One to whom an obligation is owed. In real estate, the lender in a mortgage or loan transaction. Also called the mortgagee.

obligor One who obligates. In real estate, the borrower in a mortgage or loan transaction.

offer A statement (either spoken or written) that informs one party of another's willingness to buy or sell a specific property on the terms set out in that statement. Once made, an offer usually must be accepted within a specific period (e.g., it is usually not open-ended). Once accepted, the offer by the one party and the acceptance by the other both are regarded as binding.

offeree The person who receives an offer.

Office of Interstate Land Sales Registration An agency of the U.S. Department of Housing and Urban Development (HUD) that has the responsibility of enforcing the Interstate Land Sales Full Disclosure Act.

open-ended mortgage A loan that allows the borrower to borrow further funds at a later date with the preparation (and registration) of an additional mortgage.

open listing A written authorization from a property owner to a real estate agent stipulating that the owner will pay the agent a commission if the agent presents an offer of specified price and terms. The agent does not, however, have an exclusive right to sell; in fact, the owner may have made the same arrangement with several agents, and only the successful agent will be paid the commission.

open mortgage Any mortgage that may be paid in full (or in part) at any time during the life of the mortgage without a penalty being charged to the borrower.

option to purchase leased property A clause in a rental agreement that allows the tenant the right to buy the leased property on terms and conditions that are also set out in the agreement.

original equity The owner's original down payment on a property.

original face value The principal owed on a mortgage on the day that the mortgage came into effect.

original principal value *see* original face value.

origination fee *see* commitment fee.

outbuilding A structure that is not part of the main building, such as a garage.

outstanding balance The amount owing, both principal and interest, at a given date, on a mortgage or any other kind of property loan.

owner One who has rights of ownership in a property.

owner financing *see* mortgage back.

owner's title insurance A policy that protects a property owner from any defects in title that were not apparent at the time of purchase.

P
....

package mortgage A mortgage that is secured by the borrower's personal as well as real property.

paper profit An asset, such as property, that is known to have increased in value (e.g., because comparable assets have been sold and have achieved this value) but has not actually produced a profit because it has not been sold. Therefore, the profit remains speculative.

partial interest Less than 100-percent ownership of a property.

partial release The release of a portion of property covered by a mortgage. For example, a developer of a subdivision of residential properties may obtain such a release as each house is sold and payment of a stated portion of the loan has been made.

partially amortized mortgage A kind of mortgage in which the term is actually less than the amortization period, so that, at the maturity date, the mortgage is not fully paid and either refinancing or a balloon payment is required.

participation/participating mortgage A mortgage in which the lender is owed a percentage of the income of a property or of the proceeds when that property is sold. In other words, the lender receives more than just a payment for principal and interest. This kind of mortgage is likely to be offered to a potential borrower when financing is difficult to obtain or when a real estate project requires a substantial amount of money from the lender.

party wall A shared wall, usually on the property line, such as exists between row houses, townhouses or semidetached houses.

patent The transfer of title to land from government to private ownership.

payoff/payout The payment in full (e.g., all remaining principal and interest) of an existing loan or mortgage.

payment-adjustment interval The period between changes in the amount of the payments on an adjustable-rate mortgage.

payment cap A condition of some adjustable-rate mortgages in which the level to which a monthly payment can rise is limited to a certain amount.

payment change date Under an adjustable-rate mortgage, the date on which the payment changes.

payment penalty A fee that must be paid by a borrower when she or he pays off more of the principal than is allowed under the terms of the mortgage or other loan. In effect, the lender is agreeing to receive less interest over the life of the loan and is charging a fee to make this concession. Also known as an early-payment penalty or prepayment penalty.

Payment Reporting Builds Credit A private national credit bureau. This nontraditional scoring system uses a bill payment scorecard to rate consumers' performance based on rent, child support, student loan and utilities payments.

per annum (Latin: annually). Once each year.

per diem (Latin: daily). Once each day.

per stirpes (Latin: by representation). Equal division of an estate among the heirs of the deceased.

periodic payment cap *see* payment cap.

periodic rate cap *see* rate cap.

permanent loan/mortgage A long-term mortgage.

perpetuity Forever. Many jurisdictions have laws against tying up title to a property in perpetuity.

personal property Any property belonging to an individual that is not real property (e.g., that is not real estate).

PRI *see* principal and interest payment.

piggyback loan A loan made by two or more lenders on the same mortgage. Such mortgages may indicate that the lenders believed there was risk involved or that the loan was a very large one.

PITI An acronym for principal, interest, taxes and insurance, which are the most common components of a monthly mortgage payment.

PITI reserves The amount of money that a lender requires a borrower to have in reserve to cover the cost of a mortgage's principal and interest (and, if the mortgage so stipulates, property taxes and insurance) for a set number of months.

planned-unit development (PUD) A housing development in which a homeowners' association administers common property that is owned and shared by all the owners in the project. Dwellings are often clustered together to allow for more common space, which in turn is the responsibility of the PUD. Special zoning is usually required for this kind of project.

PMI *see* private mortgage insurance.

pocket card A form of identification that is required by most states for real estate agents and brokers. It must be shown to potential clients (e.g., buyer or sellers of real estate) as evidence of the agent's or broker's professional qualifications.

point An amount equal to one percent of the principal of a mortgage. This is a fee that is charged to a borrower by a lender for originating the mortgage. It is a loan service charge that must be paid up-front when the mortgage goes into effect. Some lenders allow points to be added to the principal of the mortgage and paid over its lifetime.

power of sale This is usually the most efficient, and least expensive, method of enforcing a mortgage that is available to lenders. A clause in the mortgage agreement gives the lender the right to take over and sell the property if the borrower defaults. The sale proceeds are then allocated in the following order: principal and interest; penalties; the lender's expenses in exercising the lender's rights; and claims of other registered claimants. Finally, if there is any money left after all of these allocations, that balance is refunded to the borrower.

PRBC *see* Payment Reporting Builds Credit.

preapproved mortgage A commitment from a lender to provide a mortgage loan to a borrower on stated terms before the borrower has found a property to buy. Most real estate agents recommend that their clients who are potential buyers secure this kind of commitment because it allows them to make a firm offer when they find a desirable property; that is, they do not have to ask a seller to wait several weeks while they attempt to obtain financing. Sometimes sellers are unwilling to wait and potential buyers may lose property.

prearranged refinancing agreement An arrangement between a lender and a borrower in which the lender agrees to favorable terms for a future refinancing as an inducement to the borrower to place the original mortgage with the lender.

preclosing A meeting of the parties to a mortgage loan transaction before the actual closing date. This allows any complicated issues to be settled before closing; in addition, some of the documents can be signed in advance.

prefabricated/prefab housing Structures that are put together on a building site from components that were built off-site (usually in a factory.) Also called modular housing.

preforeclosure sale The sale of a property by a delinquent borrower that is agreed to by the lender. The sale may not produce enough money to settle the loan entirely, but the lender agrees to this kind of sale because it saves the costs of foreclosing and of the postforeclosure sale.

prepaid expenses Money, usually for mortgage costs, that has not yet been disbursed; until disbursement, the money is kept in an escrow account.

prepayment Payment of all or part of the principal of a mortgage or loan before it is actually due.

prepayment clause A statement in a mortgage that sets out the rules regarding extra payments toward principal (e.g., those in excess of what is required as part of the monthly mortgage payment).

prepayment penalty A restriction that is included in some mortgages. An extra fee is charged to the borrower for paying off the principal before it becomes due, which deprives the lender of interest that would have been collected if the mortgage had run its full course.

prepayment privilege The right, established by some mortgages, to prepay all or part of the principal amount before it becomes due.

prequalification Completion of the mortgage application process before the borrower has found a property to buy as a way of establishing how much money the borrower is qualified to obtain in a mortgage.

presale The marketing of properties that are still under construction or still in the planning stage. Condominium units and homes in a new subdivision are often sold in this way.

prescriptive easement The legal right to make use of all or part of the property of another person as a result of the continuous use of that property for a stated period. Such easements vary according to local statutes.

price-level-adjusted mortgage An adjustable-rate mortgage that uses the published rate of inflation as its index.

prime rate The most favorable interest rate charged by the largest commercial banks on short-term loans. Such loans usually are reserved for the lender's best clients. In real estate, the prime rate is not a rate that is actually charged on a mortgage, although adjustable-rate mortgages often use it as their index. Such mortgages may offer interest rates that are always, for instance, two or three percentage points above the prime rate.

principal The term has two meanings: 1) the person on whose behalf a real estate agent is acting; and 2) the amount of money borrowed (or still owed) on a loan, excluding interest.

principal and interest payment (P&I) A periodic payment, on a mortgage, that is sufficient to pay off the accumulated interest (usually that incurred over the previous month) and a portion of the principal.

principal broker The head of a real estate brokerage (also licensed as a broker), who is responsible for all the actions of that firm.

principal, interest, taxes and insurance (PITI) *see* PITI.

private mortgage insurance (PMI) Insurance that is required by a lender (and obtained from a nongovernment insurer) if the down payment on a property is less than 20 percent of its value.

property In real estate, any land or building on that land that is owned by someone.

property tax A tax that is levied on real property. The amount of tax is dependent on the assessed valuation of the property. Sometimes called realty tax.

public auction A real estate auction that is open to the public at which properties are sold to pay mortgages that are in default. Such auctions are popular with potential buyers because properties being sold at a public auction often bring less than their market value.

PUD *see* planned-unit development.

purchase agreement *see* agreement of sale.

purchase price The amount paid by the buyer to the seller in the acquisition of a property.

Q

qualification rate The rate used to calculate whether a potential borrower qualifies for a mortgage.

qualification requirements The guidelines that are set by individual lenders and used to decide whether a potential borrower will be given a mortgage.

qualified acceptance Agreement (by either party) to enter a contract provided certain conditions are met. Also known as conditional acceptance.

qualified buyer A potential purchaser who has been preapproved for a mortgage, usually to a certain limit.

quit-claim deed A conveyance in which the person doing the conveying is stating that she or he has no interest in a particular property.

R

RAM *see* reverse-annuity mortgage

rate cap The limit on how much an interest rate may change on an adjustable-rate mortgage, either for a given period or for the life of the loan.

rate commitment A written promise by a lender to lend money to a potential borrower at a stated rate of interest. Such a commitment is always for a stated period, which is noted in the agreement.

rate lock-in *see* rate commitment.

ratified sales contract A firm and binding agreement for the purchase or sale of land or property.

raw land Land in its natural state, with no improvements made to it.

ready, willing and able A term describing an individual who is in a position to complete a property contract. A broker providing an offer from a ready, willing and able buyer, which meets the price andterms of the listing, is entitled to a commission, regardless of whether the seller actually accepts the offer.

real estate The term for land and all fixtures to land, including buildings and improvements. Personal property is not usually considered real estate. A house is real estate, but the furniture in the house is not.

real estate agent Someone who works for a real estate agency and is involved in the buying and selling of property. The listing agent acts for the seller; the selling agent acts for the buyer.

real estate broker Someone licensed by the state in which he or she resides who works to engage in the real estate business in that state (e.g., to run or manage a real estate agency or brokerage). A broker may receive a commission for bringing a buyer and seller together to achieve a transfer of title; brokers may also be compensated for leasing property or for arranging an exchange of property. Brokers are responsible for the supervision of their company's associate brokers, realtors and agents.

real estate commission The amount that is paid to a real estate agent or broker on the sale of property.

real estate investment trust (REIT) A group investment in property that carries certain tax advantages for the participants. Both the federal and state governments regulate REITs.

real estate license A state license that grants an individual status as either a broker or an agent after she or he passes an examination. Some state examinations are very stringent.

real estate market The real estate activity (e.g., purchases and sales) in a particular area at a particular time.

real estate salesperson/professional *see* real estate agent and real estate broker.

Real Estate Settlement Procedures Act (RESPA) A statute adopted in 1975 that requires federally insured lenders to provide advance notice to borrowers of all the fees to be charged at closing.

real property *see* real estate.

realtor The professional designation for a member of the National Association of Realtors (or an affiliated local group). A licensed real estate agent is not a realtor unless that agent joins the association and agrees to abide by its code of ethics.

realtor's associate The professional designation of a (licensed) real estate agent who is a member of the National Association of Realtors but has not been licensed as a broker.

realty *see* real estate.

reassessment Re-estimating the value of all property in a given area for tax assessment purposes. In most municipalities, these re-estimates happen with some regularity.

recasting Adjusting the terms of a loan agreement or mortgage because of new developments, such as a change in general interest rates or a default.

receiver A court-appointed person who holds property that is either in dispute or cannot be competently administered by its owner.

reconveyance The return of property to its original owner from a trustee who has held title as collateral security for a debt.

recording fees The fee paid for recording a mortgage or other transaction.

recourse The right of the holder of a mortgage to look personally to the borrower for payment and not just to the property itself.

recovery fund An account that is made up of contributions from licensed real estate brokers and established to compensate the public for any valid claims against brokers.

red-lining The practice by a lender or lending institution of denying loans to persons in certain areas of a community (e.g., those that the lender considers to be "high risk" because of their racial or economic makeup). Red-lining specifically refers to marking up a map of a city, with red lines, to indicate to a lending staff the areas to be avoided in making loans to people who either live there or wish to buy there. This is always an illegal practice.

redeem To bring mortgage payments up-to-date after a serious delinquency in making those payments, and after the lender has started default proceedings. Once a borrower redeems, the mortgage is regarded as back in good standing.

redemption The process of canceling a title to property, such as happens in a mortgage foreclosure or as the result of a tax sale of a property.

redemption period The period during which a borrower may redeem a mortgage. The duration of this period is usually determined by local laws.

redevelop To remove existing improvements (usually buildings) on a piece of land and replace them with new, more useful or more profitable improvements.

reduction certificate A mortgage statement that is issued by a lender and outlines the amount owed on a loan as of a particular date.

re-evaluation lease *see* reappraisal lease.

refinance The situation when a borrower pays off one loan on a property and replaces it with another loan, often from the same lender. This is done most commonly when mortgage interest rates have decreased considerably from the rate the borrower is paying on the old mortgage. Thus, refinancing is a way for the borrower to reduce the amount of monthly mortgage payments.

registrar The person who is responsible for collecting, recording and maintaining instruments related to title of land. The registrar in a particular area may also be responsible for ruling on the acceptability (e.g., the legality) of any documents submitted for registration.

registration Submitting instruments relating to title in (e.g., ownership of) land or property to the public record. Different U.S. jurisdictions have different rules of submission. Once registered, documents are given a registration number, then recorded on a title abstract index.

regulation Z A U.S. Federal Reserve regulation under the Truth-in-Lending Act stipulating that a borrower must be advised, in writing, of all the costs and terms connected with any mortgage or other loan.

reinstatement Payment of the arrears on a mortgage to move it from default to good standing.

reissue rate A reduction in the cost of the title insurance on a property. It often comes into effect when there were no claims against the original policy.

REIT *see* real estate investment trust.

release/release clause That condition in a mortgage that allows the borrower to pay off the loan and have the mortgage lien removed from the title.

release of lien A document that, when it is registered, removes a claim against the title to (e.g., ownership of) a property.

renegotiation An attempt to agree on new terms to an existing contract. In real estate, there are two common examples of renegotiation: 1) when the necessary repairs to a property, as established by a home inspection, are more extensive than the seller had announced or the buyer had expected; and 2) when the appraisal of a property establishes a value or market price considerably below the price on which the parties to the contract had agreed. In both cases, the buyer will wish to renegotiate the price of sale.

repayment plan The arrangement between a borrower and a lender outlining the way in which a debt is to be paid (e.g., how much and at what intervals).

replacement cost A concept relating to insurance, this is the cost of erecting a new building to replace an existing building. It is used to determine value, in order to decide how much insurance coverage the building requires.

report A document sent by a lawyer to a bank or other lender certifying that title to a particular property is clear and marketable.

required cash The total amount of money needed to complete a real estate transaction. This may include a down payment on the purchase price, taxes, legal fees and mortgage fees.

rerecording The recording of a deed for a second (or subsequent) time to correct an error in the first recording. Also known as a correction deed, confirmation deed or reformation deed.

rescind/rescission To treat a property contract as ended or void; that is, to withdraw one's offer or acceptance of a contract. Rescission normally happens as a result of a breach of the contract by the other party to that contract.

reserve fund The fund that is maintained by a condominium corporation (or a co-operative) for future contingencies, such as unforeseen major structural repairs to the condominium building that are very expensive. A reserve fund is usually created by charging unit owners a monthly assessment that is slightly more than what is needed to cover the basic maintenance expenses of the building and placing the extra amount in the reserve fund.

reserve price The base price set before an auction that must be met in order for a particular property to sell during the auction process. For example, a house that is being auctioned with a set price (e.g., a reserve price) of $200,000 may bring $225,000 but would not be sold for $195,000.

reserves *see* escrow collections/deposit.

residential broker A real estate professional who deals exclusively with the buying and selling of homes (e.g., does not deal with commercial properties).

RESPA *see* Real Estate Settlement Procedures Act.

restraint on alienation Any limitation on an owner's right to sell or transfer property.

restriction Any limitation on an owner's right to use a property, usually as a result of zoning ordinances. For example, in an area of single-family houses, a homeowner might be disallowed from using part of his or her residence as a rental apartment.

restrictive covenant *see* restriction.

retire a debt To fulfill the obligations of a loan or mortgage such that the lender has no further claims against the borrower (e.g., to completely pay off a loan or mortgage).

reverse-annuity mortgage (RAM) A mortgage in which the equity in a home serves as collateral security for periodic (usually monthly) payments made by the lender to the borrower. RAMs are increasingly popular with elderly people who use such payments to supplement their income. The payout cannot exceed the accumulated equity in the home. If the borrower dies before all the equity is exhausted, the property is sold so that the lender may recover its investment. If any residue remains, that amount is paid to the owner's survivors.

right of first refusal Allowing someone to make an offer on a property that is for sale before it is offered to others or to the public in general.

right of redemption *see* equity of redemption.

right of survivorship The right of the surviving tenant in a co-tenancy (e.g., joint tenancy) to take title in a property upon the death of the other co-tenant.

root of title Any problem in the ownership of a property that results in a question as to who actually owns the property.

run/running with the land A rule, right or restriction that forms part of the land and is transferred to each new owner, such as an easement that allows a landlocked property owner right-of-way over the subject property.

S
....

SAIF *see* Savings Association Insurnace Fund.

sale price The amount of money that is paid by the buyer to the seller for a particular property. Also known as purchase price.

sales-assessment ratio The ratio of the assessed value of a property to its actual selling price, which is assumed to be the market value. For example, if a house were assessed at $160,000 and then sold for $200,000, it would have sold at 125 percent of its assessed value, and the market value of the house would then be $200,000 rather than $160,000.

sales associate/salesperson A real estate professional who is employed by and works under a real estate broker.

sales-comparison approach In appraisal, estimating the value of a property by comparing it with similar properties that have recently been sold.

sales contract *see* agreement of sale.

SAM *see* shared-appreciation mortgage.

satisfaction/satisfaction of mortgage Written verification from a lender that a property loan (e.g., a mortgage) has been paid in full and the borrower is released from any further obligation to the lender.

save-harmless clause *see* hold-harmless clause.

savings and loan association (S&L) An association that is chartered to hold savings and make real estate loans. These institutions are federally insured, and are a common and important source of mortgage loans in the United States.

Savings Association Insurance Fund (SAIF) An agency of the Federal Deposit Insurance Corporation (FDIC) that insures deposits in savings and loan associations.

scenic easement A right to the use of land that is given to ensure that the land is never developed and that the natural beauty of a specific area is preserved.

scheduled mortgage payment The periodic payment (usually monthly) that a borrower is obliged to pay on a loan. Depending on the terms of the loan, this payment may include amounts only for principal and interest or also for real estate taxes and insurance premiums.

search A review of public records that is undertaken to investigate whether there are any problems with the title to a particular property.

seasoned mortgage An old loan that proves that a borrower has met loan obligations in the past.

second mortgage A mortgage that ranks after a first mortgage in priority. A single property may have more than one mortgage; each is ranked by number to indicate the order in which it must be paid. In the event of a default and therefore sale of the property, second and subsequent mortgages are paid, in order, only if there are funds left after payment of the first mortgage.

secondary financing Another term for second mortgage.

secondary market The marketplace where investors buy and sell existing mortgages. The purchasers of first mortgages include banks, government agencies, insurance companies, investment bankers and independent investors. The original lender often sells mortgages in the secondary market so as to have an adequate supply of money available for new loans in the future.

security Real or personal property that is pledged by a borrower as a guarantee or protection for the lender. With a mortgage, the borrower pledges the property that the borrower is actually buying; this security is registered on the title to the property and the lender may claim the property if the borrower defaults on (e.g., fails to pay) the loan.

security instrument In real estate, this is a mortgage, which is a pledge of real property (that which is being purchased) as security that the loan made by the lender will be repaid.

security interest A legal term for the claim a lender has against a borrower's property when that property has been pledged in a mortgage-loan transaction.

self-amortizing mortgage loan Any property loan that will be paid off at the end of its term; that is, its term (its due date) is the same as its amortization period (the date on which it will be completely paid off).

seller financing An arrangement in which a seller agrees to receive payment of part or all of the purchase price over an extended period. The debt is registered on the title as a mortgage, and the seller acts as the lender, accepting monthly payments of principal and accumulated interest.

seller take-back *see* seller financing.

seller's market The situation that exists when demand for property exceeds the availability of property. In such situations, a seller may set a price for her or his property that is higher than its real market value.

semidetached housing A dwelling, usually a house, that shares one side wall with another dwelling.

separate property Property that is owned by a husband or wife and in which one of them has no legal interest or ownership.

serious delinquency The condition of being so far behind in mortgage payments that action by the lender, probably leading to foreclosure, is imminent.

servicing/servicing the loan An operational procedure having to do with the collection of home loan payments and any other payments related to mortgage loans.

servicing fee A charge made by some lenders for their costs in collecting payments on a mortgage loan as well as administering the loan.

servient estate A piece of land that is subject to an easement (the opposite of dominant estate).

settlement book A brochure or pamphlet that is given by a mortgage-loan lender to a borrower that explains the details and particulars of the loan, such as settlement procedures.

settlement costs *see* closing costs.

settlement sheet At closing, the information sheet that sets out the allocation of the various funds necessary to effect the transfer of the property.

sever/severance To divide one property from another so that each may be sold or used separately.

severalty Ownership of land by an individual.

shared-appreciation mortgage (SAM) A loan in which the lender, in return for a reduced interest rate, participates in any profits when the property is sold.

signature The act of putting one's name on a legal document. It is now legal to send a signature by electronic mail or facsimile in a property transaction.

simple interest Interest that is payable on just the principal of a loan and not on any accumulated interest.

single-family home/residence/unit A house or condominium unit that is designed for just a single family.

SRL *see* saving and loan association.

soft market The situation that exists when there is more property for sale than there are buyers to buy it; as a result, prices decrease. Also known as buyer's market.

special assessment There are two meanings: 1) the levying of an additional tax on area landowners (by the local municipality) for a specific purpose, such as to apportion the cost of infrastructure upgrades that will benefit those landowners (e.g., new sewers or sidewalks, and 2) the levying of a charge against unit owners in a condominium complex to pay for some extraordinary repair or refurbishment of such expense that it cannot be covered from the usual monthly assessments, such as the replacement of an elevator or major structural repairs to the building.

spreading agreement A property loan contract in which the borrower gives the lender a guarantee in addition to the property that is being purchased; the borrower also allows the lender to secure the loan against other property that he or she owns. This kind of agreement is sometimes made when the property being acquired is very expensive, and therefore the loan is very large and the lender believes it to carry more than the usual risk.

stamp tax Charges that are levied by governments (usually the local municipality) on the transfer of ownership of property.

standard mortgage The general description of a mortgage that involves equal periodic (usually monthly) payments and is paid in full at the end of its term.

standards of practice A professional code of behavior devised by the National Association of Realtors to guide the business practices of real estate professionals.

starter home/condominium A small house or condominium unit that is usually inexpensive and is suitable for a first-time buyer. The assumption is that the buyer will build up equity in the property and then use the equity as a down payment on a larger dwelling.

state stamps Property transfer taxes that are levied by the state.

statutory lien An involuntary lien on property that is created by law (e.g., a tax lien) and to which the owner need not agree. A mortgage, by contrast, is a voluntary lien on property.

straight-term mortgage A mortgage that requires that the principal be paid in full at the maturity of the loan.

subject to An indication (in a contract) that a property involves an obligation of some sort, such as a lien, claim or easement.

subject-to clause In a deed, a clause stating that the grantee takes title subject to an existing mortgage, which remains the responsibility of the original owner. This is different from an assumption, where one person replaces another in responsibility for the loan.

subject-to mortgage A clause in a property sale agreement stating that the buyer will assume (e.g., take over) responsibility for an existing mortgage that is registered on the title to that property.

subordinate financing *see* second mortgage.

subordination clause An agreement by a lender to allow the current mortgage to be placed in priority behind a later mortgage.

support deed An instrument that conveys ownership of land in exchange for a promise from the new owner to care for the grantor during the grantor's lifetime. Such a deed is often drawn up when an elderly person gives property to a younger relative.

surety One who voluntarily binds himself or herself to be obligated for the debt of another, such as a parent who agrees to guarantee a child's purchase of a first house by co-signing a mortgage.

surplus funds In an enforced sale of property (e.g., a foreclosure on a mortgage), any funds that are left over after the principal, interest, and penalties have been paid. Often, these surplus funds are paid to the borrower whose default provoked the sale.

survivorship Put simply, this is outliving others. Surviving joint tenants (see co-tenancy) have the right to take title to land they owned with a deceased joint tenant (e.g., they have the right of survivorship).

suspended A loan can be held in abeyance (e.g., suspended) when more information is required by the lender of the potential borrower. In such a case, the application is neither approved nor denied, and will either go forward or not when the required information has been supplied.

sweat equity A slang term for the improvements an owner makes to property through his or her own manual labor. Such improvements are expected to add to the value of the property.

swing loan *see* bridge loan/financing.

T
....

takeout commitment/takeout loan An agreement by a lender to place a long-term (e.g., takeout) loan on real property after construction is complete.

tandem plan A joint program of two government agencies, the Government National Mortgage Association (GNMA) and the Federal National Mortgage Association (FNMA), that is designed to provide low-interest home loans. In general, these loans are intended for low-income families.

tangible property Assets that have a physical existence, that can be touched (e.g., real estate).

tax A government levy against real property. If taxes are unpaid, the government may attach a lien to the property. Such liens are regarded as preeminent (e.g., they are given priority over mortgages).

tax and insurance escrow *see* escrow account.

tax assessor *see* assessor.

tax base The assessed valuation of a piece of real property. This value is multiplied by the government's tax rate to determine the amount of property tax due.

tax exemption/tax-exempt property Freedom from paying property or other taxes. This is an exemption that is granted to religious, educational and charitable institutions. In some states or with some taxing authorities, a partial tax exemption is also granted to certain classes of people, such as seniors, the disabled and military veterans.

tax foreclosure The process leading up to the sale of property to cover unpaid taxes.

tax lien A registered claim for the nonpayment of property taxes.

tax rate The assessment that is in effect; it is traditionally expressed as the number of dollars per thousand dollars of evaluation.

tax roll A list published by a local taxing authority that contains a description of each property in the area, the name of the owner (e.g., the person who receives the tax bill), the assessed value of the property, and the amount of taxes for that property.

tax sale The sale of a property by a government for nonpayment of taxes, usually at an auction.

tax search That part of a title search that determines whether there are any outstanding taxes that would constitute a lien, registered or not, on that property.

tax shelter A general term for any property that gives (or would give) the owner tax advantages, such as a house that allows the owner to deduct property taxes or mortgage interest from his or her personal income taxes, or a rental property that allows the owner to deduct maintenance costs and depreciation in addition.

teaser rate A low initial rate on an adjustable-rate mortgage, offered for a relatively short period as an inducement to potential borrowers.

term loan A loan that comes due on a particular date, regardless of whether the periodic payments have paid that loan in full.

term of a mortgage The period during which the loan contract is in effect and the borrower is making payments to the lender. The term is not necessarily the same as amortization. Amortization is the period during which, if all payments are paid on time and in full, the loan will be paid. For example, a mortgage could be amortized over 30 years but have a term of 10 years; at the end of 10 years, the borrower must pay the balance of the loan in full or refinance the loan.

termite clause A term in a sale agreement that allows the buyer to inspect for termites. If any are found, the buyer may require the seller to fix the problem; otherwise, the buyer has the right to cancel the sale agreement. Termite infestation can be a serious problem, especially in the southern United States, where the climate can be subtropical.

terms The various clauses in a lease or a purchase or sale agreement.

title The evidence an owner has of his or her right of possession of property.

title company A corporation that sells insurance policies that guarantee the ownership of (and quality of title to) property. Also known as a title insurance company.

title covenants Clauses (e.g., promises) in an instrument of conveyance that give the purchaser assurances that the title to property is good and valid.

title defect A claim against property, such as a tax lien, that affects the owner's title in that property.

title insurance policy An insurance policy that protects an owner (or lender) against loss from defective title.

title report A document that sets out the current state of the title to a specific property.

title search A review of all the recorded documents that affect a particular property. The purpose of this review is to determine the current state of title and usually also to establish whether the current owner has clear title (e.g., without liens, competing claims, mortgages, etc.).

title-theory states Jurisdictions in which property ownership is through either legal title or equitable/beneficial title. This works in the following manner: When an owner registers a mortgage, legal title is transferred to the lender and the owner retains equitable/beneficial title. When the mortgage is paid in full, legal title is then transferred back to the owner.

total debt ratio The total costs of living for a person (e.g., debt, food, travel) over a particular period compared to her or his gross income. Also called debt-service ratio.

total interest payments All the interest that will be paid over the life of a loan.

townhouse A house that is not freestanding; it shares at least one wall with a neighboring house (or houses).

transfer tax A state tax on the transfer of real property. In some areas of the United States, it is referred to as documentary transfer tax.

two-step mortgage The sort of mortgage in which the interest rate changes after a stated period. Typically, the interest rate is lower for the first part of the mortgage's term and rises later. This kind of mortgage generally reflects a purchaser's (and lender's) expectation that the purchaser's income will increase during the initial period of low interest rate.

U

underwriter This term has two meanings or uses: 1) A person who evaluates an application for a loan or an insurance policy. 2) A company that insures another, such as large title company (the underwriter) that sells insurance to a smaller title insurance company for all or a portion of the policies the smaller company issues.

undivided interest A term used in the title of co-owners (e.g., joint tenants) of a property indicating that the title cannot be separated.

unencumbered property Property that is free of any liens, claims or mortgages registered against it.

unenforceable contract An agreement that is not legal, for one of many different reasons (e.g., one of the parties to the contract was legally incapacitated, the contract was signed as a result of a threat, some of the terms of the contract are illegal).

Uniform Vendor and Purchaser Risk Act A law that says that both buyer and seller of a property are responsible for any fire damage that occurs between the signing of the agreement of sale and the closing.

uninsurable title Ownership of land that is some way flawed, to the extent that a title company refuses to insure it.

unit A single dwelling in a larger complex. The term is most often used with regard to a condominium project. It refers to a unit (or, in a rental building, an apartment) that is reserved for the exclusive use of the owner, as opposed to the common areas (e.g., lobby, sun deck, laundry room) that are intended for the use of all the owners.

unity of possession The right of each person in a co-tenancy to use and occupy the entire property.

unity of title The situation in a co-tenancy in which all the tenants are recorded under the same title.

unmarketable title A property that is not saleable because of serious defects in the public record of its ownership. Similar to uninsurable title.

unrecorded/unregistered instrument A mortgage or deed that has not been registered in any public record. It is, however, regarded as a valid contract between the parties.

unsecured loan A loan that is valid (e.g., the lender has given the borrower the requested funds) but is not secured by any asset. Such loans are virtually unknown; an exception would be a case in which the lender knows the borrower well, has had extensive business dealings with the borrower, and believes that the loan will be repaid.

V

VA *see* Department of Veterans' Affairs.

VA loan A home loan, offered to a military veteran, that is guaranteed by the U.S. Department of Veterans' Affairs. It allows the veteran to buy a home with no money down.

valuation The estimation of the worth, or likely sale price, of land or property. Also known as appraisal.

variable expenses The operating costs of a property that are not fixed, such as heating costs, which can change dramatically depending on whether a winter is mild or severe.

variable-rate mortgage (VRM) *see* adjustable-rate mortgage.

variance An indulgence that is granted by a local government authority to allow an unconventional use of property. This could be an exception granted to a homeowner that allows him or her to create a basement apartment for a sick relative in an area in which zoning bylaws ordinarily allow for only single-family homes.

voluntary lien A claim against property that is registered with the consent of the owner. The most common example is a mortgage. The lender has an enforceable claim against that property until the mortgage loan is paid.

VRM *see* variable-rate mortgage

W

walk-through inspection An examination, by the buyer, of the property she or he is purchasing. The walk-through inspection usually takes place immediately before closing and is intended to assure the buyer that no changes have taken place (and no damage has been done) to the property since the buyer agreed to buy. It also reassures the buyer that fixtures and chattels included in the sale actually remain on the property.

warehousing The process of assembling mortgages to sell to the secondary mortgage market.

warrant A legally binding assurance that title, in any transfer of ownership of property, is good.

warranty A legally binding promise that is usually given at the time of sale in which the seller gives the buyer certain assurances as to the condition of the property being sold.

weekly payments An alternative to the usual monthly payments on a loan or mortgage. Such payments result in faster reduction of the principal and therefore also the amount of interest paid overall.

without recourse A situation where the lender may look only to the property as security for the loan; the lender may not touch any of the borrower's other assets in the event of a default.

wraparound mortgage A loan in which a new loan is added to an existing first mortgage. The new money that is borrowed is blended with the money already owed and is registered on the title to the property (e.g., a second mortgage is registered as security for the new money). However, the

Index

· · · · · ·

Are You Ready to Buy a House? Your Action Plan to Make It Happen

Last Will & Testament Kit (K307)

INCLUDES INSTRUCTION MANUAL AND 17 FORMS.

Protect your loved ones, make your wishes known and award your assets as you desire. This kit contains the forms and instructions you need to plan your estate responsibly and affordably.

TOPICS COVERED INCLUDE:

- Learning how to prepare your own will
- Determining who will inherit your assets
- Designating a child guardian and executor

Buying & Selling Your Home Kit (K311)

INCLUDES INSTRUCTION MANUAL, 23 FORMS AND LEAD PAINT DISCLOSURE INFORMATION ON CD.

Purchasing or selling a home without a real estate agent can save you money, but it can be a difficult process if you don't have the know-how to do it right. Before you get started, learn how to save time, maximize your profits, reduce legal fees and make the process go smoothly from beginning to end.

TOPICS COVERED INCLUDE:

- Cleaning up your credit & financing
- Prequalification vs. preapproval
- Open houses and avoiding discrimination
- Negotiating a sale and sales contracts
- Presettlement walk-through
- Tax breaks and more

Living Will & Power of Attorney for Health Care Kit (K306)

INCLUDES INSTRUCTION MANUAL AND 12 FORMS. STATE-SPECIFIC LIVING WILL FORMS AVAILABLE FREE AT SOCRATES.COM WHEN YOU REGISTER YOUR PURCHASE.

No one wants to think about the possibility of being permanently incapacitated and unable to communicate his or her health care preferences. With a living will, you can express, while still in good health, your choice of when to discontinue treatment and life support—and who should have the power to make that decision for you.

TOPICS COVERED INCLUDE:

- Durable power of attorney for health care
- Revoking a power of attorney
- Completing your living will
- Creating your living will
- Revoking your living will

Credit Repair Kit (K303)

INCLUDES INSTRUCTION MANUAL AND 14 FORMS AND LETTERS.

A bad credit report can have a negative effect on your buying power and your life. It can make buying a car or home, obtaining a credit card, entering into leases and other agreements and building the financial future of you and your family difficult, or even impossible. You can take control and turn your credit around with this easy-to-use Credit Repair Kit. It provides everything you need to determine your credit status and repair your credit rating.

TOPICS COVERED INCLUDE:

- Understanding credit ratings and reports
- Common reasons for credit denial
- How to get a copy of your credit report
- Your legal rights
- 10-step strategy to repairing your credit
- Tax liens
- Bankruptcy

FREE

Get over $100 in forms online at:

www.socrates.com/books/ReadyHouseActionPlan.aspx

To claim your forms, register your purchase using the registration code provided on the enclosed CD.

FREE FORMS INCLUDE:

- Offer to Purchase Real Estate
- Closing Costs Worksheet
- Calculating Your Net Worth Checklist
- Mortgage Shopping Worksheet
- Community Assessment
- Property/Neighborhood Features Checklist
- Preliminary Home Inspection Checklist
- Home Maintenance Schedule
- Letter of Intent to Purchase Real Estate

Your registration also provides you with a 15% discount on the purchase of other Socrates products for your Personal, Business and Real Estate needs.